Harold Pinter
and the Language
of Cultural Power

Harold Pinter and the Language of Cultural Power

Marc Silverstein

Lewisburg
Bucknell University Press
London and Toronto: Associated University Presses

Associated University Presses
440 Forsgate Drive
Cranbury, NJ 08512

Associated University Presses
25 Sicilian Avenue
London WC1A 2QH, England

Associated University Presses
P.O. Box 338, Port Credit
Mississauga, Ontario
Canada L5G 4L8

The paper used in this publication meets the requirements
of the American National Standard for Permanence of Paper
for Printed Library Materials Z39.48-1984.

Library of Congress Cataloging-in-Publication Data

Silverstein, Marc, 1961–
    Harold Pinter and the language of cultural power / Marc
Silverstein.
        p.   cm.
    Includes bibliographical references and index.
    ISBN 0-8387-5236-5 (alk. paper)
    1. Pinter, Harold, 1930–   Knowledge—Language and languages.
2. Pinter, Harold, 1930–   Political and social views.
3. Language and culture—England—History—20th century.   4. Power
(Social sciences) in literature.   I. Title.
PR6066.I53Z816   1993
822'.914—dc20   92-54667
                                                                    CIP

PRINTED IN THE UNITED STATES OF AMERICA

To my parents,

Michael and Phyllis Silverstein,

and to my teachers and friends,

Stephen and Olga Hamilton,

who have always given me the encouragement, love of theatre, and passion for books without which this book could never have been written.

Contents

Acknowledgments   9

1. "The Pinter Problem" Re-Problematized   13
2. "You'll Be Integrated": Subjectivity as Subjection in
   The Birthday Party   26
3. "It's Part of Their Nature": Woman's Truth in *The
   Collection*   50
4. "The Structure Wasn't Affected": *The Homecoming* and
   the Crisis of Family Structure   76
5. "I'll Be Watching You": *Old Times* and the Field of
   Vision   108
6. Conclusion: "In the Light (or the Shadow) of Power"   141

Notes   161
Bibliography   167
Index   178

Acknowledgments

I want to thank the first readers (and first critics) of this book in its earliest stages, John Emigh, Paula Vogel, and Victor Cahn, for their insightful comments and suggestions. I know that I could not have written the book without them.

I have also profited from exchanges with colleagues, friends, and students concerning a variety of topics directly bearing upon the issues I explore in this book. Discussions with my colleagues in the Auburn University Department of English have provided me with the opportunity to think out loud and clarify my position on many of the topics at the heart of this book. At the very earliest stages of this project, I had the good fortune to have many valuable conversations concerning Irigaray and feminist theory with my friend and colleague Elizabeth Huergo. Since professors frequently lament the disjunction between their teaching and research, I consider myself lucky to have taught a number of students with whom I could raise and explore the questions at the heart of this book. Among their number, I want to single out Juanita Gale, whose lively intelligence and keen interest in the subject of power relations allowed me to pursue further the implications of the notion of power at the center of this work. Finally, I want to thank Nikki Graves for her invaluable assistance in the laborious task of proofreading.

I want to thank Harold Pinter, Faber and Faber, and Grove Weidenfeld for permission to quote from the published editions of Pinter's work. Parts of this work have previously appeared in print: portions of Chapter 2 appeared in different form under the title "Keeping the Other in its Place: Language and Difference in *The Room* and *The Birthday Party*" in *The Pinter Review* (1993), and portions of Chapter 6 appeared in different form under the title "*One for the Road, Mountain Language* and the impasse of Politics" in *Modern Drama* 34, no. 3 (1991). I thank the editors of these journals for permission to reprint this material.

Harold Pinter
and the Language
of Cultural Power

1
"The Pinter Problem" Re-Problematized

On 19 May 1958, *The Birthday Party,* Pinter's second play and the first to receive a London production, opened at the Lyric Theatre, Hammersmith. Failing to find either an audience or sympathetic critical response (the notable exception, Harold Hobson's defense of the play, did not appear in the *Sunday Times* until after the production closed), the play ended its run five days later. The following extract from the review in *The Manchester Guardian* is representative of the overwhelmingly negative response to the play: "What all this means, only Mr. Pinter knows, for as his characters speak in non-sequiturs, half-gibberish and lunatic ravings, they are unable to explain their actions, thoughts, or feelings."[1]

It is one of the ironies in the rise of Pinter's critical fortunes that the source of much of the hostility to *The Birthday Party* has now become a source of the fascination not only with this play, but with Pinter's *oeuvre* as a whole: I refer, of course, to the dramatist's relation to and utilization of language. A further irony lies in the fact that many of those who praise Pinter subscribe to the same implicit view of language function, what I would term the expressive view, informing the *Guardian* review. Consider the following examples from three critics who would certainly repudiate the negative response to *The Birthday Party.* "Pinter employs language to describe the failure of language; he details in forms abundant the poverty of man's communication; he assembles words to remind us that we live in the space between words" (J. R. Hollis).[2] "Underneath the web of cliches, repetitions, interjections, anecdotes, we can understand what the characters are feeling far more profoundly than if they had tried to put it into words themselves" (Adrian Brine).[3] Pinter's language enacts "the complete contradiction between the words that are spoken and the emotional and psychological *action* which underlies them . . . the language has almost totally lost its rhetorical, its informative element" (Martin Esslin).[4]

While Hollis, Brine, and Esslin obviously do not subscribe to the *Guardian's* annonymous reviewer's estimate of Pinter's achievement, all four critics share the view that the central function of language is or should be defined in terms of expression, whether of emotional/psychological states, ideas, or self-definitions. For these writers (indeed, for the great majority of those who write on Pinter), language constitutes a structure of re-presentation—a system that, when it works, can translate pre-existing interior states into public discourse, thus guaranteeing the speaker's self-presence, his or her status as the transcendental signified of the utterance.

Thus, the *Guardian* reviewer excoriates Pinter for transgressing the law of language by peopling his plays with characters who "are unable to explain their actions, thoughts, or feelings." Rather than considering that Pinter may utilize language for purposes other than expression, or interrogating the viability of conceptualizing language as an expressive structure, the reviewer faults the playwright for creating characters who possess linguistic incompetence, proving incapable of exploiting the expressive potential inherent in language.

Unlike the reviewer, Hollis, Brine, and Esslin suggest that the "inability" to express "actions, thoughts, or feelings" may point to a fundamental problem with language that they see Pinter exploring. Thus, according to Hollis, the "non-sequiturs, half-gibberish and lunatic ravings" represent Pinter's use "of language to describe the failure of language . . . the poverty of man's communication." Pinter himself has voiced strenuous opposition to those critics who approach his works as the standard-bearers of "that tired, grimy phrase: 'Failure of communication,'" suggesting that it is not the failure of, but the willful retreat from, communication that interests him: "Communication is too alarming. . . . To diclose to others the poverty within us is too fearsome a possibility."[5]

The problem with Hollis's comments upon which I wish to focus, however, lies in his willingness to privilege the expressive function of language, a privileging implicit in his equation of "the failure of language" with "the poverty of man's communication." The sense of loss conveyed by "failure" and "poverty" testifies not only to Hollis's yearning for a language that could directly express the human essence now precariously situated "in the space between words," but also to his Platonic belief in an ideal, i.e., expressive, language, of which the "failed" language we employ in the phenomenal world provides at best a dim copy, at worst a perversion. Such a belief underwrites his further observation that Pinter's language "note[s] that the most important things are not being said,"[6]

and will remain unsaid as long as language continues in its fallen
state.

What interests me about this latter comment of Hollis's is the
manner in which, making a virtue of necessity, he manages to sal-
vage a version of the expressive theory of language function even
while decrying "the failure of language." I am referring to the implications of his claim that Pinter's language can "note" those things
that "are not being said." Hollis here appeals to a kind of modernist
aesthetic (reminiscent of Virginia Woolf or the Wittgenstein of the
Tractatus Logico-Philosophicus) that both recognizes the limits of
the sayable and sees in those limits evidence of the "existence" of
the unsayable. To phrase this another way: according to this view,
"the failure of language" expresses not *what* it cannot express, but
that it cannot express. Just as Wittgenstein locates the reality of
the aesthetic, the ethical, and the mystical in language's inability
to contain them, so Hollis perceives the reality of the unsayable—
which is also the realm of value, since it is only "the most *important*
things" that escape articulation—through the failure of utterance.

Brine also regards the fallen state of language that he claims
Pinter explores as testifying to the existence of a non-discursive
realm located "underneath the web of cliches, repetitions, interjections, anecdotes." Indeed, he goes even further than Hollis. While
the latter claims that "the failure of language" allows us to perceive
"that the most important things are not being said," he does not
state that we can actually gain access to what those "things" are.
Brine argues, however, that once we move "underneath" language,
"we can understand what the characters are feeling far more profoundly than if they had tried to put it into words themselves." As
the Platonist apprehends the essence, the Idea, only by moving
through the materiality of phenomena, so Brine asserts that only
by journeying through the imperfect materiality of language will
we arrive at the ineffable, the non-discursive realm of emotional/
psychological reality.

Esslin conceptualizes the relationship of language to the extra-
linguistic in Pinter's plays in terms of "the complete contradiction
between the words that are spoken and the emotional and psychological *action* which underlies them." Once again, "the failure of
language" to play its expressive role—what Esslin calls the loss of
"its informative element"—becomes transformed into another *kind*
of expression. Despite Esslin's reference to the irresolvable contradiction between words and action, his ability to discern this
action suggests that it is the very inadequacy of language that
points to and expresses that which resides beyond its limits. As

Austin Quigley observes, "it is surely obvious that if Esslin can perceive the 'emotional and psychological action' underlying the words, then the language is very informative."[7]

To summarize: the four critics I have cited (and in this respect they represent a recurring pattern in commentary on Pinter) all implicitly accept a metaphysical theory that defines language's central function in terms of its communicative, expressive, or "informative element." I say metaphysical because such a theory predicates itself both upon a split between the linguistic and the extra-linguistic and the granting of a privileged status to the latter. This split does not necessarily have to assume the form of a contradiction between the sayable and the unsayable, as it does in Hollis, Brine, and Esslin's writing. It can also inform the claim that the extra-linguistic takes *temporal* precedence over the linguistic, a claim with which the *Guardian* reviewer would sympathize. Unlike the other critics I have discussed, s/he not only thinks language should play an expressive role, but that it does play this role. The criticism that Pinter creates characters who "are unable to explain their actions, thoughts, or feelings" implies that "actions, thoughts, . . . feelings," rather than discursively constituted, precede and exist outside of the language that gives voice to them in a process of articulation that remains subordinate to the material being expressed.

I have already mentioned Pinter's own objections to this kind of approach to his work, his unequivocal assertion that he does not concern himself with issues of expression or communication. This raises the question, does Pinter refrain from dramatizing such issues because he simply wants to focus on other aspects of language or, more radically, because he rejects the kind of metaphysical assumptions underlying the expressive theory of language function, i.e., belief in an extra-linguistic realm that enjoys the status of a transcendental signified?

This question underlies arguably the most significant and certainly the most extensive study of the role of language in Pinter's plays, Austin Quigley's *The Pinter Problem*. Quigley devotes almost the first quarter of this book to an exhaustive survey of the criticism that addresses tiself to Pinter's use of language (a survey to which much of my preceding discussion owes a considerable debt). He critiques the linguistic/extra-linguistic dichotomy elaborated in much of this criticism because it allows critics to deflect their attention away from language to some fuzzily-defined area variously identified, in the examples I have employed, as "the space between words" or the space "underneath" words. Quigley reads such dichotomizing as symptomatic of an impasse not only in Pinter criticism, but in any kind of work in linguistics that clings to what he terms "the reference theory of meaning"[8] (to which the phenomenon I have called the expressive theory of language roughly corresponds).

Of particular importance here is the manner in which Quigley identifies the recurring presence of an unacknowledged, problematic linguistic theory underwriting the majority of Pinter criticism. Quigley calls for a self-conscious acknowledgement of the kind of linguistic theory that informs the writing on Pinter's use of language, since recognizing the presence of such theory would hopefully lead to an interrogation of the viability of that theory and an awareness of alternative theoretical models that would not only be more responsive to how language functions in the plays, but would also foreground Pinter's rejection of the very concept of language that has been paramount in the explication of his texts.

For his own theoretical paradigm, Quigley turns to Wittgenstein—the later Wittgenstein of the *Philosophical Investigations* rather than the Wittgenstein of the earlier, more metaphysically-oriented *Tractatus*. Quigley quotes approvingly and takes as his guiding principle Wittgenstein's dictum, "Look at the sentence as an instrument, and at its sense as its employment."[9] Wittgenstein's importance for Quigley lies in the philosopher's refusal to separate meaning and use; unlike the expressive theory of language that conceptualizes meaning as both pre-and extra-linguistic, Wittgensteinian linguistics theorizes meaning as a product of language—not an inherent property of words, but an effect of how those words are used. (Esslin makes a tentative move in this direction when he writes that "what matters . . . [in Pinter's use of language] is more what people are *doing* to each other through it rather than the conceptual content of what they are saying."[10] Esslin, however, still preserves the dichotomy between meaning—"the conceptual content"—and use that Quigley rejects.)

In order to identify the meaning of meaning within Pinter's dramatic world, Quigley asks how language is employed and deployed in the texts. He finds the answer to this question by examining how the characters use language to negotiate positions of power within the various relationships into which they find themselves thrust. In a passage worth quoting at some length, Quigley states,

This battle [i.e., the battle for position within a relationship], in the Pinter world, is grounded in the power available in language to promote the responses that a speaker requires and hence the relationship that is desired. It is here that the link between language and relationships is established, and it is here that we must concentrate our attention. The language of a Pinter play functions primarily as a means of dictating and reinforcing relationships. This use of language is not, of course, exclusive to a Pinter play and is a common component . . . in all language; but, in giving this use such extensive scope, Pinter has . . . made his work unavailable to any critical analysis based on implicit appeals to the reference theory of meaning.[11]

Quigley terms this kind of linguistic activity the "interrelational function" of language, choosing "interrelational" rather than "interpersonal" because the latter "tends to suggest that the personalities, the identities of those participating, are given in advance. In the Pinter world, however, the considerable prominence of developing relationships is in large part dependent on the ways in which relationships function in the development of a self-concept."[12]

Quigley's rejection of "the reference theory of meaning" leads him, via the route of Wittgensteinian linguistics, to a semiotic understanding of Pinter's use of language. If "self-concepts" develop through relationships that are themselves developed and negotiated through language, then subjectivity, rather than "given in advance," becomes the effect of signifying practices, produced through a perpetual inscription and reinscription within language.

While Quigley's approach marks a significant advance over earlier studies of Pinter's use of language and produces some insightful and suggestive readings, it remains limited by an almost exclusive focus on what Saussure calls *parole* (the individual speech-act), without sufficient attention to *langue* (language as a codified system) and its relationship to the *parole*. Quigley wants to conceptualize the subject as an effect of language, spoken as well as speaking, rather than an entity "given in advance" that language merely re-presents, but his failure to consider how the system of language both allows for *and* places certain constraints upon individual utterance tends to resituate the subject outside of the language to which it remains superior.

To clarify my point, and to demonstrate that this problem is inherent in the linguistic paradigm Quigley adopts, I want to consider the implications of Wittgenstein's comment that provides the foundation for Quigley's theory of meaning: "Look at the sentence as an instrument, and at its sense as its employment." To regard language solely as an instrument is to define it in terms of an absolute agency with the speaker assuming the position of an absolute or free agent. Furthermore, since the "being" of instruments depends upon their use, they do not effectually exist until becoming engaged in some kind of activity; that is, until *someone* utilizes them, someone to whom they are subordinate, someone who stands as their point of origin.

In the most obvious sense, of course, Wittgenstein and Quigley are correct. When I speak a sentence, the words leave *my* mouth and may have never previously assumed quite this form. While the actual sentence may have been uttered by someone else (as the individual words certainly have), I will perform the act of articulation with an intonation, rhythm, gesture, and facial expression that are uniquely mine—perhaps. Even if this proves to be the case, however, I can only claim the utterance as inalienably and eternally my property by neglecting the category of history, as does Quigley. One does not have to subscribe to "the reference theory of meaning" to acknowledge that, no matter how arbitrary the process of linguistic signification, words accrue a good deal of semiotic baggage—the various desires, meanings, and values they encode— that we cannot simply erase when we appropriate them for our utterances. As Mikhail Bakhtin observes, "only the mythical and totally alone Adam, approaching a virgin and still unspoken world with the very first discourse, could really avoid altogether"[13] the limits that *langue* imposes upon the *parole*. Unlike Adam, we are born into a world and into a language that confront us with the always-already-said. Wittgenstein and Quigley's transfer of meaning from the word as sign to the "employment" of language (thus assuming an unproblematic intentionality) attempts to confer upon *parole* the status of "the very first discourse." No matter how we may wish to employ a particular utterance, however, we cannot ignore the traces of other voices (and the Other's voice) inhabiting the words constituting that utterance.

The preceding comments raise a question of central importance both within Pinter's plays and within much of the current theoretical work on the relationship between language and cultural power: who (or what) speaks through the voice that articulates (it)self? In other words, how can we as speaking beings fashion our subjectivity through a language marked by the otherness that comes to locate itself within that subjectivity? Throughout his works, Pinter examines in a manner both complex and compelling the sometimes fraught relationship between this speaking subject and language, giving dramatic shape to one of the central insights of both structuralist and post-structuralist linguistics: no speaking subject "can ever find words in the language that are neutral, exempt from the . . . evaluations of the other. . . . he receives the word by the other's voice and it remains filled with that voice. He intervenes in his own context from another context, . . . find[ing] a word already lived in."[14]

What exactly is the nature of this linguistic "otherness"? As Quigley notes, the relationships in these plays often emerge from pitched verbal battles between at least two speakers attempting to impose their terms (in both a linguistic and contractual sense) upon each other. For Quigley, then, language's "interrelational function" assumes the presence of a speaking subject and a definite other. Enlarging the scope of our focus to include *langue* as well as *parole*, we must introduce a third term: the speaking subject, an other (or others), and *the* Other, i.e., the symbolic order, the locus of language as a system encoding the dominant cultural values. Anthony Wilden defines the Other in the following terms: "The Other is not a person, but a principle; the locus of the 'law of desire' . . . the only place from which it is possible to say 'I am who I am'. . . . [The Other] puts us in the position of desiring what the Other desires: we desire what the Other desires we desire."[15]

This "law of desire" is also a law of language, since language serves as the medium in which the Other materially embeds its desire: the language models that allow us to identify ourselves, "to say 'I am who I am,'" create us in the image of the Other, thus ensuring that we will desire not only *what* the Other desires but *as* the Other desires. To illustrate this point, let me briefly turn to *The Birthday Party,* the Pinter play that, perhaps more than any other, takes as its central concern the cultural construction of subjectivity, the socializing process through which the "I" emerges in the discursive field of the Other. Pinter dramatizes this process most forcefully in the second-act "interrogation" scene and the third-act "brainwashing" scene—sequences containing some of the most powerful examples of verbal violence in the Pinter canon—in which Goldberg and McCann expropriate Stanley from "his" language, transforming him into an empty vessel waiting to be filled with the cultural codes that will allow him to speak with the Other's voice, embrace the Other's values, desire the Other's desire.

These two scenes echo an earlier moment in the play between Stanley and Meg, his "symbolic mother":

Stanley. What about some tea?
Meg. Do you want some tea? (Stanley reads the paper.) Say please.
Stanley. Please.
Meg. Say sorry first.
Stanley. Sorry first.

Meg. No. Just sorry.
Stanley. Just sorry![16]

This exchange both parodies and enacts the process through which the mother constructs the child as an "appropriate" cultural subject on the ideological terrain of the family. Meg structures and effectually creates Stanley's desire by channeling it through the language model she imposes. As long as he claims desire as inalienably his, articulating it through his own mode of speech ("What about some tea?"), Meg withholds recognition. Only when Stanley has been successfully assimilated to the Other's language will his desire receive "official" sanction.

This exchange would appear to provide a perfect illustration of Quigley's thesis. The "meaning" of the dialogue has less to do with the cup of tea than with the relationship between Meg and Stanley, and the question of who will dictate the terms that structure that relationship. Rather than rejecting Quigley's sense of how language operates in these plays, I want to extend the range of his definition to include *langue* as well as *parole,* the Other as well as the subject and an other. Viewed from this perspective, we can say that while Meg wins this round, the language model she forces Stanley to adopt reveals the controlling presence of the Other. When Meg tells Stanley to "say please," she invokes the highly coded discourse of etiquette, words and conventions strongly marked with the Other's evaluations, its judgments, its ability to sanction acceptable language and desire and withhold recognition from any mode of speech or desire failing to conform to its specifications. That Meg should uncritically appeal to this discourse reveals the extent of her own subjection to the Other, her own status as a mouthpiece for the codes that allow her to inhabit the place of the Other, desiring its desires, speaking its language, enacting its scenarios.

As these comments suggest, cultural power, the power of the Other, does not so much inhere in individual words as in the larger discourses to which those words belong—or, to be more precise, in these discourses' conventions and codes, termed by Roland Barthes the cultural codes: "the utterances of the cultural code are implicit proverbs. . . . [They allow] the discourse to state a general will, the law of a society, making the proposition concerned ineluctable or indelible."[17] The proverbial is closely related to and at times indistinguishable from the clichéd, and clichés play a central role in Pinter's work. I am referring not only to clichéd sentiments (e.g., Goldberg's "Never, never forget your family, for they are the rock, the constitution and the core"[18]), but also to what I would call, at the risk of tautology, clichéd conventions (e.g., Meg's "Say please") and clichéd representations (e.g., the patriarchal construction of acceptable femininity in terms of silence and powerlessness, as opposed to the equivalence of masculinity, language, and power, that speaks through Deeley's comment, in *Old Times*, that Kate's "virtue" inheres in her "silence"[19]).

Much Pinter criticism, particularly the attempts to discuss his plays under the rubric of "Theatre of the Absurd," has followed Esslin's lead in seeing these clichés as instancing how an atrophied, attenuated language contributes to the failure of communication. Esslin includes Pinter in the ranks of those "absurdists" engaged in a project to liberate humanity from "ossified cliches," replacing them with "a living language" that will inspire "man's reverence toward the spoken or written word as a means of communication."[20] Leaving aside Esslin's tendency to generalize when he writes about the "absurdists," as though there were no fundamental differences between Beckett, Ionesco, Genet, and Pinter, it is rather difficult to see Pinter clad in the vestments of a priest of "a living language" at whose altar he exhorts his audience to kneel and offer "reverence."

The real problem with Esslin's opposition between the "ossified cliché" and "living language" when applied to Pinter's plays, however, is that, far from constituting a dead mode of speech, these clichés serve as the locus of cultural power, of the "law of desire," of the Other. As Pinter's works illustrate, it is through these clichés—and again, I am using "cliché" in the broadest sense of the term, as synonymous with Barthes's cultural codes—that the Other fashions the subject positions we inhabit, and that we are able "to say 'I am who I am,'" whether we define this "I" in ontological terms (the "I" as self) or in social terms (the "I" as a gendered, ethnic, class-bound entity). Throughout his plays, Pinter explores the necessarily contingent status of this "I," the subjectivity that can only establish itself at the price of remaining subject to the Other, perpetually reinscribing this subjectivity/subjection within that utterance that marks us as with the brand of the Other.

As the preceding discussion suggests, in this study I propose to re-problematize "the Pinter problem," to rethink the question of how Pinter utilizes language by broadening the scope of Quigley's "interrelational function" to examine how the viarious battles for power enacted in these plays are fought on the terrain of the Other's discursive field with weapons consisting of the codes that speak the various forms of cultural power. In Pinter's works, the process of negotiating relationships is inseparable from the process through which the subject attempts to anchor itself firmly within the symbolic order, the cultural space organized and maintained by the codes, structures of representation, and ideological apparatus that speak (from) the Other.

To argue, as I shall, that questions of cultural power and the subject's relationship to that power are of central importance to these plays is to claim that Pinter's work explores some fundamental political questions. Not only, then, in plays like *One for the Road* and *Mountain Language* that directly concern themselves with the state, or in plays like *The Birthday Party, The Dumb Waiter,* and *The Hothouse* that, in Pinter's own words, offer a "political metaphor"[21] of an authoritarian political order, but throughout his works Pinter focuses on questions of power, marginalization, sexuality and gender, the ideological status of the family, the relation of violence to the coercive power of language—all of which are essentially political questions.

Esslin makes a similar point at the very beginning of his study of Pinter: "Behind the highly private world of his plays, there also lurk what are, after all, the basic political problems. . . . Only very superficial observers could overlook this social, this political side of the playwright."[22] Esslin promises more here than he eventually delivers, however, for the category of the socio-political is largely absent from the book. Since we obviously cannot attribute this absence to Esslin's ignorance of the political dimension of Pinter's work, we must trace its source to what Esslin means by politics. Esslin ranks "the use and abuse of power"[23] as chief among "the basic political problems" that Pinter explores. While I fully agree that Pinter's examination of the dynamics of power raises political questions, the "political" is a product of *how* he conceptualizes power rather than a quality that inheres in power. Despite the very significant differences between them, for the most part Esslin, like Quigley, divorces the battles for power within the relationships he discusses from the cultural space in which they are fought. For Esslin, at stake in these battles is the question, who will control this relationship?

For Pinter, however, "personal" power is both an effect of and vehicle for cultural power, and it is the integrity of the cultural order that ultimately is at issue in the various struggles for authority he dramatizes. To illustrate this point, consider *The Collection, The Homecoming,* and *Old Times,* three plays that depict struggles for power between husband and wife. We might think of these plays, concerned as they are with power relations within the "domestic" sphere, as social dramas (as opposed to the overtly political *One for the Road*), but they contain serious political implications. If we want to discuss such implications, then we must see the struggles for power they dramatize as placing in question not only the structure of *one* particular family or of *the* family as a strictly social institution, but the status of the family as an ideological apparatus for the reproduction of patriarchal power relations.

In my discussion of these three plays, I will argue that Pinter views familial relationships as mediated by ideological representations; that "husband" and "wife" do not so much refer to actual people as designate discursively constituted subject positions that exceed their inhabitants; that through the battle for power within the family, Pinter engages in the project advocated in another context by Althusser: "We must also work out the ideological formations that govern . . . 'husband-and-wife-being' . . . in the modern world."[24] I will argue, in other words, that we can only fully grasp the political resonance of the power struggles in these plays if we see the question of who will occupy the dominant position within the marriage as inseperable from the larger question of whether the family will serve as a stable site for the articulation of patriarchal power or as the vanishing point that works to undermine that power and the cultural order it supports. My analysis of Pinter's plays, then, takes as one of its guiding principles the recognition that political questions do not, in Esslin's words, "lurk . . . behind," but pervade the very heart of Pinter's dramatic world.

As my references to cultural codes and the Other indicate, I will be enlisting the aid of a certain theoretical apparatus in my analysis. I am not claiming that Pinter has been influenced by Althusser, Lacan, or any of the other theorists discussed in these pages at any stage in his career, but rather that the kind of conceptual lens through which I will examine these plays can contribute to the project of rethinking the role of language in Pinter's works.

I would emphasize "rethinking" in the preceding sentence. Reading through the not inconsiderable amount of commentary devoted to Pinter's use of language, one cannot help experiencing an overwhelming feeling of *deja vu;* in the introduction to *The Pinter Problem,* Quigley notes the impasse Pinter criticism has reached, and little has changed in the intervening years. It is symptomatic of this impasse that a recent collection of essays containing a variety of differing methodological interventions within the field of Pinter criticism—*Harold Pinter: Critical Approaches,* edited by Steven H. Gale—includes only one piece, John Fuegi's "The Uncertainty Principle and Pinter's Modern Drama," that addresses the question of language. Unfortunately, Fuegi's main thesis—that Pinter uses language to create the aura of "instability, ambiguity, [and] uncertainty"[25] that dominates his dramatic universe—is another example of that eternal return of the same that haunts Pinter criticism.

My use of theory, however, has not been guided by the desire to say something different about Pinter's use of language for the sake of saying something different. I fully endorse Quigley's position that we can no longer rely on impressionistic accounts of the function of language in general if we are to understand its function within Pinter's theater. Implicit in such a view is the belief that if contemporary theory can help focus some of the issues in Pinter's plays, then Pinter's plays can help focus some of the issues in contemporary theory. When I invoke the names of Irigaray, Lacan, et cetera, in these pages, then, I do so not only instrumentally, but because I see Pinter's dramatic practice, like their theoretical investigations, aiding us in articulating and thinking through complex questions about the relation of language to subjectivity; about the relation of the subject to the Other; about whether the subject can become an agent or must remain subject(ed) to the language that voices cultural power.

I propose, then, to offer a new perspective on a perennial problem in Pinter criticism. The question of the role of language in these plays has been posed many times, but, as this introduction suggests, I am convinced that it remains open to reexamination and reformulation. It is almost impossible to exaggerate the importance of this question to an understanding of Pinter, since many of the issues these plays explore—issues of power, issues of identity, issues of sexuality—repeatedly return us to the problem of language. Richard Gilman once remarked that in Pinter's world, language *is* the play;[26] while such a sweeping observation tends to overstatement, I would certainly agree that language provides the lens that brings these other issues into focus. In the analyses that follow, I attempt to bring language itself and its relation to subjectivity into focus; to offer one path out of the impasse in which commentary on Pinter's language currently finds itself; to describe with some degree of thoroughness those conditions which, as Pinter remarks, render language an highly complex, "highly ambiguous business."[27]

2

"You'll be Integrated": Subjectivity as Subjection in *The Birthday Party*

In the preceding chapter, I argued that we can only fully grasp what is at stake in the struggle for power that forms the quintessential action of a Pinter play if we focus on how subjectivity emerges and finds itself contained within the cultural space organized and supported by the ensemble of codes, structures of representation, and ideological discourses that speak (from) the Other. I begin my discussion of this issue with a reading of *The Birthday Party,* which, although only Pinter's first full-length play, provides perhaps his most intensive exploration of the process through which subjectivity slides into subjection to a coercive Law of Culture. With its demystifying exhibition of the operations of cultural power, *The Birthday Party* stands as a kind of dramatized "theory" of power, a "theory" fundamental to an understanding of Pinter's *oeuvre.* We will see that what he dramatizes in an "abstract," almost allegorical manner in this play informs his more "concrete" explorations of both the patriarchal construction of gender relations *(The Collection, The Homecoming, Old Times)* and the ideological underpinnings of the authoritarian state *(One for the Road, Mountain Language).* In this chapter, then, I will identify the specific characteristics of the concept of cultural power elaborated in *The Birthday Party* by focusing on how the formation, de-formation, and re-formation of Stanley's "identity" dramatize the conscriptive process through which we are inserted within the cultural order, a process that raises the question, can we talk about the subject as controlling power, or does power inevitably exceed even those figures who seem to embody it?

As the title of this chapter indicates, I will argue that Pinter's vision of cultural power implicitly equates subjectivity with subjection. The inseparability of these terms recalls the fundamental ambiguity that Althusser sees as characterizing the concept of the subject: "Subject in fact means: (1) a free subjectivity, a centre of initiatives, author of and responsible for its actions; (2) a subjected being, who submits to a higher authority, and is therefore stripped of all freedom except that of freely accepting his submission."[1]

For Althusser, the ideological field in which our subjectivity emerges does not so much resolve as mystify this ambiguity. Through its various codes and discourses, ideology supports and ensures the reproduction of the cultural order by serving as a "mirror" in which we find consolingly unified and coherent images of the self with which to identify. These images, however, are little more than lived fictions generated from within the Other's discursive field, guaranteeing that all our actions will be socially appropriate, i.e., actions that never challenge the dominant values, desires, imperatives, and prohibitions that constitute the Law of Culture. The power of ideology thus resides in its ability to produce subjects who (mis)recognize themselves as "centres of initiatives," without understanding that their illusory autonomy is merely a sign of their subjection to and thorough internalization of the Other's Law. For Althusser, then, the kind of freedom and authenticity that existentialism and other philosopies of individualism privilege cannot be opposed to the Law since they are the most fundamental images produced by the ideological machinery of the Law.

Like Lacan, upon whose theory of the mirror stage he draws for his sense of how ideology works, Althusser utilizes the identification of subjectivity with subjection to deconstruct the categories of the individual and the self. If "the self" is nothing more than an illusory effect of our positioning within the cultural order, then we cannot conceptualize our subjection to the Other and our interpellation within the dominant ideology as a tragic scenario in which the individual suffers defeat by some "external force."[2] Rather, to claim individuality as an human characteristic, an ontologically real category of human experience, is to announce that we always already speak from within the Other's territory, that we are always already subjected to that Law whose power consists in its ability to obscure its status as Law.

Althusser's equation of subjectivity and subjection and his sense of the thoroughly ideological nature of the rhetoric of "free subjectivity" provide the necessary theoretical groundwork for a discussion of *The Birthday Party's* dramatization of the process through which the Other "integrates" its subjects. This is a particularly important issue for an understanding of Pinter's vision of cultural power, and one that has most often been discussed (by critics such

as Esslin, Dukore, Gale, and Gordon) in terms of the tragic scenario (the autonomous self crushed by "external force") that, like
Althusser, Pinter's work rejects. Such discussions ground themselves in a reading of Stanley's account of his ill-fated career as a
concert pianist. I would agree that Stanley's narrative suggests
what is at issue in the play, not because it supports what I have
termed the tragic scenario, but because it reveals the extent to
which such a reading mystifies the connection between subjectivity
and subjection.

The narrative projects an image of Stanley as a latter-day Ro-
mantic artist/genius, a rebel and nonconformist, an individualist
whose reliance on his "unique touch [, a]bsolutely unique" (p. 32)
constitutes a sin for which he must be punished, first by unmerited
persecution—being prevented from giving a second concert—then
by being returned to the path of conformity. Such a reading implicitly invokes the tragic conflict between individual and society, so
that the work is "about," according to Gale, "the death of Stan as
an individual."[3] Gordon goes even further, seeing the play as part
of Pinter's continuing anatomization of civilization and its discon-
tents: "Pinter's assault is levelled at . . . civilization itself. . . .
There is something about the nature of the individual that is incom-
patible with the communities of men."[4] The problem with such
readings is their refusal to interrogate the concept of the individual—even the claim that the play enacts the death of the individual assumes that "individual" denotes a "real" existential category
that can be destroyed. When critics introduce "the individual" into
their discussion of the play, they "posit an entity that is both autonomous and stable"[5]—a self that enjoys the status of foundational irreducibility rather than ideological image. This assumption
means that whether or not Stanley's story possesses literal truth[6]
we must regard it as symbolically true, for it is through his narrative—through Stanley's vision of himself as the "absolutely
unique" pianist persecuted because he *is* unique—that he creates
the image of himself as the play's representative of individualism.

We could find no better example than Stanley's narrative, however, with which to disturb the kind of reading that bases itself
upon an uncritical acceptance of "the individual" as a meaningful
concept in Pinter's world. Morrison claims that Stanley's narrative
fails "because his fear quickly changed it from a tale of success
to one of unmerited persecution."[7] If Stanley's first concert is a
"success," however, it also entails defeat, for it marks an ominous
and ineluctable process of self-estrangement through which Stan-

ley is seduced into (mis)recognizing the "truth" of his "individuality."

Stanley describes his concert as follows:

> I once gave a concert. . . . Yes. It was a good one, too. They were all
> there that night. Every single one of them. It was a great success. Yes.
> A concert. At Lower Edmonton . . . I had a unique touch. Absolutely
> unique. They came up to me. They came up to me and said they were
> grateful. Champagne we had that night, the lot. (pp. 32–33)

While Stanley offers this account as a token of his personal triumph, the image of the concert he describes essentially reproduces
the process of ideological (mis)recognition through which the subject comes to apprehend itself *as* a subject. The narrative clearly
reveals the contingency of Stanley's identity as a pianist, his vulnerability before the Janus-faced gaze of the Other that can either
assume the benevolent aspect of the Other as mirrored self, or the
menacing, "sinister aspect of the Other . . . what makes your hair
stand on end,"[8] termed "the enemy" by Herbert Blau. In both
cases, the Other wields absolute power—the power either to bestow or withhold the recognition that creates identity.

The audience at Stanley's concert may not display the features
of the enemy, but it does demonstrate the extent to which the
"self," rather than some core of being inhering within the subject,
issues from the Other. If we ask what defines Stanley's identity as
pianist, the answer is not his "unique touch," but the Other, whose
gaze and actions become a mirror in which Stanley sees reflected
his "essence": "They came up to me. They came up to me and
said they were grateful."

This moment of triumphant (mis)recognition arrives charged
with all the complexity and ambiguity of the Lacanian mirror stage,
the model upon which Althusser draws for his theory of the subject's ideological interpellation within the cultural order. For Lacan, the mirror stage occurs when the infant, confronting its own
image in the mirror—an image of spatial coherence and unified
form—identifies with and introjects that image, imagining itself as
possessing a physical and existential integrity that masks what
Lacan calls its "discordance with [its] own reality."[9] Like the process through which ideology creates the effect of an "absolutely
unique" self that mystifies our subjection to the Other, the mirror
stage mystifies the extent to which the "I" it engenders is an "Ideal-
I," a self with only "the illusion of autonomy"[10] and cohesion.
Thus, as both Lacan and Althusser argue, this experience of self-

discovery precipitates self-estrangement—the process of identification that constitutes identity situates that identity in a line of
fiction and alienation.

Stanley's account of his concert provides a dramatic analogue
of the mirror stage, with the approving gaze of the audience serving
as the mirror in which he both finds and loses himself. Stanley's
definition of identity in terms of an (illusory) "absolutely unique"
essence confines him in "the armour of an alienating identity,"[11]
alienating to the extent that it grounds itself in an image and bars
him from perceiving his truth: the primacy of the Other in producing his subjectivity.

Stanley's narrative reveals the paradox at the heart of both Lacan's version of the mirror stage and Althusser's grafting of the
dynamics of the mirror stage onto his theory of ideology. Though
the experience of identification signals the formation of Stanley's
"I," he discovers this "absolutely unique" identity in the externality of the not-I (the approving gaze of his audience) that conditions and ultimately possesses him. At the same time he loses
himself through capture by the Other, Stanley has the chance to
save himself from what Lacan terms that "primordial Discord[,]
. . . the effect in man of an . . . insufficiency in his . . . reality"[12]—
the sense of fragmentation that engulfs him when he is denied the
possibility of (re-)experiencing his "self" through the Other at his
second concert: "Yes. Lower Edmonton. Then after that, you know
what they did? They carved me up. Carved me up . . . My next
concert . . . when I got there, the hall was closed, the place was
shuttered up, not even a caretaker" (p. 33).

What Stanley's narrative refuses (or is unable) to address directly is the question of *why* this possibility is denied him; what
causes "them" to withhold recognition; what transforms the Other
from the mirrored self into the enemy. In order to answer this
question, we must consider the point at which Stanley's narrative
threatens to collapse, the point of transition that transforms his
tale from a celebration of autonomous subjectivity into a bitter
account of subjection: "My father nearly came down to hear me.
Well, I dropped him a card anyway. But I don't think he could
make it. No, I—I lost the address, that was it" (p. 33).

In order to understand why this reference to the father disrupts
the coherence of both Stanley's narrative and the image of "free
subjectivity" inscribed within that narrative, we need to conceptualize the father in Lacanian and Althusserian terms, i.e., we need
to consider "the father" in its symbolic (rather than biological)
dimension as the most powerful signifier "of the Law, the fantasy

image of all Right."[13] For Lacan and Althusser, the Father," who Is Law . . . [represents] the Order of the human signifier . . . the Law of Culture . . . [the] discourse of the Other."[14] As the signifying space from whence issues "the order of objectifying language that . . . allows[s] [the subject] to say: I . . . that will therefore allow the small child to situate itself"[15] within the cultural order, the Father occupies the point of origin of the cultural codes that instill the appropriate values, discipline, behavior, and responses in the subject.

As the symbolic embodiment of the Other, the Father denies the validity of the subject's claim to existential self-sufficiency. Stanley may (mis)recognize the mirror image, taking the reflection for the real, as he (mis)recognizes his "absolutely unique" self in the valorizing gaze of his audience, but he can never extricate himself from subjection to the Father-as-Other, whose Law is invoked whenever the subject utters his or her name. We tend to regard the name as the most rudimentary signifier of self-presence, while in fact it indicates the insistence of the Other *within* the "self." Bakhtin, who, like Lacan and Althusser, focuses on the otherness inscribed at the heart of subjectivity (albeit assigning a more positive reading of that otherness than do the two French theorists), remarks *a propos* of names, "I receive my name from the other, and this name exists for the other (to name oneself is to engage in usurpation)."[16] Stanley engages in such "usurpation," only to have the Father confront him with his transgression:

Goldberg. Webber! Why did you change your name?
Stanley. I forgot the other one.
Goldberg. What's your name now?
Stanley. Joe Soap.
Goldberg. You stink of sin. (p. 60)

Stanley's "sin," his usurpation of the Father's prerogative, can only end in failure, for such a project aims at nothing less than his liberation from the cultural order itself. The Other, however, never releases its subjects from the demand for adherence to its Law— as Stanley himself observes, "there's nowhere to go" (p. 36) that resides beyond the Other's gaze. The Other insists upon making itself heard, even through a silence for which Stanley's narrative cannot account, an omission that declares itself as an omission: "My father nearly came down . . . But *I don't think* he could make it." As the Other's representative, the Father dislodges Stanley from the illusory subject position of an "absolutely unique" self, revealing the truth of his subjectivity as subjection, contingency, centerlessness, dislocation.

The account of the concerts provides the audience with a narrative that effectually deconstructs the subject position Stanley inhabits—the ideologically-generated position of the "absolutely unique" self—revealing his confusion between the orders of linguistic and "natural" reality. As Althusser argues, ideology can only maintain its position as a form of cultural power by inducing such confusion, by foreclosing the epistemological operations through which we could distinguish the imaginary structure of "identity" from the reality of subjection. Lacking the capacity to make this distinction, the subject remains irremediably subject(ed), and never more so than when locating the source of its actions in an unique, autonomous, and foundational self.

While Stanley's narrative offers the audience a kind of X-ray vision through which emerges the shadowy lineaments of the subjection inhering in subjectivity, it also suggests a problematic aspect of the Althusserian paradigm I have invoked. For Althusser (and here he departs from Lacan), once the subject identifies (it)-self in an image, it achieves a coherence which, although traversed by alienation, keeps it firmly anchored within the imaginary order of (mis)recognition. For Lacan, on the other hand, the subject of the imaginary retains a measure of instability and discordance precisely because "the illusion of autonomy" can never completely erase its status as illusion. The subject's division is at its most apparent when the imaginary order of identification clashes with the symbolic order of language; that is, when the subject attempts to secure authenticity for its "identity" through an act of narrative self-definition. Rather than self-presence, however, the subject discovers the "frustration inherent in [its] very discourse. . . . For in this labor which he undertakes to . . . construct [a narrative] *for another,* he rediscovers the fundamental alienation . . . which has always destined it to be taken from him *by another.*[17]

Lacan's observation provides an apt description for what happens during the course of Stanley's narration. As I have argued, the narrative commences by demonstrating the imaginary status of the "absolutely unique" self to which Stanley lays claim. By the end of the narrative, Stanley encounters the kind of "frustration" to which Lacan points—the frustration of an inability to sustain those identifications through which subjectivity emerges. In his discussion of Stanley's account of the concerts, Steven Gale makes this point in terms that are particularly instructive. The narrative "seems to be just the opposite of the existential idea that 'man makes himself,' for Stanley is certainly *unmaking* himself as his story progresses."[18] As Gale emphasizes, it is not merely the story and its rhetoric of authenticity, but the very structure of Stanley's subjectivity that collapses.

This collapse, however, takes the form of a forced dispossession. As Lacan writes, we are "destined" to suffer the disintegration of our subjectivity through the very force that initially produces it. Because we construct the discourse in which our subjectivity comes to rest "for another," that discourse can be appropriated "by another." In other words, since it serves as the site from whence issue the codes, images, and language that constitute our "identity," the Other can recall those codes, forcing the subject to at least tacitly acknowledge that its idealized image of a self-determined being was merely a "construct in the imaginary."[19]

In *The Birthday Party,* this de-formation of subjectivity provides the occasion for its re-formation, as Stanley must submit to displacement from the (illusory) subject position of the unique self and re-placement within the circumscribed space of subjection. The de(con)struction of his "identity," commencing with the Other's dismantling of Stanley's narrative through the disruptive figure of the Father, enters a new phase during the interrogation conducted by Goldberg and McCann, the symbolic "fathers" who act as the Other's spokesmen. While the extent to which the Other controls the subject's discourse remains hidden from the speaker during the moment of articulation (which, as Lacan and Althusser emphasize, represents yet another example of ideology's ability to mystify its own operations), Goldberg establishes control over Stanley by unveiling this power; by ordering Stanley to answer the fundamental existential question, "Who do you think you are" (p. 58), in terms acceptable to the Other; by forcing Stanley to create himself *for* the Other and, therefore, *in the image of* the Other.

With each new question that Goldberg and McCann hurl at him, Stanley "become[s] engaged in an ever-growing dispossession of . . . being,"[20] as he finds himself incapable of producing a coherent discourse that could answer the kinds of contradictory accusations to which he must respond.

> *Goldberg.* Why did you kill your wife? . . . How did you kill her?
> *McCann.* You throttled her.
> *Goldberg.* With arsenic. . . . Why did you never get married? (p. 59)

Like the narrative of the concerts, the irresolvable contradictions introduced by Goldberg and McCann undermine the rhetoric of authenticity by leaving Stanley with neither the image of an unified self nor a stable position from which to speak. Bereft of his (illusory) sense of being, Stanley lapses into the silence of the *infans,* the child lacking the linguistic forms in which to express its subjectivity. When Goldberg and McCann reduce Stanley to this silence, they commit a form of murder:

> *Goldberg.* What makes you think you exist?
> *McCann.* You're dead.
> *Goldberg.* You're dead. You can't live . . . You're dead. You're a plague gone bad. There's no juice in you. You're nothing but an odour! (p. 62)

What gives Stanley the impression of existence is language. Language may be, as Pinter writes, "a highly ambiguous business,"[21] but it is the only medium for establishing subjectivity, even if we purchase that subjectivity at the cost of subjection. Without language, Stanley is "nothing but an odour," the fading trace of a voice disintegrating within a prison-house of silence.

Goldberg and McCann must imprison Stanley in this silence, removing him from the field of language, before they can "save" (p. 92) him by offering him a new subjectivity (and a new access to language)—one defined by the Other which Stanley must "recognize" (p. 60) and to which he must submit. The (re)construction of Stanley's "identity" begins during the interrogation. As Stanley proves increasingly unable to answer their questions, Goldberg and McCann begin to shift from question to assertion and declaration, generating an image that both offers him a subject position to fill and displays the power wielded by the Other in the formation of subjectivity. We see language structuring experience as the accusations begin to form the outline of the "character" Stanley will play at the party. The significance of these charges, however, does not lie in any truth value they may contain, but in the way they combine to form Stanley's new "identity" as criminal/sinner.

Accusations of crimes against women run through the charges like a leitmotif: "He's killed his wife! . . . You throttled her . . . You contaminate womankind . . . Mother defiler!" (pp. 59–61). At the party, Stanley displays his introjection of this image as he tries to throttle Meg and "contaminate" Lulu. Pinter's staging of this moment gives powerful dramatic expression to the play's vision of identity as a product of identification with the mirror:

McCann finds the torch on the floor, shines it on the table and Stanley.
Lulu is lying spread-eagled on the table, Stanley bent over her. Stan-
ley, as soon as the torchlight hits him, begins to giggle. Goldberg
and McCann move towards him. He backs, giggling, the torch on
his face. They follow him upstage, left. He backs against the hatch,
giggling. The torch draws closer. His giggle rises and grows as he
flattens himself against the wall. Their figures converge upon him.
(pp. 75–76)

At this climactic moment, Stanley has reached the final stage in
the "dispossession" of his being, the recognition of his misrecognition—his giggling dissolution into a kind of madness tacitly ac-
knowledging that his illusion of autonomy *is* only an illusion. This
"madness" objectifies the alienation resulting from the mirror-stage
identification that forms the "I."

Presiding over this enactment of an alienating identity, Goldberg
and McCann's shining flashlight, trapping Stanley in its field of
"vision," functions as a kind of inquisitorial gaze. The stage direc-
tions indicate that Stanley begins to giggle and fall into the condition Goldberg describes as a "nervous breakdown" (p. 81) *only*
when the light hits his face. The light/gaze has transformed itself
from the mirror reflecting an image for identification into the
Medusa-like gaze that "has the effect of arresting movement and
. . . of killing life."[22] Stanley becomes the puppet of the light, his
movements dictated by the advance of the beam that will not let
him escape. With this transformation from the human into a puppet
whose every action and gesture—indeed, whose very physicality—
are at the disposal of the Other, Stanley undergoes the final stage
in the dismantling of his "identity." As a puppet, he lacks the illusion of consciousness and autonomy, and even his body forsakes
him. At the party's conclusion, he has become the image of Goldberg's words: "You're dead. You can't live, you can't think, you
can't love. You're dead" (p. 62).

In the third act, we witness the beginning of Stanley's rebirth,
his assumption of an identity created by and *in the image of* the
omnipotent Other. Like Peter Handke's Kaspar, Stanley does not
so much assimilate language as he becomes assimilated and subjected to language and the types of values expressed in that language. Handke's comments about Kaspar's transformation from
inarticulate clown to model speaker apply equally as well to the
promised transformation Stanley will undergo at Monty's: "This
was a model of conduct, building a person into society's course of
conduct by language, by giving him words . . . he is reconstructed
by voices, by language models."[23] Although we never actually see

his accession to speech as we do Kaspar's, the promise that Stanley will "give orders . . . make decisions" (p. 94) indicates that he will be "reconstructed . . . by language models," and will in turn give birth to others through those same models.

Pinter dramatizes the process of "building a person into society's course of conduct by language" in Goldberg and McCann's third-act litany of salvation. They create a new image with which Stanley can identify, an identity demonstrating the role language plays in the social construction of desire:

> *Goldberg.* You'll be re-orientated.
> *McCann.* You'll be rich.
> *Goldberg.* You'll be adjusted.
> *McCann.* You'll be our pride and joy.
> *Goldberg.* You'll be a mensch.
> *McCann.* You'll be a success.
> *Goldberg.* You'll be integrated.
> *McCann.* You'll give orders.
> *Goldberg.* You'll make decisions.
> *McCann.* You'll be a magnate.
> *Goldberg.* A statesman.
> *McCann.* You'll own yachts.
> *Goldberg.* Animals. (pp. 93–94)

Pinter sees language producing consciousness, but he uses the rapid-fire verbal performance of Goldberg and McCann to suggest the fundamentally coercive nature of a language that constrains consciousness in the act of shaping it. The third-act litany parodies the socialization experienced in infancy. As the parents shape the child's consciousness through assimilation to a language that encodes and communicates a particular matrix of values, while disallowing others.

Bakhtin comments on the process of socialization:

> All that touches me comes to my consciousness . . . from the outside world, passing through the mouths of others, with . . . their values. . . . The very being of man (both internal and external) is a *profound communication.* . . . . To be means to be for the other, and through him. . . . Man has no internal sovereign territory . . . looking within himself, he looks *in the eyes of the other* or *through the eyes of the other.*[24]

Goldberg and McCann's imposition of their language (which is no more "their" language than it will be "his" language) on Stanley dramatizes that act of "profound communication" through which the cultural order seeks above all else to ensure the reproduction of those forms, values, and institutions it finds ideologically indispensible.

In the mirror of Goldberg and McCann's language, Stanley will see his subjectivity "through the eyes of the other," through the Other's codes and categories of evaluation. If, as Lacan writes, "man's desire is the desire of the Other,"[25] Goldberg and McCann use language to direct Stanley's desire towards what the Other posits as the object of desire. Anthony Wilden's discussion of the Lacanian conception of desire provides a valuable insight into how Goldberg and Mccann employ language to position Stanley in the field of the Other:

> The Other is not a person, but a principle; the locus of the "law of desire" . . . the only place from which it is possible to say "I am who I am." The paradox of identity and autonomy which this involves— identical to or identified with what?—puts us in the position of desiring what the Other desires: we desire what the Other desires we desire.[26]

As Goldberg, McCann, and Monty transform Stanley from inarticulate *infans* stage to speaking subject, his accession to language will entail accession to the Other's desire. After his treatment at Monty's, Stanley may speak again, may desire, may adopt particular values, but the language, desire, and values will never be his.

Once socialization has been completed, once he becomes subjected to the Other's desire, the Other will bestow infinite value upon Stanley. In return for the gift of "his" desire, Stanley will "be re-orientated . . . adjusted . . . integrated" into the symbolic order of culture, where, under the now-approving gaze of the Other, he will become "our pride and joy . . . a mensch . . . a success." The exchange of the Other's approbation for the subject's desire lies at the heart of the process of socialization through which the cultural order maintains and perpetuates its dominance. In effect, the process is not an exchange at all, but a manifestation of the Other's power to reduce difference to identity, the heterogeneous to the homogeneous, the dialogic to the monologic. By revealing the essentially coercive nature of the social construction of desire, Pinter demystifies socialization and the ideological apparatus primarily responsible for carrying out socialization—the family. If Goldberg and McCann sound like parodic fathers when they promise Stanley that he will be "our pride and joy . . . a mensch . . . a success," Pinter can employ the comic effect of the lines to reveal the effects of the socialization carried out within the family. Pinter emphasizes the status of the family as an institutional support of the cultural order and not an autonomous private realm by underscoring the similarity of Goldberg as "father" and Meg as "mother." The linguistic construction of Stanley's "self" in the third act echoes a moment from early in the play:

> *Stanley.* What about some tea?
> *Meg.* Do you want some tea? *(Stanley reads the paper.)* Say please.
> *Stanley.* Please.
> *Meg.* Say sorry first.
> *Stanley.* Sorry first.
> *Meg.* No. Just sorry.
> *Stanley.* Just sorry! (pp. 27–28)

Despite the comic effect produced by watching an "old washing bag" (p. 28) treat a man in his late thirties as if he were a child, this exchange enacts the same kind of linguistic alienation we see when Goldberg and McCann forecast the progress of Stanley's reconstruction. Like Goldberg, Meg structures and effectually creates Stanley's desire by channeling it through the language model she imposes. As long as he claims desire as inalienably *his*, articulating it through his own mode of speech ("What about some tea?"), Meg withholds recognition. Only when Stanley has been successfully assimilated to the other's language will his desire receive "official" sanction. Whether the object of desire is a cup of tea or a social identity is irrelevant. Indeed, placed in the context of the play as a whole, Meg's treatment of Stanley is neither as innocuous nor as ideologically neutral as it may appear. We are dealing with more than the question of similarity between Meg and Goldberg. The kind of socialization we see enacted in the exchange about the tea authorizes and is itself an integral part of the more overtly pernicious form of socialization and cultural programming carried out by Goldberg and McCann. What is really at issue is the inscription of a power relation in which Stanley is the linguistic subject *of,* hence subjected *to,* the Other's master language and overmastering desire.

If Stanley's de- and re-construction dramatize the relationship between subjectivity and subjection, what are we to make of Goldberg? While Stanley's "self" emerges as an effect of cultural power—a totalizing power inscribing itself within his subjectivity but over which he can exercise no control—Goldberg appears to "own" power, to possess his language rather than it possessing him.

Paradoxically, our sense of both Goldberg's power *and* Stanley's powerlessness stems from the same source: the subject's disappearance and discontinuity within its speech. While the interrogation ruthlessly annihilates the presumed unity of the speaking subject by forcing Stanley to produce his "I" as a contradictory and discordant being, Goldberg appears to embrace such discordance and dispersal across a range of discursive registers. Where, for example, can we locate a core of being that embraces the different "I"s that emerge in the following passages:

> The main issue is a singular issue and quite distinct from your previous work. Certain elements, however, might well approximate in points of procedure to some of your other activities. All is dependent on the attitude of our subject. . . . I can assure you that the assignment will be carried out and the mission accomplished with no excessive aggravation to you or myself. (p. 40)

> I had a wife. What a wife. . . . "Simey," my wife used to shout, "quick, before it gets cold!" And there on the table what would I see? The nicest piece of rollmop and pickled cucumber you could wish to find on a plate. (p. 69)

Goldberg's power depends to a great extent on the irreconcilability of the discursive territories in which his "I" emerges. The noncoincidence between the "I" of the two passages—the former "spoken" through the linguistic code of the bureaucrat, the latter "spoken" through the code of the Jewish paterfamilias—denies us access to Goldberg by denying Goldberg's status as an unified subject to which we *can* gain access. We never know who Goldberg is; we only know that he is *not* in his utterance. The phrase recurring like a leitmotif through his speeches, "Don't talk to me about . . . ," by refusing to allow us to seize him through his voice, removes him from his language, locating him in the silence that always attaches itself to vocalization, the silence that Pinter says we hear "when perhaps a torrent of language is being employed."[27] The monologic denial of any other utterance, as much implicit in the opacity of Goldberg's discourse as it is in his command, "Don't talk to me," denies rather than affirms presence, producing power in the silence sustained in his speech.

The mastery of discourse Goldberg displays, however, bears its equivocations. Goldberg's absence from his speech produces a kind of power, but power for whom? If Goldberg does not inhabit his voice, who (or what) does? If there is always an Other in the voice when speech occurs, if otherness is the fundamental condition of utterance, then Goldberg, no less than Stanley, remains subjected to language. The language models used to build Stanley into society's course of conduct have also placed Goldberg "in the position of desiring what the Other desires."

Given the play's vision of an "interiority" in which the Other linguistically inscribes itself, we can say that Goldberg's speeches do paradoxically constitute a "transparent" medium through which we can fix him, not as an unified self but as the Other's spokesman, shaped by the very cultural codes that he disseminates. This Other(ness) articulates itself most forcefully in the torrent of cliches and platitudes behind which "Goldberg" recedes:

> The secret is breathing. Take my tip. It's a well-known fact. Breathe in, breathe out, take a chance, let yourself go, what can you lose? . . . What's happened to the love, the bonhomie, the unashamed expression of affection of the day before yesterday . . . I believe in a good laugh, a day's fishing, a bid of gardening. . . . All my life I've said the same. Play up, play up, and play the game. Honour thy father and thy mother. All along the line. Follow the line, the line, McCann, and you can't go wrong. (pp. 37, 66, 87)

In Goldberg's speech, we confront the impossibility of appropriating language and making it one's own. An extreme form of language as always already spoken, the cliche severs self and voice, effacing the self *in* the voice. The figure we identify as Goldberg mouths the words, but the voice belongs to the Other. The cliche denies difference, merging all separate voices into an univocality that dissolves the limits of the self. It exemplifies the kind of linguistic strategy through which the Other pursues its imperative to suppress all potential social conflict by reducing heterogeneity to an undifferentiated totality.

The maxims and cliches that run throughout Goldberg's speeches provide the play's most conspicuous manifestations of cultural coding. He utters the proverbial formulas "by which the discourse states a general will, the law of a society, making the proposition concerned ineluctable or indelible."[28] If Goldberg acts as the agent of this law, however, he also remains subject to its strictures. "All my life I've said the same"—through *saying* the same, Goldberg has *become* the same, which, in *The Birthday Party*, means becoming the Other and losing the self. Goldberg's words are double-edged: his utterance signals an arrival on the scene of power, while unmooring him, turning against him the voice that speaks power.

The various stories Goldberg relates foreground the alienation of "his" voice. The narrative voice itself has bifurcated, split between the Other's voice transmitting the maxims of the master cultural codes and an identifiably ethnic voice that, while situating Goldberg on the periphery of the cultural order, appears to grant him an identity that is "his" rather than a product of the Other's desire and language. These narratives emphasize Goldberg's Judaism in their content (specifically Jewish family life, *e.g.*, excursions with Uncle Barney "after lunch on Shabbuss" [p. 37]), diction ("Mazoltov! And may we only meet at Simchahs!" [p. 66]), and mimetic reproduction of the speech rhythm and intonation associated with a "Jewish" accent ("Culture? Don't talk to me about culture. He was an all-round man, what do you mean?" [p. 38]).

Goldberg initially seems to succeed in finding a voice that places him beyond reach of the Other's compulsion to integrate all its subjects. His distinctively Jewish voice is a voice of cultural difference that, by virtue of that difference, should find itself necessarily opposed to the voice of centrality, the voice articulated through the hegemonic cultural codes. Rather than asserting itself against these codes, however, the voice proclaiming Goldberg's identity as a Jew becomes an extension of them. As "the only place from which it is possible to say 'I am who I am,'" the Other allows Goldberg to identify himself as a Jew by producing Judaism in its own linguistic image. The Other accommodates Judaism within the cultural network, eliding the contradictions between speaking as a Jew and speaking from the locus of society's law.

Goldberg's narratives function in a manner similar to his cliches: two disparate voices—the voices of centrality and marginality—merge in a monolithic form of utterance that neutralizes Judaism as a form of difference:

> When I was an apprentice yet, McCann, every second Friday of the month my Uncle Barney used to take me to the seaside, regular as clockwork. . . . After lunch on Shabbuss we'd go and sit in a couple of deck chairs. . . . Uncle Barney. . . . Respected by the whole community. Culture? Don't talk to me about culture. He was an all-round man, what do you mean? He was a cosmopolitan. (pp. 37–38)

The reference to "Shabbuss" promises a narrative that will allow an audience to fix Goldberg, at least in terms of ethnicity, but the "ritual" visits to the seaside bear no connection to the religious rituals that characterize observance of the Jewish Sabbath. The narrative similarly divorces Uncle Barney from any recognizably Jewish characteristics. As "an all-round man . . . a cosmopolitan," he is a man of "culture"—not only cultured but, like Goldberg and (after his "treatment" with Monty) Stanley, Cultured, speaking what the Other speaks, desiring what the Other desires.

Goldberg's narratives do not so much negate Judaism as redefine and transform it into a vehicle for eliciting desire of the Other. In the terms of the play, Uncle Barney is never more "Jewish" than in his cosmopolitanism, his lack of either an individually or an ethnically "absolutely unique" self. Baker and Tabachnick assert that "Uncle Barney reflects . . . [the] conflict between assimilation and assertion of . . . Jewishness,"[29] but the narratives *ideologize* Jewishness, veiling the conflict between assimilation and Jewish identity, defining Jewishness as a *form* of assimilation. To be a Jew in *The Birthday Party* means being "re-orientated . . . adjusted . . . integrated"; to speak as a Jew means speaking the maxims and proverbials tatements, the "fragments of ideology,"[30] that constitute the Other's discursive field:

> Honour they father and mother. All along the line. Follow the line, the line, McCann, and you can't go wrong. What do you think, I'm a self-made man? No! I sat where I was told to sit. I kept my eye on the ball. School? Don't talk to me about school. Top in all subjects. And for why? Because I'm telling you, I'm telling you, follow my line? Follow my mental? Learn by heart. Never write down a thing. And don't go too near the water. (p. 87)

Who is speaking here? "Honour thy father and mother" suggests that Goldberg speaks to aaffirm his Jewishness, but, since the speech equates this sacred text with such cliches as "keep your eye on the ball" and "don't go near the water," the "Jewish voice" dissolves into the Other's monologic Voice. He counsels McCann to "follow *my* line," but the "line"—the tag phrases encoding the law of society—is *his* only to the extent that "his" voice is ex-centric. In the play's dramatic world, Goldberg is not "a self-made man," but a creation of the texts that he has "learn[ed] by heart."

Goldberg is the figure in the play that we tend to think of most in terms of voice, yet his absence from that voice leaves obscure who he is and where he is in his discourse. If this absence initially seems to define the nature of Goldberg's power, by the end of the play it marks his subjection to that power. His mastery of a wide discursive range has less to do with the suppression of his own narrative—a narrative that would allow us to retrieve him from his disappearance in the Other's voice—than with the impossibility of any such narrative, the impossibility of articulating an "I" outside the range of the Other's discourse. Pinter dramatizes the absence of a self-determined identity (both linguistic and ontological) as we watch Goldberg's one attempt to fashion an autonomous "I" fade into the silence of depletion: "You'll find—that what I say is true. Because I believe that the world . . . *(Vacant.).* . . . Because I believe that the world . . . *(Desperate.).* . . . . BECAUSE I BELIEVE THAT THE WORLD . . . *(Lost.)*" (p. 88).

Goldberg suffers from the same ontological laryngitis afflicting Stanley, the laryngitis defining the fundamental condition of the speaking subject. Lacking a voice to act as the source of self-present speech, Goldberg and Stanley can never cast themselves as the unitary origin of their narratives. Neither can they escape bearing the traces of the Other's power speaking in and through them. I have referred to Goldberg as the Other's spokesman, but it would be more precise to say that he and Stanley function as what Derrida calls "mouthpieces". "Like the alphabetic signifier, like the letter, the [mouthpiece] himself is not inspired or animated by any particular language. He signifies nothing. He hardly lives, he lends his voice. It is a mouthpiece."[31] As "mouthpieces," Goldberg and Stanley do not merely filter other words through their own voices; rather, the voices become Other in the act of utterance. Stanley exits the play in silence, led off to Monty for the treatment that will grant him a voice (although not *his* voice). Similarly, Goldberg exits the play having regained speech, but only after receiving a "blow in [his] mouth" (p. 89)—after the empty space of the mouth has been filled by the Other's voice. These exits into an area beyond the stage to which we are denied access reproduce visually what has occurred orally—a disappearance so complete as to exceed the power of recall.

It may appear that my aligning Stanley and Goldberg in this manner ignores the power Goldberg exercises over him at the end of the play. I would not deny that this power exists, but, as I have argued, when Goldberg moves his lips, the Other speaks: the barrage of words hurled against Stanley, words that reduce him to silence, come from Goldberg, but only in his capacity as "mouthpiece" for the Other. As Wilden observes, "The Other is not a person, but a principle"—Goldberg serves but is not identical to the Other. If we wish to assign the Other a name, we can call it "Monty"—palpably absent yet always present; situated in no one location yet enclosing the play's dramatic universe; standing behind yet speaking through the figures on the stage; an inescapably pervasive form of power inscribed within each subjectivity as its information structure.

In *The Birthday Party,* then, power is always power of and for the Other (a point whose implications I will address in the conclusion to this study). To speak from the field of the Other, as Goldberg does, is also to be subject to an "external force" that is no longer only external. For Pinter, power is not a matter of having a voice but of voicing, becoming a conduit and "mouthpiece," an equivocal position that allows entrance into the field of power at the cost of suppression and effacement. Commenting on the importance of this sacrifice for establishing a cultural "order-principle," J. F. MacCannell writes, "Anything can look like a benefit from the point of view of the totality. . . . The surplus value gained by culture is experienced solely as loss for the self."[32] Goldberg promises Stanley the power to "give orders . . . make decisions . . . be a magnate. A statesman," but the orders and decisions will issue from the Other's voice, phrased in the Other's language, encoding the Other's desire. "From the point of view of the totality," this dissemination of power to one who speaks from within the field of that power, confirming Stanley's subjection to the "order-principle," can only "look like a benefit." Similarly, granting Goldberg a "Jewishness" in which difference slides into sameness—giving him the verbal codes that define him as a Jew in his culture's discursive universe—also promotes the "order-principle":

> *McCann.* You've always been a true Christian.
> *Goldberg.* In a way. (p. 39)

To be a Jew is to be "a true Christian"—Goldberg rejects any sense of contradiction between speaking as a Jew and speaking as "a true Christian", between the Other as the source of identity and the difference that marginalizes him:

> *McCann.* Simey!
> *Goldberg (opening his eyes, regarding McCann).* What—did—you— call—me?
> *McCann.* Who?
> *Goldberg (murderously).* Don't call me that! *(He seizes McCann by the throat.)* NEVER CALL ME THAT! (p. 86)

Goldberg's violent rejection of his name—the signifier of an ethnic difference that threatens to sever his ties to the Other—betrays a fear that he can never locate himself within "the totality" from which recognition issues. As "a true Christian"—but only "in a way"—Goldberg faces the threat that he may be excluded from the codes through which "the subject is constituted, which means that it is from the Other that the subject receives even the message he emits."[33] Only through the agency of the message can Goldberg and Stanley "say 'I am who I am.'" In saying "I," however, they name themselves as creatures of the Other, spoken rather than speaking, voicing but voiceless.

Despite his subjection to the Other, Goldberg (mis)recognizes the source of linguistic authority, locating it in the speaker rather than the speech, basing his refusal of dialogue on an appeal to absolute enunciative authority: *"Don't talk to me about school. . . . And for why? Because I'm telling you, I'm telling you, follow my line?"* Goldberg's claim introduces a paradox: if language confers authority only on those who have the authority to use such language, then some form of power must ultimately reside outside and function as a precondition of semantic authority. Goldberg speaks from an extra-linguistic site of power conferring authority on his speech, although we cannot assign either the authority or the speech to him in any ultimate sense. At issue here is the question of where the play locates authority: does the Other's discursive field—the field from which Goldberg speaks— draw potency from its ability to encode "the law of a society," or does that "law" depend on an extra-discursive force for recognition of its status as law?

To answer this question, we must not only consider Goldberg's "position" (p. 41) as Monty's emissary, the Other's "mouthpiece," but also how McCann's presence reinforces this "position." Goldberg himself raises the issue of his need for McCann: "You know what I said when this job came up. I mean naturally they approached me to take care of it. And you know who I asked for? . . . You. . . . You're a capable man, McCann" (p. 39). Initially, McCann seems little more than Goldberg's double. Like Goldberg's Judaism, his Irish Catholicism, rather than signifying cultural difference, proclaims itself as an extension of the Other's code, values, and law. The Other allows McCann to speak as an Irishman (as it allows Goldberg to speak as a Jew) as long as it can produce Irish Catholicism in its own image and veil the contradictions between speaking from a site of difference and speaking from a site of cultural centrality, the locus of the law.

If McCann were only another version of Goldberg, we would still have to ask why Goldberg needs him and what this need reveals about where the play situates power. Pinter provides an answer to this question at the beginning of Act Two, the first time the audience encounters McCann without Goldberg: *"(McCann is sitting at the table tearing a sheet of newspaper into five equal strips)"* (p. 47). The image figures both the psychic "carving-up" Stanley will receive at the hands of Goldberg and McCann and the manner in which this attack will take as its immediate object Stanley's language, with its pretension to self-authenticating transparency.

Perhaps the most significant aspect of this image, however, lies in its suggestion of McCann's potential for violence—not the kind of metaphorical linguistic violence we frequently encounter in Pinter (*e.g.*, during Stanley's interrogation), but the physical violence that supports and in a sense authorizes Goldberg's verbal assault. This potential becomes transformed into actuality during the party when McCann breaks the blindfolded Stanley's glasses and causes him to fall over the drum. While such acts may appear insignificant when compared to the offstage torture and rape in *One for the Road*, they nevertheless emphasize the relationship between the more ideological form of linguistic domination practiced by (and against) Goldberg and the more tangible physical brutality reinforcing if not actually creating the power of the discursive field from which Goldberg speaks. Just as Goldberg cannot commence the interrogation until McCann successfully threatens Stanley into sitting down, so in Pinter's dramatic universe the cultural codes constituting subjectivity draw potency from the violence that produces the body as subject to "external force." The menace of disappearance threatens the body as well as the "self," and places Stanley entirely at the Other's disposal. The violence McCann directs against Stanley provides the ultimate proof of our vulnerability as embodied creatures, of the body's capacity to forsake us when confronted with pain and punishment. Physical and linguistic violence combine, transforming Stanley into a victim of ontological and corporal disjuncture, revealing the implications of Goldberg's promise to "bring [Stanley] out of himself" (p. 43).

That "Monty" must employ a McCann as well as a Goldberg does not invalidate the power the text ascribes to the "fragments of ideology" mouthed by Goldberg. Rather, the Goldberg–McCann relationship allows Pinter to explore the coercive pressure that, no matter how veiled, always accompanies and supports the process of socialization constituting subjectivity. If violence and the threat of violence demarcate the discursive field from which the Other exercises its enunciative authority, it is also true that the discursive field sets the limit of violence. Violence empowers the Other's Word, as the implied threat of McCann's looming presence forces Stanley to submit to the interrogation. Violence creates discontinuity between "self" and body, transforming the body into a text that displays the visible signs of the Other's power. Violence cannot, however, perform the task Peter Handke refers to as "building a person into society's course of conduct." The power to constitute the subject as a receptable for the Other's desire and "a mouth-piece" for the Other's word belongs, as Handke asserts, to the "voices" and "language models" that engage in their own form of violence. McCann's violence enables Goldberg's linguistic violence, but the play never suggests the interchangeability of these two forms of violence. The power to integrate Stanley and Gold-berg into the cultural order—the form of power on which the play chiefly focuses—inheres, finally, in the codes and messages that confer "identity" by interpellating them within the Other's ideo-logical field.

What emerges most palpably from *The Birthday Party's* explora-tion of how the Other constructs subjectivity is a sense of the totalizing and monolithically unassailable nature of cultural power. There is never any question of the Other's capacity to foreclose the possibility of resistance, to manage all social conflict out of existence before it even has a chance to emerge. Like Marcuse, Pinter conceptualizes the cultural order as a seamless and self-regulating system, totalitarian as well as totalizing in its ability to embrace and structure every aspect of human experience.

I mention Marcuse to indicate a certain Frankfurt School ele-ment in Pinter's vision of cultural power. When Stanley makes his final appearance as the "one-dimensional man," dressed in dark suit and bowler hat (the uniform of the conservative English busi-nessman), and receives assurances that he will become "rich . . . a success . . . a magnate"; when Goldberg mouths the codes of social homogeneity or speaks with the voice of the impersonal bureaucrat, we can see that the specific object of Pinter's focus is not simply the process of integration, but integration within the reified, bureaucratized order of advanced capitalism. In this con-text, the play becomes dramatic *Ideologiekritik,* whose unmasking of the rhetoric of authenticity and the autonomous self, and identi-fication of the identity principle (the principle demanding that dif-ference yield to an inexorable logic of the same) through which the Other perpetuates and reproduces its power, aligns it with the cultural criticism produced by the Frankfurt School. Like Marcuse and a certain defeatist strain in Adorno, Pinter sees the entrench-ment of the capitalist order as a kind of cultural fascism, an exten-sion of the ideological universe of totalitarianism. While this vision receives compelling dramatization, the play (again, like Marcuse as well as Althusser) tends to collapse the distinction between Western capitalism's totalizing ideological project and its real ideological conditions.

To clarify this last point, we must remember that ideology never openly declares its totalizing impulse; that even as the cultural order may work to impose the identity principle, Western (or, more to the point in Pinter's case, English) capitalism often has recourse to a liberal humanist ideology that at least pretends to validate difference. By foregrounding the "reality" underlying such ideological rhetoric, Pinter reminds us just how spurious such rhetoric is. At the same time, however, by putting this kind of rhetoric into discursive play, capitalist culture places itself at a certain risk. The language of difference can become the site of hegemonic struggle, lending itself to appropriation as a kind of critical yardstick with which to measure the extent to which the cultural order fails to organize its practices in terms of the ideological concepts it invokes.

For example, when McCann calls Goldberg "a true Christian," the very unproductive irony of the latter's response ("in a way") signals the impossibility of salvaging a notion of difference *as* difference in Pinter's world. I am not claiming that there exists some ahistorical essence of Judaism, a self-present Jewish identity that Goldberg can invoke. What is at issue here is the ability to appropriate "Jewishness" as an object of self-representation, articulated through codes that construct difference as a category of experience in opposition to the Other's codes of social conformity. If such an option never presents itself as a possibility in *The Birthday Party*, if the ideological rhetoric of difference never puts in a discursive appearance that could allow for its appropriation, we can ascribe this absence to the play's foregrounding of the "real" operations of cultural power that ideology obscures. Such a strategy, however, risks reifying the very form of power that the play puts on display and anatomizes. While there is no question of Pinter endorsing the kind of power he dramatizes, there is a sense in which the play "validates" it by taking it at its own estimation, by showing the infinite recuperability of a cultural order in which resistance and oppositional practices never fail because they never arise.

I will return to this issue in my concluding chapter. For now, I simply want to point out that the absence of resistance is as much a product of the play as of the cultural power the play examines, which leaves *The Birthday Party* precariously balanced between unmasking and reifying the operations of power. As an audience in the 1990s, we can attribute our sensitivity to such an absence, at least in part, to the emergence throughout the last thirty years of the various social and theoretical movements that have placed questions of difference and oppositional practices squarely on the political agenda. Perhaps no movement—or ensemble of movements—has raised these questions with more urgency than the various feminisms, and it may not be entirely fortuitous that those plays in which Pinter engages with issues of feminist concern are also the plays that take up the issue of resistance.

Plays like *The Collection, The Homecoming,* and *Old Times* (the subjects of the following chapters) examine how patriarchal culture attempts to secure a stable ideological identification of masculinity with power and femininity with powerlessness. Unlike *The Birthday Party,* however, these plays reveal a potentially disabling contradiction within the ideological field—a contradiction located in the figure of the woman who is simultaneously constructed as both docile body and site of potentially threatening difference. The possibility of resistance situates itself precisely in the gap that such a contradiction insinuates within the dominant ideology. At the same time, however, the plays raise the troubling question as to whether or not what announces itself as resistance is the product of a (mis)-recognition that only reinforces ideological power. This is the question that will inform my discussion of the following three plays.

3

"It's Part of Their Nature": Woman's Truth in *The Collection*

I concluded the preceding chapter by suggesting that the contradiction I will examine between woman as docile body and woman as site of threatening difference is located in the figure of the woman herself. It would be more precise, however, to see this contradiction as residing within the ideological field, within the mutually exclusive subject positions that women are "allowed" to inhabit within patriarchal culture. In terms of *The Collection*, we can identify these positions as "wife" and "whore." On the one hand, patriarchy demands that women recognize masculine authority by becoming wives so that they may become mothers, reproducing the dominant culture both physically and ideologically, transmitting the socially legitimated desires and values that will transform their children into appropriate social subjects. On the other hand, patriarchal ideology insistently constructs women as whores, sexually transgressive beings who refuse either to acknowledge the imperatives of masculine desire or recognize the "natural" legitimacy of masculine power. Patriarchal culture needs to maintain a sharp distinction between these categories, for the wife's slide into a whore would undermine the status of the family as a site for the reproduction of both the dominant ideology and the dominant economy of power relations. My discussion of *The Collection* will focus on how the play dramatizes the inherent instability of a patriarchal order unable to maintain the opposition between wife and whore. I will argue that the collapse of wife and whore into each other not only threatens the ideological role of the family, but also threatens to confront patriarchy with the fundamentally *homosexual* desire that it must never acknowledge as constitutive of its social reality. Finally, I will argue that the particular cultural instability the play dramatizes creates the opportunity for the kind of resistance to ideological pressure that Luce Irigaray terms "mimicry."

The Collection is essentially a mystery—less a whodunit than a did-she-do-it—concerning James's attempts to discover if his wife, Stella, had an adulterous liaison with Bill. Like all mysteries, the play involves a quest for truth, a quest to discover Stella's "truth"—not her personal, existential truth, but the truth that proclaims her identity as Woman. Bill's assertion that "every woman is bound to have an outburst of . . . wild sensuality at one time or another. . . . It's part of their nature,"[1] suggests the specific "truth" at issue in the play. As a mouthpiece for the patriarchal Other, Bill sees Stella's "truth" inscribed in her "nature"—*i.e.*, in the essence determining female desire, female identity, female sexuality, the essence that all women reflect and from whence all women emanate. To figure Woman in this manner, however, is itself an act of representation. Bill's comment thus participates in a specific discursive project—the cultural construction of female sexuality.

To regard Bill's comment as both a "reading" of Stella and an act of representation is to say that it posits a truth and is "about" how truth is posited. Bill explains Stella's threatening excess sexuality—her "outburst of . . . wild sensuality"—by appealing to the "truth" of woman's essence: "It's part of their nature." At the same time, if we accept this definition of female nature, then Bill's statement itself becomes an index of truth, and representation becomes (mis)recognized as reality. In other words, as an interpretation of Stella, Bill's reading posits a truth that, whether susceptible to capture or forever elusive, exists autonomously, independently of his utterance. As a discursive construction of femininity, however, the utterance's representational "truth" lies in the speaker's ability both to suppress the epistemological gap separating representation from the real and to promote the illusion that Truth is a metaphysically absolute category divorced from discursive practice. Such representational "truth" is less a statement of truth than an exercise of power: the ideological power to assimilate reality to representation; to make the subject participate in its discursive capture and containment by (mis)recognizing its position within the cultural order as natural rather than inscribed within a structure of representation; to construct an image of the "truth" with which the subject must identify.

While Bill's interpretation/construction of the "truth" of female sexuality voices ideological power, the play asks if patriarchy can

ultimately accommodate such power. To represent women as naturally sexually transgressive is to say that they can never assume
their "proper" role as the figures who guarantee both the physical
and ideological reproduction of patriarchal culture. Given this
problem, we might assume that James would attempt to prove
Stella's innocence. Yet such is not the case; the play reveals his
most obsessive need to verify Stella's guilt, to see her embodying
the "truth" of female sexuality. This need may seem understand-
able when we recall that, according to James, Stella admits to having an affair (an admission that Pinter refuses to dramatize).
Matters become more complicated, however, when Stella declares
both that she never slept with Bill and, even more importantly,
that she never *confessed* to sleeping with Bill. According to Stella,
James "dreamed up such a fantastic story, for no reason at all"
(p. 148).

If James has "dreamed up" Stella's confession, the obvious question is, why should he want to cast his wife in the role of "whore"?
To pose the question in this way assumed a rigidly fixed opposition
between "wife" and "whore" at the level of the signified as well as
at the level of the signifier. As Saussure observes, meaning can
only emerge through the play of these differences within a closed
sign-system: "In language, as in any semiological system, whatever
distinguishes one sign from the other constitutes it. Difference
makes character just as it makes value and the unity in it."[2] In
Saussurean terms, the sign "wife" derives its value and significance
from whatever distinguishes it from and opposes it to the sign
"whore." Because, as Stephen Heath writes, the wife in patriarchal
culture must recognize her role as "reproductive agent and identity
of the husband whose legal and symbolic authority she must confirm,"[3] promulgating the wife/whore opposition assumes a central
importance for patriarchy's ideological project. If the woman
evinces a desire exceeding the bounds of matrimony, if she trans-
gresses the significative boundaries separating "wife" from
"whore," the resulting confusion of categories confronts patriarchy
with the threat of its own undoing.

James appeals to the "absolute" distinction of linguistic and conceptual space differentiating wife from whore when he reports
Stella's confession to Bill: "When you treat my wife like a whore,
then I think I'm entitled to know what you've got to say about it"
(p. 131). The distinction, however, begins to dissolve even as James
sets it in place. The dangerous proximity of "wife" and "whore"
in his comment invites comparison as much as it does contrast,
and the simile linking the two words suggests that if a wife can be

treated "like a whore," then she *is* like a whore; that "wife" and "whore" are linked by shared identity rather than separated by difference.

The indistinction of place represented by the sliding between the categories "wife" and "whore" points to a fundamental ideological contradiction at the heart of patriarchy. The same culture that defines the wife as guaranteeing the hegemony of masculine power also constructs feminine desire in terms of excess, the "outburst of . . . wild sensuality" into which women always threaten to erupt. Of central importance to the reproduction, both physical and ideological, of patriarchal culture, the family (and, specifically, the identity of the husband) is always subject to the threat of division and fragmentation posed by the wife's sexuality—a sexuality that transforms wife into whore and adulteress simply by virtue of being a wife.

In a passage worth noting, Stephen Heath discusses the collapse of difference adultery precipitates:

> Adultery . . . turns essentially on confusion, confusion around the figure of the woman. . . . Adultery, in fact, is . . . the slide from identity to indifference. . . . What guarantees identity is the woman who is then equally the weak point in its system: if she gives, everything gives; moving from *her* right place, the adulterous woman leaves no place intact. . . . As mother the woman is sure, as wife always potentially unsure.[4]

"The slide from identity to indifference"—adultery undermines both the closed system of marriage, in which identity finds its guarantee in the woman's assumption of "her right place," and the closed system of language that defines that place. If the wife is "always potentially unsure," then what does it mean to declare that the signification of "wife" derives from its opposition to the signification of "whore"? If "the adulterous woman leaves no place intact," then what does it mean to assert that the signification of "husband" derives from its opposition to (while finding its support in) the signification of "wife"?

The collapse of linguistic difference places in doubt the knowledge and "truth" predicated on that difference. Bill's question to James, "Do you know her [Stella] well" (p. 136), echoed later by Harry's observation, "Women are very strange. But I suppose you know more about that than I do; she's your wife" (p. 154), foregrounds the disruption of knowledge—both carnal and epistemological—adultery effects. Knowledge of one's wife arises from accepting the cluster of terms, definitions, and ideological codes that constitute the sign "wife." This kind of knowledge bases itself on a fundamental (mis)recognition, since it conceives of a natural bond linking signifier and signified. Adultery, however, reveals the conventions governing both the relationship between signifier and signified and the play of linguistic differences in which meaning inheres. Adultery illustrates Saussure's dictum, *"The linguistic sign if arbitrary."*[5] If "wife" can become "whore," then there is no reason to assume any natural or necessary relationship between "wife" as a signifier and the ensemble of values that patriarchal ideology assigns "wife" as a signified.

I offer these remarks on adultery in an attempt to suggest an answer to the question I posed some pages back: If James "dreamed up" Stella's confession, why should he want to cast his wife in the role of "whore"? In one sense, the question is irrelevant. Whether or not Stella confessed and whether or not she had an affair with Bill ultimately are of no consequence since, as a wife, she is "always potentially unsure," susceptible of being treated and becoming "like a whore." As Heath's comments suggest, the wife is always already an adulteress by virtue of being a wife.

In another, albeit paradoxical, sense, James *needs* Stella's guilt; needs to actualize her potential for adultery in order to reinsert her into the patriarchal family plot; needs to re-position her as the wife who guarantees her husband's identity. James must both acknowledge the radical indeterminacy that defines the woman's status as wife and recuperate that status, cleansing it in order for Stella to confirm his "symbolic authority": the self he erects on his identity as husband. Ascribing guilt to Stella becomes the necessary first stage in the process of purification to which James attempts to submit her—a process purging her of her excess sexuality in order to be rendered fit for her place in the patriarchal order. This process consists of Stella's progress from crime to punishment to rehabilitation. Beginning the play marked as a "whore," Stella must (mis)recognize the "truth" of her unlawful desire, a "truth" reflected in the ideological mirror of the Other's cultural codes, a "truth" she must repent before being returned to "her right place" as guarantor of patriarchal stability.

This attempt to "save" both Stella and the patriarchal order, however, falls prey to what I have previously referred to as an inherent contradiction in patriarchy itself. As I have argued, patriarchal culture depends for its perpetuation on the woman's assumption of her role as wife, "reproductive agent and identity of the husband." At the same time, a kind of masculine anxiety in the face of feminine desire promotes the construction of women's sexuality in terms of a natural "wild sensuality." With an unconscious irony that undercuts his own need to ascribe guilt to Stella, James reveals the extent to which this essentialist view of feminine sexuality is a discursive creation when, after recounting Bill's version of the events at Leeds to Stella, he remarks, "Typical masculine thing to say, of course. . . . You know what men are" (p. 143).

A cultural fiction (mis)recognized as Truth, the conception of feminine sexuality as naturally transgressive, hence absolutely irrecuperable, provides the structuring contradiction undermining James's attempt to secure patriarchy by domesticating Stella. The play registers this sense of contradiction through an insistence on linking Stella with sexual betrayal even when seeking to proclaim her innocence. Looking beneath the surface contrasts of the play's multiple realities, the various versions of what occurred at Leeds, we discover that all the accounts (with the exception of Stella's claim that James "dreamed up" her confession) represent Stella as an adulteress in thought or word if not in deed.

> *Bill.* You should have her seen to. . . . I'm dreadfully sorry, really, I mean, I've no idea why she should make up all that. Pure fantasy. Really rather naughty of her. Rather alarming. (pp. 131, 136)

> *Harry.* What she confessed was . . . that she'd made the whole thing up. She'd made the whole damn thing up. For some odd reason of her own. They never met, you see, Bill and your wife; they never even spoke. . . . Women are very strange. But I suppose you know more about that than I do; she's your wife. (p. 154)

> *James.* You didn't do anything, did you? *(Pause.)* He wasn't in your room. You just talked about it, in the lounge *(Pause.)* That's the truth, isn't it? *(Pause.)* You just sat and talked about what you would do if you went to your room. That's what you did. (p. 157)

The wife who indulges in a "pure fantasy" of adultery is as "alarming," as much in need of being "seen to," and as much a threat to the stability of patriarchal culture as the wife who has committed adultery. With these considerations in mind, the final passage quoted above takes on an ambiguous shading. On the one hand, for Stella to confess her innocence would secure the husband's identity. On the other hand, if Stella admits that she and Bill "talked abut it," she would declare her inevitable transgression of the boundaries within which patriarchal culture seeks to ensconce her. In this final encounter between James and Stella, containment faces the shadow of subversion. If she has committed a kind of verbal adultery once, she may do so again—"always potentially unsure," the wife continues to resist (en)closure, her entombment within patriarchy's family plot.

I now want to consider at some length one particular moment in the play that crystallizes the various issues I have discussed— the ideological construction of a naturally lawless female sexuality; the unstable opposition between "wife" and "whore"; the obsessive need to see Stella as in some sense guilty. The verbal insistence on her guilt finds its support in ocular proof—her positioning within the play's visual field in relation to the audience's gaze. Is the wife a whore? Does Stella "slide from identity to indifference"? Is she possessed of the "wild sensuality" that defines the "truth" of women's "nature"? Consider the "evidence":

> [Stella] goes to the record player, and puts on a record. It is 'Charlie Parker.' She listens, then exits to the bedroom. . . Stella comes back into the room with a white Persian kitten. She lies back on the sofa, nuzzling it. . . . Fade flat to half light. . . (pp. 127–28)

As Elin Diamond observes, "Stella is identified with her white kitten, suggesting a feline seductress who guards claws under a guise of softness and fragility. . . . When she puts on a Charlie Parker record in her darkened apartment, then lies back on the sofa stroking the kitten, she creates an impression of . . . sexual readiness."[6]

Diamond's analysis appeals implicitly to the power of the gaze to penetrate the illusion "of softness and fragility" and discover the "truth" of feminine sexuality that attempts to escape the eye. Sign of epistemological mastery, the gaze Pinter invites his audience to turn on Stella forms an integral part of what Michel Foucault terms "the structure . . . of visible visibility. . . . [The gaze] chooses a line that instantly distinguishes the essential; it therefore goes beyond what it sees; it is not misled by the immediate forms of the sensible, for it knows how to traverse them; it is essentially demystifying."[7] Foucault here describes the doctor's medical gaze, and it is with this clinical eye that we are asked to regard Stella. The power of this gaze arises from the same extreme essentialism articulated in Bill's assertion that "wild sensuality" is part of woman's "nature." This gaze despecularizes and, somewhat paradoxically, de-eroticizes Stella's body, transforming it into a "symptom" of the sexuality that resides in the realm of Woman's Nature, beyond the confines of the individual female body, yet transforming the body into an emanation of that Nature. Under the gaze, the body is less an independent, self-contained entity than a visible signifier pointing to an invisible signified, an enigmatic text, yet susceptible to decipherment.

The gaze transforms our vision of Stella lying on the couch into a moment of truth, a moment in which we grasp the "truth" of Woman's transgressive sexuality. At this moment, the gap between stage and audience expresses itself through the privileging of the audience: we and *only* we are granted the power of the "demystifying" gaze; we and *only* we are permitted to lift Stella's veil and gaze upon the truth it would obscure. James may not "know" Stella, but the gaze allows us the knowledge denied him—a knowledge both epistemological and carnal.

I stated previously that the gaze paradoxically deeroticizes the female body. It would, however, be more accurate to say that the locus of the erotic is displaced from the body onto the structure of the gaze itself. I do not mean to suggest that the gaze invests the body with an erotic content, but rather that the act of looking is a form of sexual activity. As Sartre observes, "What is seen is possessed; to see is to *deflower . . .* [to] *violat[e] by sight.*"[8] Like Foucault, Sartre focuses on the gaze as an instrument of power, but a power bound up with an implicitly masculine sexual desire, precisely the desire that focuses our gaze on Stella.

Applied to the particular truth at issue in *The Collection*—the "truth" of feminine sexuality—Sartre's remarks place in question the epistemological certainty offered by our vision of Stella, since they suggest that "truth," rather than yielding itself up to visual capture, is produced through the act of perception. The "demystifying" gaze allows the audience to recognize Stella's appearance as a (dis)guise masking the truth of her "wild sensuality"—the whore lurking within the wife. Yet, if the gaze constitutes a kind of defilement, a "deflowering," then it is *through the agency of the gaze* that Stella slides from wife to whore. If Bill's reference to Stella's "wild sensuality" represents, in James's words, a "typical masculine thing to say," then the gaze that converts Stella's body into a signifier of this sensuality represents a typical masculine mode of perception. That the "wild sensuality" ascribed to Stella inheres in the logic of the gaze rather than in the "nature" the gaze claims to penetrate indicates the gaze's status as one among a multitude of practices designed to encode and effect a certain ideological construction of Woman as other—an other who possesses a dangerous, transgressive sexuality; an other who (like Stanley) must undergo purification before she can assume her proper place within the cultural order.

Because the "demystifying" gaze is itself in need of demystification if we are to understand its role in the cultural construction of the feminine, it seems only appropriate to ask how *The Collection* participates in that construction. Does the play endorse the conception of a feminine essence and a feminine sexuality determined by women's "nature"? Does the play reify the power of the gaze? We might initially be tempted to answer yes to both questions. As I have argued, the play appears to insist on Stella's guilt, enlisting the services of the audience's gaze in the case against her. This moment of perception also functions as a kind of mirror stage for the audience. (Mis)recognizing the "truth" that Stella is a "feline seductress" possessed of a "wild sensuality," (mis)recognizing the "truth" that her otherness derives from nature rather than from the gaze patriarchal culture casts upon women, the audience will confirm its position within that culture. This (implicity male) gaze sets in place an interior/exterior dichotomy, discerning in the otherness that sets Stella outside the bounds of patriarchy a reflection of its own centrality within those bounds.

As Bill warns James, however, mirrors are "deceptive" (p. 146)—perhaps never more so than when the "mirror" is a stage, a representational site "tainted" by the distortion requisite to all representation. If *The Collection* were simply one example of the discursive practices contributing to the construction of Women as other, then we might expect the text to suppress the epistemological gap separating representation from reality and constructed truth from "natural" truth. Whether or not the play wants to effect this suppression, however, it cannot help foregrounding its status as a theatrical representation that is necessarily a misrepresentation, thereby allowing the audience to question if the "truths" underwriting patriarchy are true or if they are ideological fictions deriving their force not from any inherent content, but from the cultural power to promulgate these fictions as truth. As Anthony Wilden observes, "Whoever defines the code or the context, has control . . . and all answers which accept that context abdicate the possibility of redefining it."[9]

Most noticeable among the play's ostensive features is Pinter's utilization of the split stage: "The stage is divided into three areas, two peninsulas and a promontory. Each area is distinct and separate from the other. Stage left, Harry's house in Belgravia. . . . Stage right, James's flat in Chelsea. . . . Upstage centre on promontory, telephone box" (p. 120). Unlike *The Birthday Party,* Pinter originally wrote *The Collection* for television before adapting it for the theater. The divided stage allows him to solve the problem of how to reproduce in the theater, without unwieldly pauses dissipating the play's tension, the kind of continuous cutting between the house and the flat that television can achieve without any temporal lag.

Quite apart from the role it plays in translating *The Collection* from one medium to another, however, the staging ultimately challenges the hegemony of the gaze and its ability to render visible the essence of any object in its field of vision. I want to suggest that we can use the staging to problematize the antithesis between man as specular subject and woman as specular object, an antithesis central to the organization of patriarchal power relations.

In order to examine how the staging both elicits and problematizes the gaze, let mc return to the scene in the flat with Stella lying on the couch, nuzzling her kitten. This sequence commences with the flat lit only by moonlight. After the preceding blackout, the appearance of even this dim light ensures that all eyes fasten on the space Stella will occupy. Perhaps the most significant aspect of this beginning is that while Pinter could have opened the scene with Stella in the flat, he chooses, albeit momentarily, to delay her entrance until *after* the lighting has indicated where the audience should direct its vision. It is almost as if, when Stella does appear, she is less an "autonomous" character than an image conjured up by the interplay between our gaze and the theatrical apparatus.

When Stella finally enters, we observe her switch on a lamp, remove her gloves, put her handbag down, place a Charlie Parker album on the phonograph, and exit into the bedroom. Immediately after Stella leaves the stage, lights fade up on the house and direct our gaze towards Bill, who *"goes to the drinks table and pours a drink, then lies on the floor with a drink by the hearth, flicking through a magazine"* (p. 127). Stella returns with the kitten and assumes the position on the couch she will maintain until her exit. Our gaze now divides its focus between her and the events in the house—Harry's exit, James's approach to the door of the house, and Bill's going to answer the door. Throughout this silent action, the play of light, forcing our gaze to shift between the two "peninsulas," indicates a point of connection, not yet readily apparent, between house and flat—a point of connection that only the gaze, transcending the spatial division of the two playing areas, can discover.

This process of discovery commences as our gaze fastens upon

Stella, seeing through the surface exterior to the interior "truth" of her "wild sensuality." The act of seeing, however, is neither natural nor spontaneous. Perhaps nowhere else in the play do we have a stronger sense of the intrusiveness of the theatrical apparatus (specifically, the lighting), with its power to direct our gaze and create the object of perception, than when James and Bill begin their dialogue. It is at this moment that Pinter fades the flat to half light, thus drawing our eyes irresistibly towards the shadowy and mysterious space inhabited by Stella, even as the equally mysterious dialogue draws our ears towards James and Bill. Rather than impending vision, however, the relative darkness of the flat demands the "demystifying" gaze by alerting us to the presence of an essential kernel of truth that attempts to evade the eye. To the extent that it lends an aura of danger and menace to Stella, creating the image of the *femme fatale,* the half light, following the logic of Foucault's "structure of invisible visibility," both proclaims the "truth" of her sexuality by its very attempt at concealment and transforms Stella's body into a specular space regulated and mastered by our perception.

The final mark of this mastery occurs after Stella leaves the stage and *"the flat fades to blackout"* (p. 130). Immediately following her exit, James begins to question Bill concerning the events at Leeds, and it is only now that the audience can perceive the connection between what we have witnessed in the flat and the continuing scene in the house. Armed with the "evidence" of Stella's corporeal confession, we can judge the different truths advanced by James and Bill, weighing them against the "truth" of Stella's sexuality to which the epistemological structure of the gaze grants us access. We "know" Stella is "like a whore" (if not actually a whore); we "know" she possesses a "wild sensuality"; we "know" the "feline seductress" lurks within her.

We come away from this scene, then, convinced that we "know" Stella's "truth" because the theatrical apparatus structures the scene precisely so that the audience can claim to have plucked out the heart of her mystery. Yet we may ask why our sense of epistemological and visual mastery of Stella depends on our recognizing her as sexually lawless; why, in other words, the play seems to insist at some level on representing Stella as guilty, "like a whore." If the wife poses a threat to patriarchy because she is "always potentially unsure," always liable to move "from her right place," we might expect the play's action to distance Stella as much as possible from any lingering suspicion of guilt rather than to equate the "truth" of her sexuality with adulterous transgression.

Are we allowed to discover this "truth," then, in order that a more disturbing "truth"—a "truth" perhaps even more damaging to patriarchal stability—remain concealed?

To discover the nature of this problematic "truth," we can return to the scene with Stella alone in the flat. I have suggested that the dynamics of this scene operate to create the impression of Stella as a "feline seductress." Such terms, however, assume that Stella remains incomplete without an object over which she can exercise sexual mastery. As she lays with her cat on the sofa in the half-light, however, we see the image of a self-contained sensuality, an eroticism that does not admit of division into subject and object, a sexual relationship between Stella and her own body. The presence of the cat—an animal conventionally associated with independence from, if not indifference to, man—both reinforces our sense of Stella's self-sufficiency and raises the possibility that it is precisely this self-sufficiency, rather than her "inevitable" move from wife to whore, that constitutes Stella's greatest threat to patriarchy.

To link or compare women with cats may appear banal enough, but I propose to look at one such comparison from Freud's essay "On Narcissism" in order to clarify what is at stake at this point in the play, and to suggest why we have been encouraged to think of Stella's sexuality as transgressive and object-oriented—Stella as the "feline seductress" in need of someone to seduce—rather than narcissistic.

In this essay, Freud declares that because women preserve the original narcissism that men must renounce, they "develop a certain self-contentment. . . . Strictly speaking, it is only themselves that such women love. . . . Nor does their need lie in the direction of loving."[10] While "such women have the greatest fascination [*Reiz*] for men,"[11] they also (perhaps because of this fascination) create anxiety in the male lover who fears their self-sufficiency. It is in a passage focusing on this ambiguity that Freud compares the female narcissist and the cat:

> The charm [of these women] . . . lies to a great extent in . . . [their] narcissism, . . . [their] self-contentment . . . and inaccessibility . . . just as does the charm . . . of certain animals which seem not to concern themselves about us, such as cats. . . . It is as if we envied . . . them for maintaining . . . an unassailable libidinal position which we ourselves have since abandoned. The great charm . . . of narcissistic women has, however, its reverse side; a large part of the lover's dissatisfaction, of his doubts of the woman's love, of his complaints of her enigmatic nature . . . has its root in [female narcissism].[12]

In this essay, Freud represents woman as enigmatic and ineluctably other, but, rather than ascribing this otherness to the psychical consequences of her anatomical "lack"—*i.e.*, the castration complex and penis envy—as he does in "Femininity," he equates "female otherness" with an independence from and indifference to masculine authority that terrifies even as it fascinates. In what amounts to a departure from and reversal of the Freudian model of sexual difference, "On Narcissism" defines *woman*—the narcissistic, feline woman—in terms of wholeness and plenitude and *man* in terms of lack and deficiency.

By the essay's conclusion, Freud extricates himself from this dangerous reversal by identifying narcissism with an egoism that must be transcended in favor of object love of the attachment type, *i.e.*, loving like a man. For the purposes of my discussion of *The Collection*, what interests me here is Freud's need for such an argument, for a defensive strategy in order to avert his gaze from the troubling figure of the narcissistic woman. I am suggesting that we can see a similar strategy operating in *The Collection*. James exhibits all the "dissatisfaction . . . doubts of the woman's love . . . [and] complaints of her enigmatic nature" that Freud asserts characterize the narcissistic woman's lover. James repeatedly links Stella with the guilt of a lawless, transgressive "wild sensuality," however, rather than confront the possibility that her erotic and ontological self-sufficiency lies at the base of his anxiety. While both the narcissistic woman and the adulterous woman threaten to undermine the stability of patriarchal power, there always exists the possibility that the latter type of woman can be recuperated and reinserted in her proper place. What I referred to earlier as the process of purification to which James would submit Stella constitutes such an attempt at recuperation, at restoration of the wife to her position as "identity of the husband" and guarantor of his "symbolic authority."

What authority, however, can the husband exercise over the narcissistic woman? If the adulterous woman terrifies because she reveals the in-difference between wife and whore, the narcissistic woman terrifies because she appears irremediably other, situated in an inaccessible elsewhere, exceeding the reach of patriarchal power. As Freud remarks, narcissistic women, like cats, "seem not to concern themselves about us." Such lack of concern, with its concomitant suggestion of existential completeness, foregrounds the inherent weakness in the system of patriarchal power: while the narcissistic woman apparently possesses her own identity, the patriarchal husband *needs* the wife to provide him with his "identity." James could regain his "identity" by reclaiming an adulterous wife, but, having refused to be claimed, the narcissistic woman cannot be reclaimed. James's insistence on defining Stella's "truth" in terms of a transgressive sexuality and the urgency with which he attempts to establish his identity at the expense of her subjectivity betray a need to see her as guilty rather than confront the "truth" of a narcissism that forms the vanishing point both of the husband's "symbolic authority" and the identity that depends on recognition of that authority.

The scene in the flat stages the encounter of these two "truths," an encounter that finds its locus in the figure of the cat. I have already quoted and elaborated on Diamond's assertion that Pinter utilizes the cat to suggest the "truth" that Stella is "like a whore," a "feline seductress" possessing "wild sensuality." As the preceding discussion suggests, however, we can also read the cat as imaging the independence and inaccessibility that characterize the self-sufficient woman and not the seductress in search of an object. Rather than legislating one of these readings, the image of the cat accommodates both, thus placing Stella's "truth" in question at the very moment that our gaze seemingly captures that "truth."

If the cat possesses multiple and contradictory associations, then perhaps what we (as well as James and Bill) identify as the "truth" of Stella's transgressive sexuality is a representation, a construction, rather than a revelation of her essential Truth. Pointing to the kind of self-contained independence in Stella that James neither will nor can acknowledge, the figure of the cat (like the mise-en-scene) permits us to question what is at stake in the various representations of Stella as an adulteress, and why the male characters—as mouthpieces of the patriarchal Other—insist with an almost paranoiac urgency on foreclosing any reading of Stella that would define her "truth" in terms other than those denoting a guilty "wild sensuality."

I have paused at such length over the scene in the flat because it both provides a theatrical correlative of the cultural construction of woman and allows the audience to critique that construction's dependence upon the categories of the natural and the essential, thus questioning its claims to truth. At the same time, we can utilize the mise-en-scene and the image of the cat to denaturalize the power of the gaze, revealing its status as a construction of the theatrical apparatus that focuses it and produces its field of vision. *The Collection* thus permits the audience to engage in a process of demystification that, by unmasking the "truth" of feminine sexuality as ideological fiction, raises the question, why does patriarchy need this particular myth?

As I have argued, the construction of Stella's sexuality as naturally transgressive forms the pretext for James's attempts to domesticate her, to render her fit for her proper role. This project seems doomed to failure since the wife is always inherently unstable, always "like a whore," always the abyss into which patriarchy threatens to sink. To claim that the wife possesses a subversive potential because she slides into the role of whore may appear a questionable strategy for mounting a critique of patriarchy. There is a difference, however, between asserting that the whore's "wild sensuality" is part of woman's "nature"—a claim informed by patriarchy's reification of the woman as sexually threatening other—and asserting, as does Luce Irigaray, that, within patriarchy, "wife" and "whore" share certain characteristics; that they are both *"social roles imposed on women"*; that both these roles constitute "women as 'objects' that emblematize the relations among men."[13] I want to pursue Irigaray's elaboration of these remarks in "Women on the Market" and "Commodities among Themselves," two essays containing implications that can aid us in exploring the structure of patriarchy as we see it emerging in *The Collection.*

Irigaray defines patriarchy as a sociocultural order that ascribes to woman the value of the sign and the commodity, the value derived from the exchange between men that she makes possible in her role as "material alibi for the desire for relations among men."[14] Whether cast as wife or whore, the woman finds her role organized in accordance with this desire, thus ensuring the continued stability of the culture that valorizes exchanges among men. Wife and whore share the fundamental trait of making exchanges among men possible—the latter by being an object of that exchange, the former by maintaining and reproducing the social order structured by the logic of exchange.

While patriarchy promotes exchanges among men and valorizes men's needs and desires, specifically "the desire for relations among men," these relations, according to Irigaray, must remain hidden. Irigaray's explanation for the disavowal of such desire provides the link between these essays and *The Collection.* She suggests that patriarchal culture, organized around the family and, therefore, apparently valorizing heterosexuality, finds its support in the very homosexual desire it must prohibit and marginalize. Because women "are the objects of transactions among men and men alone . . . [T]his means that the *very possibility of a [patriar-*

chal] order requires homosexuality as its organizing principle."[15]
While, in Irigaray's view, homosexual desire functions as the base
upon which the superstructure of patriarchal culture erects itself,
it must remain hidden from the social gaze, expressing itself "not
in an 'immediate' practice, but in its 'social' mediation."[16] The need
to maintain the pretense of heterosexuality accounts for the taboo
patriarchy places on the unmediated expression of homosexual
desire, which, if allowed to take the form of an "immediate" sexual
practice, would jeopardize the very culture that privileges the masculine. The "'immediate' practice" of homosexuality would "lower
the sublime value of the standard, the yardstick. Once the penis
itself becomes merely a means to pleasure, pleasure among men,
the phallus loses its power."[17]
Irigaray's identification of the truth of homosexual desire at the
heart of patriarchal societies suggests why these societies enforce
the play of differences separating wife from whore. For the wife
to commit adultery, reinserting herself within the circuit of exchange as both subject and object, would effect a transformation
of her body from the mirror in which the husband sees reflected
his "symbolic authority" into a palimpsest on which he finds displayed the traces of other men. Possessing a whore's body, the
adulterous wife threatens to confront the husband with his own
homosexual desire. It is precisely this threat that even the suspicion Stella has committed adultery poses—the threat to name the
unnameable, to make visible the invisible, to expose the desire
both required and forbidden by a phallocentric culture.
Along with its demystification of the essentialism that underwrites both the construction of feminine sexuality as naturally
transgressive and the reification of the (male) gaze as a naturalized
mode of perception, *The Collection* also undermines the heterosex-
ual/homosexual dichotomy from which the patriarchal "mode of
'semblance'" draws its support. Once again, Pinter's staging plays
an essential role in the critique. The playwright's insistence that
James and Stella's flat remain "distinct and separate from" the
house shared by Harry and Bill reproduces patriarchy's absolute
line of demarcation dividing the centrality of heterosexuality from
the marginality of homosexuality in terms of the disposition of
theatrical space. As the implications of Irigaray's argument suggest, this line, allowing patriarchy to disclaim all knowledge of its
structuring desire, never compeletely transcends the danger of being traversed. No matter how "distinct and separate" flat and house
remain from each other, James moves with relative ease between
the two locations. As his status in the house changes from "in-

truder" to "guest" (p. 129), James develops an ambiguous relationship with Bill. The two men come to form a "couple" that links
the flat and the house, the heterosexual (James and Stella) and the
homosexual (Harry and Bill). By the end of the play, the fixed
division of the stage has been undermined by the trajectory of an
(albeit mediated) desire that "merges" the two spaces.

James himself indicates the relation between heterosexual practice and homosexual desire when he thanks Stella for bringing him
and Bill together in a passage that reduces her to the "material
alibi" for that desire:

> I can see it both ways, three ways, all ways . . . every way. . . . I've
> come across a man I can respect. It isn't often you can do that, that
> that happens, and really I suppose I've got you to thank. *(He bends
> forward and pats her arm.)* Thanks. *(Pause.)* He reminds me of a bloke
> I went to school with. Hawkins. Honestly, he reminded me of Hawkins.
> Hawkins was an opera fan, too. So's what's-his-name. I'm a bit of an
> opera fan myself. Always kept it a dead secret. . . . I think I should
> thank you, rather than anything else. After two years of marriage it
> looks as though, by accident, you've opened up a whole new world for
> me. (pp. 143–44)

Like many of the speeches in Pinter's work, this passage creates
its effect through implication and insinuation, circling around a
subject without ever naming it, therefore making it impossible to
state unequivocally exactly what that subject is. James's assertion
that he can see marital relations "three ways"; his reference to the
school acquaintance with whom he (and Bill) share a dark, "dead
secret," followed by the comically implausible identification of that
secret; his enthusiasm for the "whole new world" to which Stella
has introduced him—all these hints point to a desire that resists
disclosure even in the process of its articulation.

Gale asserts that, regarding James and Bill's relationship, "there
are no overt proofs of homosexuality in the play," although he does
acknowledge the presence of "homosexual implications."[18] His remarks suggest the frankly ambiguous status of homosexuality in
the play—the same kind of ambiguity that Irigaray discovers in a
patriarchal culture that must prohibit the "immediate" manifestation of the desire it requires. Yet homosexual desire pervades patriarchy, in its guise of "'social' mediation." It is precisely through
mediation—through "implication" rather than "overt" sexual practice—that this "dead secret" makes its presence felt in *The Collection*. As the relationship between James and Bill develops,
language itself, specifically another version of the kind of interroga-

tion scene we witness in *The Birthday Party,* assumes a complex mediative role to which I shall now turn my attention.

Throughout the two scenes in which James attempts to learn the "truth" about Stella from Bill, power and desire encircle each other so completely that the audience finds itself compelled to question what kind of power we see being exercised. No less ambiguous than the nature of power is the source of that power: who controls the interrogation?

> *James.* Did you have a good time in Leeds last week?
> *Bill.* What?
> *James.* Did you have a good time in Leeds last week? . . .
> *Bill.* What makes you think I was in Leeds.
> *James.* Tell me all about it. See much of the town? Get out to the country at all? (p. 130)

In this exchange, James's power expresses itself through the questions that both compel Bill to "tell . . . all about it" and set boundaries to the range of that telling. When James refuses to answer Bill's question, "What makes you think I was in Leeds," he asserts his control by denying Bill's power to pose questions.

Once James declares that he knows Bill was in Leeds for a fashion show, however, a curious role reversal and shift in power occurs. Now Bill has become the interrogator and James the subject who must confess:

> *James.* You were down there for the dress collection. You took some of your models.
> *Bill.* Did I?
> *James.* You stayed at the Westbury Hotel.
> *Bill.* Oh?
> *James.* Room 142.
> *Bill.* 142? Oh. Was it comfortable?
> *James.* Comfortable enough. . . . [y]ou had your yellow pyjamas with you.
> *Bill.* Did I really? What, the ones with the black initials?
> *James.* Yes, you had them on you in 165.
> *Bill.* In what?
> *James.* 165.
> *Bill.* 165? . . .
> *James.* You booked into 142. But you didn't stay there.
> *Bill.* Well, that's a bit silly, isn't it? Booking a room and not staying in it?
> *James.* 165 is just along the passage to 142; you're not far away. . . . You could easily nip back to shave.

Bill. From 165? . . . What was I doing there?
James. . . . My wife was in there. That's where you slept with her.
   (pp. 130–31)

Moving towards yet postponing its inevitable conclusion by lingering over details, this exchange leaves the audience suspended in
an almost unbearable state of tension that, nevertheless, engenders
the pleasure associated with the eventual satisfaction of desire, a
pleasure shared not only between Pinter and his audience, but
between James and Bill as well. The shift in roles; the questions
that move towards revelation while prolonging that movement;
Bill's refusal to confess after James declares that he knows Bill
was in Leeds; James's refusal to directly accuse Bill—all of these
imply a pleasure in the process of confession that unites the two
men even as each attempts to dominate the other. While relations
of power are very much at issue here, and while we can detect the
threat of violence rippling under the surface of the dialogue, we
also feel that James and Bill share the pleasure that arises from
discursive intimacy.
   What is the nature of the power and pleasure that James's interrogation of Bill brings into such perilous contact? Foucault's description of the power dynamics informing the ritual of confession
(and it is just such a confession that James hopes to extract from
Bill) suggests an answer:

> The pleasure that comes of exercising a power that questions, monitors,
> watches, spies, searches out, palpates, brings to light; and on the other
> hand, the pleasure that kindles at having to evade this power, flee from
> it, fool it, or travesty it. The power that lets itself be invaded by the
> pleasure it is pursuing; and opposite it, power asserting itself in the
> pleasure of showing off, scandalizing, or resisting. Capture and seduc-
> tion, confrontation and mutual reinforcement.[19]

Pursuit, evasion, flight, resistance, capture, seduction—Pinter
seizes upon the charged eroticism Foucault discerns surrounding
the confessional ritual, an eroticism all the more dangerous in *The
Collection* (from a patriarchal perspective) because of its homosexual character. As "power . . . lets itself be invaded by the pleasure
it is pursuing," the line separating the two participants in the interrogation becomes transformed into a bond of a desire.
   While thus engendering desire, James's interrogation of Bill also
mediates and contains that desire by transforming it into discourse.
Pinter illustrates this discursive capture of desire by having James
repeat the "confession" he claims to have received from Stella:

"She wanted you to go, you wouldn't. She became upset, you sympathized, away from home, on a business trip, horrible life, especially for a woman, you comforted her, you gave her solace, you stayed" (p. 132). That James speaks from the structural position of the one who confesses in order to produce this narrative raises the possibility that what we hear constitutes *his* "confession," and not merely a repetition of Stella's text. Through narrative, he not only (re)enacts the alleged seduction, but, since the reality of the affair possesses only a discursive existence within the play, its "truth" solely a matter of narrative representation, he participates in the seduction as well. This "confession" mirrors its content, aligning Bill, who treats Stella "like a whore" by seducing her, and James, who treats her "like a whore" by representing her as an adultress.

At issue here is not the "truth" of James's account, but how the narrative creates Stella as a whore; how the narrative brings James and Bill into erotic proximity by allowing them to *share* Stella; how the narrative both acknowledges the framework of desire within which James's relationship with Bill develops and contains that desire, displacing it onto an account of heterosexual seduction. James's "confession" thus serves as a kind of safety valve, allowing him to articulate his desire, yet in so thoroughly mediated a form as to make possible disavowal of that desire, thus preserving the heterosexual fiction patriarchal culture (mis)recognizes as its truth.

Despite this mediation, the play never loses sight of the possibility that "masculine" desire will exceed its discursive perimeters, a threat that materializes in the second scene between the two men, when James, declaring that he "get[s] a bit tired of words sometimes" (p. 152), proposes the "mock duel" (p. 152) with the knives. Moving beyond the safety of verbal containment, James's desire erupts into the violence of the duel, a violence that, with its blatant homoerotic overtones, registers the threatening intensity of his desire even as it attests to his need to dominate Bill.

> *James.* Go on! Swallow it! *(James throws a knife at Bill's face. Bill throws up a hand to protect his face and catches the knife by the blade. It cuts his hand.)*
> *Bill.* Ow!
> *James.* Well caught! What's the matter? *(He examines Bill's hand.)* Let's have a look. Ah yes. Now you've got a scar on your hand. You didn't have one before, did you? (pp. 152–53)

James's final comment refers back to his earlier claim that Stella initially resisted her seduction and had scratched Bill, to which the latter replies, "She scratched a little, did she? Where? *(Holds up a hand)* On the hand? No scar. No scar anywhere. Absolutely unscarred" (p. 133). By abandoning words in favor of enactment, James can verify his account of the events at Leeds by forcing Bill to play the role of the scarred seducer.

We in the audience must balance our sense of James's victory against one of the few facts in our possession: we *know* that Bill's hand remained unscarred until James threw the knife. This knowledge, however, allows us to see the duel, like James's interrogation of Bill, as both violent confrontation and seduction—a seduction initiated by Bill, brandishing the fruit knife and emphasizing its phallic associations in a "rather unsubtle" (p. 152) way when he invites James to "try it. Hold the blade . . . grasp it firmly up to the hilt" (p. 150). At the same time that the duel/seduction appears to undermine the heterosexual/homosexual opposition that plays such an integral role in patriarchy's ideological self-representations, however, it operates according to what we might call the rules of patriarchal binary thought. Wielding the knife that will "violate" Bill, James assumes the role of the "masculine," active, aggressive sexual partner, while Bill finds himself thrust into the passive, acquiescent, "feminine" role.

If, as both Irigaray and *The Collection* suggest, homosexuality serves as the structuring principle of patriarchal culture, it is hardly surprising that the feminine should be associated with otherness and powerlessness in James and Bill's relationship. We can discover the same kind of associations informing the more "overt" homosexual relationship shared by Harry and Bill. Like James, Harry finds himself confronted with the threat of his partner's "adultery." Also like James, Harry can only regain control of the relationship by reducing his partner to an acceptable, *i.e.,* unthreatening, femininity. Harry establishes his authority and Bill's "feminine" powerlessness in a speech that provides one of the richest examples of Pinter's rhetoric of insult:

> There's something faintly putrid about [Bill], don't you find? Like a slug. There's nothing wrong with slugs in their place, but he's a slum slug; there's nothing wrong with slum slugs in their place, but this one won't keep his place—he crawls all over the walls of nice houses, leaving slime, don't you, boy? . . . All he can do is sit and suck his bloody hand and decompose like the filthy putrid slum slug he is. (p. 155)

Along with Harry's overt appeal to the mastery his social status confers on him in relation to Bill, the speech appeals, through implication, to the kind of binary thinking arising from the underlying opposition man/woman in patriarchal culture. Reducing Bill from "a slum boy" (p. 154) to "a slum slug," Harry excludes him from the realm of the human, opposing and subordinating him to the civilized world "of nice houses." This rhetorical move conflates class antagonism and the Culture/Nature dichotomy in which we can trace the hidden contours of the male/female opposition with its attendant positive/negative evaluation.

As "a slum slug," an example of "feminine" Nature, Bill shares with Stella the woman's "essential" radical instability. As she putatively slides from wife to whore, he "won't keep his place," but slides from the slum to "the walls of nice houses, leaving slime." Harry accuses Bill of polluting the "masculine" world of culture, thus linking defilement and Bill's "femininity." Watching Bill suck his wounded hand, his powerlessness exposed by James, Harry sees him victimized by his defiling femininity. It is not the "masculine" world "of nice houses," but the "feminine" Bill who will sink into his own "slime" as he "decompose[s] like the filthy putrid slum slug he is."

By asserting that the relationships of the play's three "couples" share a similar power structure in which the "masculine" enjoys a privileged status and the "feminine" becomes associated with powerlessness, I want to suggest that *The Collection* gives dramatic expression to the kind of connection that Irigaray discerns between homosexuality and heterosexuality within patriarchal culture. At the same time, it should be noted that not all revelations of homosexual desire pose the same threat to this culture. Because we can consider Harry and Bill's relationship overtly homosexual, it proves susceptible to being relegated to the role of the other against which the "heterosexual" regime of patriarchy can define and (mis) recognize itself. On the other hand, because James's marriage sustains the appearance of heterosexuality, his developing relationship with Bill carries with it the threat of dismantling patriarchy, confronting it with the "dead secret" that authorizes its cultural existence.

By transforming James's desire from narrative displacement to ritually symbolic enactment, the duel becomes the locus of this threat. Extending the conflation of the desire for power and the power of desire running throughout James and Bill's confrontation, the outburst of violence allows James to affirm his authority while also, through its suggestion of violation and deflowering, measuring the intensity of a desire that refuses containment. It is only *after* the duel, after desire surfaces (albeit in the form of a "game" [p. 152]), that James will accept the "truth" of Bill's claim that he and Stella "never touched . . . we just talked about it" (p. 157). James's acceptance of this account results in the removal of the taint of adultery from Stella, since Bill offers this final version of the "truth" after James and Harry have exposed the "femininity" that proclaims the impossibility of his being Stella's lover. From an Irigarayan perspective, we can see why the logic of patriarchal culture demands that James accept this "truth": as long as Stella remains under suspicion of being a whore, patriarchy will find itself in danger of being undermined as James and Bill's "relations" move closer to direct, immediate expression and further from "'social' mediation." To reinstate Stella as a wife and reintroduce the play of differences that separate "wife" from "whore" would preserve the appearance of heterosexuality while returning homosexual desire to its function as patriarchy's hidden base.

Bill's final version of his meeting with Stella reveals the extent to which woman functions as the axis around which patriarchal culture turns. In order for Bill's narrative to achieve the status of truth, Stella must acknowledge it as true; must "confess" her innocence; must use her voice only to lose it by assimilating it to James's voice, confirming his word and his control of the codes and contexts that determine truth. Such a confirmation would provide patriarchy with its ultimate ideological triumph—the woman recognizing her "truth" in a culturally constructed image.

Stella's response to James's demand for confirmation frustrates the desire for this triumph, exposing the epistemological gap that patriarchy seeks to suppress between truth as apodictically given and truth as construction.

> *James.* You didn't do anything, did you? *(Pause.)* He wasn't in your room. You just talked about it, in the lounge. *(Pause.)* That's the truth, isn't it? *(Pause.)* You just sat and talked about what you would do if you went to your room. That's what you did. *(Pause.)* Didn't you? *(Pause.)* That's the truth . . . isn't it? *(Stella looks at him, neither confirming nor denying. Her face is friendly, sympathetic.)* (p. 157)

Stella's power in the play, like that of Ruth *(The Homecoming)* and Kate *(Old Times),* finally lies in her refusal to utter the speech that patriarchy would impose on her; her refusal of construction; her refusal to speak with her "master's" voice and become the instrument of her own betrayal; her refusal to accept the imposition of (en)closure within the patriarchal family plot. Resisting James's speech, her silence strikes at the very heart of patriarchy's self-fashioning project that locates the "identity of the husband" in the figure of the wife.

Stella's implacable silence suggests the political strategy of mimicry advocated by Irigaray. How, asks Irigaray, are women *"to work at 'destroying' the discursive mechanism"*[20] that effects their subjection without granting them subjectivity?

> There is, in an initial phase, perhaps only one "path," the one histori-cally assigned to the feminine: that of *mimicry*. One must assume the feminine role deliberately. Which means already to convert a form of subordination into an affirmation, and thus to begin to thwart it. . . . To play with mimesis is thus, for a woman, to try to recover the place of her exploitation by discourse, without allowing herself to be simply reduced to it.[21]

Wedded to silence at the end of the play, Stella "deliberately" assumes the woman's role as the voiceless presubject, transforming that role into an index of subjectivity, of an interiority that she refuses to violate. James's attempt to render Stella fit for her role as "identity of the husband" takes the form of an assault on her voice, first turning that voice against her by claiming she has con-fessed to adultery, then unleashing a violent, mocking verbal as-sault that, at one point, reduces her to tears, leaving her unable to speak (pp. 142–43). This attack is designed to reduce her to the silence and exclusion from enunciative authority that remand women to the margins of patriarchal culture. Choosing silence at the precise moment when James commands her to speak, when patriarchal power needs the voice of the woman in order to ensure its stability, Stella denaturalizes women's silence, exposing the en-semble of "discursive mechanisms" and instruments of vocal era-sure combining to create that silence, to create (the) Woman defined by that silence.

Stella's strategy of silence forces the audience to reevaluate her relative silence throughout most of the play. An imposed silence may situate women in the place of the ex-centric, but, as the final moments of *The Collection* indicate, we cannot always equate the ex-centric with the powerless, the negative, the absent. Even pas-sivity may paradoxically engender a sense of empowerment if it is actively and "deliberately" assumed, *i.e.,* mimed. James's repeated encroachment into and reduction of Stella's vocal field appears to invite an unequivocal opposition between his activity and her passivity. If, however, mimicry "make[s] 'visible' . . . what was supposed to remain invisible"[22]—women's "exploitation by discourse"—then Stella's "silencing" by James may be less an index of her victimization than a mimetic performance denaturalizing that victimization. Masking its subversive mimicry, Stella's "passivity"—her apparently total subjection—seduces James into unmasking both his own cruelty and the discursive practices through which patriarchy denies women access to the voice. Indeed, her ability to resist James's coercive power when he demands she "confess" her innocence raises the possibility that her original confession (and for the moment I am accepting that James speaks the truth when he claims she has confessed), like her silence early in the play, may represent the woman's subversive "play with mimesis."

According to Irigaray, for a woman to become a mimic "means to resubmit herself . . . to 'ideas,' in particular to ideas about herself that are elaborated in/by a masculine logic, but so as to make 'visible' . . . what was supposed to remain invisible."[23] Through her act of confession, Stella both "resubmit[s] herself" to "ideas" about female sexuality "elaborated in/by a masculine logic"—a "masculine" system of representation—and challenges patriarchy to reveal from what source "masculine logic" derives its legitimating authority. Stella's confession would seem to provide that authority: her acknowledgement of guilt allows patriarchal culture to (mis)recognize the "truth" of its representations of female sexuality and to deny their status *as* ideas, myths, cultural fictions.

Yet this confession is a double-edged sword—if it empowers the "masculine logic" that defines woman as threateningly other, it also reveals that power's contingency upon the very women it would subject. If the construction of a naturally transgressive female sexuality inscribes women as always already guilty, then Stella's mimicry demystifies the process of inscription that attempts to disappropriate her from her relation to herself. If, as Irigaray asserts about patriarchy, "the 'feminine' is never to be identified except by and for the masculine,"[24] then Stella's mimicry reveals the operations of power subtending the process of identification.

While we can never state unequivocally why (or even if) Stella has confessed adultery to James, or what might be the truth underlying this confession, what interests me here is the possibility that Stella may *perform* her confession, theatricalizing the ritual in order to assert what Foucault refers to as the confessional subject's "power . . . of showing off, scandalizing, or resisting." Stella's confession, as an act of resistance, enables her silence at the end of the play, enables her to see that silence carries the greatest threat to a cultural order that needs women to verify the "truths" by which it marginalizes them. Stella thus transforms confession from an instrument of patriarchal power to a weapon in the mimic's arsenal, from a discursive ritual ensuring women's subjection to a site from which the woman-as-mimic can resist her containment within the boundaries of the definitions and constructions "elaborated in/by a masculine logic."

Like the contradictions that undermine the ideological opposition between "wife" and "whore," and like the staging of the scene in the flat that foregrounds the representation of a dangerous female sexuality as a representation, Stella's silence problematizes the status of truth claimed by patriarchy's representations and constructions of the feminine. By exposing the fictive nature of these "truths," Stella's mimicry indicates the problem of power shadowing patriarchy's attempts at cultural self-fashioning. Through its suggestion that women's "meaning" does not correspond to the "truth" of their cultural consruction, that, indeed, women do not possess "meaning" if we understand that word to denote an irreducible, definable core or essence, Stella's silence exposes the representational structure constituting women's reality. This silence points to a "self" that exists only by not being articulated, that refuses to accept the masculine definitions that the patriarchal order would impose. According to Irigaray, "if women are such good mimics, it is because they are not simply resorbed in this function. *They also remain elsewhere.*"[25] *The Collection* situates this "elsewhere"—a space from which to resist ideological subjection—in Stella's silence: a silence that, converted from a mark of subjection into an instrument of assertion, transforms her from an object of patriarchal representation into the subject of self-representation.

While mimicry succeeds as a subversive strategy for Stella, are we justified in positing it as the fundamental base from which all oppositional feminist politics arises? Is mimicry the kind of panacea Irigaray imagines it to be, or does its effectiveness depend upon the position from which the mimic speaks (or remains silent)? I will explore these questions in the following discussion of *The Homecoming,* a play that problematizes the inherently disruptive powers Irigaray associates with the mimic.

4

"The Structure Wasn't Affected": *The Homecoming* and the Crisis of Family Structure

As a mimic, Stella appears to escape the kind of ideological incorporation that subjects Stanley and Goldberg to the Other's power. Yet the mimic always runs the risk of overacting, of playing her role so well that, paradoxically, she may reinforce the very cultural order against which her subversive gestures are directed, thus undermining her contestatory strategy. It is instructive that immediately after defining what she means by mimicry, Irigaray goes on to distinguish it from "a direct feminine challenge to . . . [patriarchy that] means demanding to speak as a (masculine) 'subject,' . . . [and] postulat[ing] . . . a relation to the intelligible that would maintain"[1] the play of patriarchal power relations. That Irigaray feels the need to make this distinction at the outset of her argument points to a certain anxiety that mimicry might very well degenerate into this "direct feminine challenge" that, at best, would invert cultural norms while preserving the forms of the larger patriarchal order—the order privileging the masculine subject even if a woman should occupy the place of that subject. The mimic cannot, then, simply by virtue of her mimicry, escape the problem of subject position. When the mimic speaks, or (as Stella does) maintains silence, "is she speaking *as* a woman, or *in the place of* the . . . woman, *for* the woman, *in the name of* the woman,"[2] or, alarmingly, in the place of the masculine subject? As Toril Moi asserts, "It is the . . . *context* of such mimicry that is surely always decisive"[3]— it is the position whether mimicry challenges or reinforces the discursive mechanism it would dismantle.

I offer these observations as a context for my discussion of *The Homecoming,* a play in which the mimic comes to inhabit a masculine subject position. Pinter places Ruth's struggle for dominance within and over Teddy's family at the heart of the play, and while general critical consensus grants her the victory, some of the play's commentators have raised questions concerning the decisiveness of this victory. Austin Quigley declares that "for Ruth, . . . the ending is of uncertain value,"[4] and Elin Diamond cautions, "To say Ruth has won is to ignore the ambiguities that resonate in the last moments of the play."[5] Identifying the source of these ambiguities necessitates asking how the subject position from which Ruth speaks and acts impacts on the victory she wins over the family.

As I will argue, *The Homecoming* concerns itself specifically with the subject position Lacan terms the "symbolic father"—a position which we must distinguish from the actual, biological father. As a subject position, the "symbolic father" is an ideological representation, an "identity" articulated through the cultural codes and master tropes of patriarchy, the privileged signifying position in which patriarchal ideology locates what Roland Barthes terms "the hallucinatory attributes of the Father: power, fascination, instituting authority, terror, power to castrate."[6] It is this subject position of the "symbolic father" that Ruth's victory over the family allows her to occupy. Indeed, as I will argue, Ruth successfully undermines the patriarchal family structure *because* she comes to embody what patriarchal ideology defines as the "attributes of the Father." That Ruth (rather than any of the males) should possess these attributes provides the source both of the ironic inversions and subversions of patriarchal norms the play dramatizes *and* of the ambiguity to which Quigley and Diamond respond—the ambiguity of a "matriarchal" order establishing itself through the exercise of a peculiarly phallic power.

I want to begin my discussion of how the play problematizes mimicry by examining Pinter's own reading of Ruth's victory over the patriarchal family:

> [Ruth is] used by this family. But eventually she comes back with a whip. She says "if you want to play this game I can play it as well as you." She does not become a harlot . . . if she [becomes a prostitute for the family], she would not be a harlot in her own mind.[7]

How are we to understand Pinter's claim that, if Ruth does become a prostitute, "she would not be a harlot in her own mind"? We might answer this question by observing that Pinter here describes a kind of mimetic practice, a deliberate assumption of the role to which patriarchy consigns women that transforms subjection into empowerment. Another reading of Pinter's remarks suggests itself, however. A woman who engages in prostitution while refusing to recognize herself as "a harlot in her own mind"—might this not serve as the definition of what patriarchy considers an acceptable, unthreatening, even desirable woman? As Irigaray argues, the prostitute represents the position of all women in patriarchy, for she finds herself "in a situation of *specific exploitation*."[8] She goes on to assert that it is precisely because women are denied even the illusion of autonomy within partriarchy that the possibility of resistance arises: "This situation of specific oppression is perhaps what can allow women today to elaborate a 'critique of the political economy,' inasmuch as they are in a position external to the laws of exchange, even though they are included in them as 'commodities.'"[9]

Ruth's articulation of the law of exchange in the play's climactic "contract scene" may dislodge the men from their "natural" position of enunciative authority, but does this fundamentally alter her status as a commodity? If, as Pinter asserts, Ruth would not think of herself as a prostitute even as she engaged in prostitution, then how could she recognize the exploitation that finally marks her as subject to patriarchal power? Irigaray asserts that in order to disrupt the play of patriarchal power relations, women must leave "behind their condition as commodities—subject to being produced, consumed, valorized, circulated, and so on, by men alone— and t[ake] part in elaborating and carrying out exchanges."[10] Ruth engages in such an exchange, but, as the contract scene illustrates, this exchange reaffirms her commodification:

> *Ruth.* I would naturally want to draw up an inventory of everything I would need, which would require your signatures in the presence of witnesses.
> *Lenny.* Naturally.
> *Ruth.* All aspects of the agreement and conditions of employment would have to be clarified to our mutual satisfaction before we finalized the contract.
> *Lenny.* Of course.[11]

This exchange compels us to ask from what position Ruth speaks. Does she speak as the mimic attempting to demystify the processes that effect women's exploitation? Does she, on the other hand, speak as one of those commodities that, in Irigaray's words, "*share in the cult of the father, and never stop trying to resemble, to copy, the one who is his representative . . . [so] that their remarks* confirm the exchangers' plans for them?"[12] As an example of mimicry, Ruth's "performance" foregrounds the same dangerous prox-imity between the terms "wife" and "whore" that had proved so threatening to the maintenance of patriarchy in *The Collection*. In *The Homecoming*, however, the "representatives" of the father (Max and Lenny) themselves become instrumental in suspending the play of difference between these categories. If such a move seemingly runs counter to the demands of patriarchal ideology, then we might remember, as Irigaray writes, "In fact [wife and whore] are joined together in traditional monogamous marriage, a legal form of prostitution that is not declared as such."[12]

If the legal and contractual apparatus veils the extent to which marriage institutionalizes women's commodification, then Ruth's appropriation of the Word-as-Law, her manipulation of legal and economic discourse, foregrounds this exploitation. Max may re-proach Lenny for "concentrating too much on the economic con-siderations [when] [t]here are other considerations . . . the human considerations" (p. 87), but Ruth's position as the subject (as well as object) of exchange—a position that quite literally deconstructs the opposition between wife and whore—reveals that it is precisely the sentimental rhetoric of "human considerations" that mystifies how marriage functions as a culturally sanctioned form of prostitu-tion. Warning Lenny that "you would have to regard your original outlay simply as a capital investment" (p. 93), miming the "mascu-line" elaboration of the laws of exchange, Ruth forces the men to become economically dependent upon her, to assume that role that phallic economy traditionally reserves for women.

Irigaray speculates that "if commodities could speak; they might possibly give an opinion about their price, about whether they consider their status just, or about the dealings of their owners."[14] The contract scene grants the commodity a voice: "I would want at least three rooms and a bathroom. . . . A personal maid . . . You'd supply my wardrobe. . . . I'd need an awful lot. Otherwise I wouldn't be content" (pp. 92–93). Because this commodity substi-tutes the language of contracts and investments, exchange-value and use-value, for the mystifying language of "human considera-tions," she can reveal the ideological rhetoric and social practices that produce women's subjection within the patriarchal family.

If Ruth's language demystifies this rhetoric, however, it produces its own form of mystification by allowing Ruth to equate her posi-tion as subject of exchange with an inversion of values that hollows out and redefines the category of the prostitute. Dictating her "con-ditions of employment," Ruth may seek to transform prostitution from a form of exploitation into an instrument of empowerment, but she can only achieve such empowerment by acquiescing to her commodification.

In a pasasge worth quoting at some length, Irigaray addresses the same ambiguity concerning women's empowerment that the contract scene dramatizes. When women challenge

> the contemporary play of powers and power relations, they are in fact working toward a modification of women's status. On the other hand, when . . . [they] aim simply for a change in the distribution of power, leaving intact the power structure itself, then they are resubjecting themselves, deliberately or not, to a phallocratic order. This latter gesture . . . may constitute a more subtly concealed exploitation of women . . . [since it] plays on a certain naiveté that suggests one need only be a woman in order to remain outside phallic power.[15]

Appropriating the power of the Word-as-Law, declaring that she will not only set her terms but also "draw up" the contract herself, and inverting the terms of the relationship that leaves the wife/ prostitute dependent on the husband/client (or husband/pimp), Ruth unquestionably effects a redistribution of power. Whether or not she "leav[es] the power structure intact," however, depends on the subject position from which she speaks.

While *The Homecoming* resists resolving the kinds of ambiguities I have discussed, the play quite clearly focuses on a crisis within patriarchy that Pinter locates at the level of the family. To regard Ruth's initial entrance as heralding the invasive appearance of a disruptive force that threatens the totality of social relations on which the patriarchal family depends and which it must therefore reproduce is to ignore the radical instability of the family that manifests itself from the play's opening scene, an instability through which Pinter explores the cracks and fissures developing in the structure of the patriarchal family.

Family structure plays a crucial role in the two plays I have discussed so far. *The Birthday Party* casts Goldberg and Meg as Stanley's surrogate parents, whose role in the play—giving Stanley a language that channels his desires into a socially acceptable form—points to the family's cultural role as an ideological apparatus for the management of social subjectivity. *The Collection* explores the paradox of the patriarchal family that vests symbolic and legal authority in the figure of the husband while leaving him dependent upon the wife for recognition of this authority. The husband's "self," his role as the representative of patriarchal power, can never completely surmount this contingency, this dependence on the wife's conforming to the ideological imperatives that mediate her role in the family.

As in these plays, the family constitutes a site of ideological production in *The Homecoming,* a site for producing appropriate gendered subjects, ready to assume their place in the system of social relations that supports the perpetuation of patriarchy. Wally Secombe elaborates on the mother's role within the ideological apparatus of the family: "The mother . . . produces willing participants for the social order. . . . Young adults must be produced who have internalized a repertoire of attitudes and perceptual structures that enables them to self-actualize willingly in an adjusted manner within [patriarchy]."[16] Within the family, it is the mother who becomes the agent for the transmission of ideology, recruiting "individuals" for the subject positions articulated through the symbolic network of patriarchal culture. As Max tells Ruth, it was *Jessie* who "taught those boys everything they know. She taught them all the morality they know. I'm telling you. Every single bit of the moral code they live by—was taught to them by their mother" (pp. 61–62).

In the context of what the audience has already witnessed of this "moral code," Max's comment possesses a good deal of irony, but it also foregrounds Jessie's absence—an absence that, repeatedly inscribed within the male characters' dialogue, paradoxically grants her a verbal presence. This presence speaks through the non sequitur that invades Teddy's description of the changes in the room: "We knocked [the wall] down . . . years ago. . . . The structure wasn't affected. . . . My mother was dead" (p. 37). Teddy verbally (re-)situates Jessie within the boundaries from which the men have attempted to banish her through a kind of architectural de-feminization of space. Similarly, Max's reminiscence of the night the children "knelt down at our feet, Jessie's and mine" (p. 62), finds its clichéd, almost Victorian, vision of unity disrupted by a troubling absence: "I came downstairs and I made Jessie put her feet up on a pouffe—what happened to that pouffe, I haven't seen it for years—she put her feet up on the pouffe and I said to her, Jessie, I think our ship is going to come home" (p. 62). Max's narrative of family harmony—the same narrative that praises Jessie for her role in socializing the children—attempts to "save" her, to efface her image as "a slutbitch of a wife" (p. 63) and install her securely within the patriarchal realm of the docile wife. Projecting a fantasized image of Jessie, the narrative must displace her absence onto the pouffe, must ask "what happened to that pouffe" in order to avoid asking "what happened to that wife." Such displace-

ment, however, undoes the narrative's recuperative work: in order
to avoid naming Jessie as unnameable, as the unexplained absence,
Max's story resorts to a metaphoric identification of the pouffe
with Jessie, an identification so tenuous as to foreground rather
than resolve the problem of her absence.

Why should Max want to avoid asking "what happened to that
wife?" What connection exists between Jessie and the crisis of
family structure Pinter dramatizes? Sam provides *an* answer if not
the answer: "MacGregor had Jessie in the back of my cab as I
drove them along" (p. 94). The suspicion that Jessie may have
committed adultery confronts Max with the same paradox that
troubles James in *The Collection:* patriarchy depends for its reproduction on achieving a fit between the actual wife and the ideological function of the wife. At the same time, however, the conception
of the wife's natural instability, her refusal to remain anchored
within her "appropriate" subject position, represents a constant
threat to both the physical and ideological reproduction of patriarchal social relations. If wives must in one sense lose their status
as commodities by being excluded from further exchange, such
exclusion stems from the need to ensure the orderly transmission
from father to (legitimate) son of the laws, discursive codes and
social structures that maintain the patriarchal order.

If Jessie committed adultery, Max's description of his family as
"three bastard sons, a slutbitch of a wife" (p. 63) may represent
more than just another example of Pinter's comic rhetoric of insult.
Lenny's verbal assaults on Max repeatedly cast doubt both on his
mother's fidelity and his "father's" biological paternity. When Max
refuses to cook for Sam and Joey with the telling line, "Go and
find yourself a mother" (p. 32), Lenny responds by calling into
question Max's right to assume and speak in the Name-of-the-
Father:

> *Lenny.* What the boys want, Dad, is your own special brand of cook-
>   ing, Dad. . . .
> *Max.* Stop calling me Dad. Just stop all that calling me Dad, do you
>   understand?
> *Lenny.* But I'm your son. (p. 33)

Lenny's mockery, however, cuts two ways: If Jessie's infidelity
forecloses the possibility of identifying Max with the "symbolic
father," then Lenny's own accession to the Name-of-the-Father will
remain extremely problematic. If the mother's adultery denies her
son the opportunity to occupy the place of the "symbolic father,"

and if Lenny cannot identify with the father as possessor of the phallus and all the cultural privileges it signifies, he will remain subject to the *mother's* desires, become appropriated by *her* and marked with *her* name. His rejection of "Leonard," "the name my mother gave me" (p. 49), reveals Lenny's sense of his own ex-centricity to the paternal space that patriarchal logic demands he come to occupy.

This sense of dislocation from his "natural" subject position prompts him to question his origins:

> That night . . . you know . . . the night you got me . . . that night with Mum, what was it like? Eh? When I was just a glint in your eye. What was it like? What was the background to it? I mean, I want to know the real facts about my background. I mean, for instance, is it a fact that you had me in mind all the time, or is it a fact that I was the last thing you had in mind? . . . I should have asked my dear mother. Why didn't I ask my dear mother? Now it's too late. She's passed over to the other side. (pp. 52–53)

Lenny's comment that "I was the last thing you had in mind," with its suggestion that Max may not be his father, points to the havoc wrought when the wife/mother refuses to guarantee the husband/father's "symbolic authority." More than just another attack on Max, Lenny's desire for "the real facts" reveals the extent to which the possibility of Jessie's infidelity has rent a hole in the family cell, disrupting the (imaginary) equivalence between the members of the family and the ideological subject positions that shape the experience of paternity and maternity within patriarchal culture.

If *The Homecoming* registers a greater anxiety than does *The Collection* concerning the suspended play of difference between "wife" and "whore," we must remember that by extending the family structure Pinter raises the stakes. If Stella guarantees (or fails to guarantee) the identity of the husband, Jessie must act as guarantor for the identity of the family. She proves indispensible to the ideological reproduction of patriarchal relations because, as Secombe notes, the mother not only bears children, she produces those children as subjects who can assume their proper place within the dominant cultural order. As Secombe's argument implies, for the mother to play this socializing role, she must herself have "internalized" the codes, desires, and values that allow her to identify with the ideological imperatives that define the "mother" within patriarchy.

I would emphasize that the crisis Pinter explores does not concern an actual mother and father, but the ideological stability of the subject positions we designate by the terms "mother" and "father," terms that (like "wife" and "whore") derive meaning from their differential relation to each other in the closed system of familial signification, terms that encode the values of patriarchal culture. Max may withhold "the real facts" concerning Jessie's sexuality from Lenny, but he cannot hide from the consequences of her refusal to remain anchored in the place to which patriarchal ideology, embedded in the discourse of the family, would remand her.

We witness these consequences from the play's opening moments:

> *Max.* Do you hear what I'm saying? I'm talking to you! Where's the scissors?
> *Lenny (looking up, quietly).* Why don't you shut up, you daft prat? . . .
>   Plug it, will you, you stupid sod, I'm trying to read the paper. . . .
> *Max.* [G]et out! What are you waiting for? *(Lenny looks at him.)*
> *Lenny.* What did you say?
> *Max.* I said shove off out of it, that's what I said.
> *Lenny.* You'll go before me, Dad, if you talk to me in that tone of voice.
>   (pp. 223–27)

Diamond notes that Lenny undermines "Max's authority, . . . respond[ing] not to what Max asks but to the noise he makes."[17] As this remark suggests, to undermine the father's authority, one must reduce his speech to "noise," a concatenation of sounds lacking the signifying power of the Father's Word. Lenny's violently dialogic intervention not only withholds recognition of the father's utterance, but refuses to grant Max the enunciative authority of the "symbolic father" whose speech possesses the monologic power of the law—an omnipotent Word that disallows any response other than compliance.

Rather than a decisive assertion of the "self," however, Lenny's response marks his subjection to the (m)other. As Lacan observes, recognizing the father's word becomes the mother's fundamental ideological task within patriarchy: *"The father is present only through his law, which is speech, and only in so far as his speech is recognized by the mother does it take on the value of law. If the* position of the father is questioned, then the child remains subjected to the mother."[18] In Lenny's refusal to regard Max as the representative of the Law, we can discern the traces of Jessie's own refusal to subordinate herself to the father's law, to recognize Max's word as law. This refusal foregrounds Max's (mis)recognition of fatherhood as a natural rather than cultural category. For Max, "fatherhood" constitutes a reflection of the "self" rather than an ideological representation governing paternity, and power vests itself not in the "symbolic father" but in the actual father: "I used to knock about with a man called MacGregor. . . . We were two of the worst hated men in the West End of London. I tell you, I still got the scars. We'd walk into a place, the whole room'd stand up, they'd make way to let us pass. You never heard such silence" (p. 24). Max locates value in individual force, a belief that has become untenable within a cultural order that defines power in terms of subject position rather than in terms of individual essence. Max may have been, as he claims, "a tearaway . . . [who] could have taken care of [Lenny] twice over" (p. 24), but reliance upon individual force cannot confer upon him the linguistic mastery that constitutes a specifically patriarchal form of power.

Pinter carefully orchestrates the play's opening sequence so that the more Lenny challenges Max's speech, the more Max attempts to ground the father's power in his "self." As Lenny continues to mock his Word, Max attempts to reassert his image as "a tearaway," the castrating father who wields "the chopper and the slab" (p. 63) and threatens to "chop your spine off, [if] you talk to me like that" (p. 25). Lenny's response, a parodic performance of the terrified and subjected child, further undermines Max by exposing the comically inflated nature of his claims to embody patriarchal power:

Oh, Daddy, you're not going to use your stick on me, are you? Eh? Don't use your stick on me Daddy. No, please. It wasn't my fault, it was one of the others. I haven't done anything wrong, Dad, honest. Don't clout me with that stick, Dad. (*Silence. Max sits hunched. Lenny reads the paper.*) (p. 27)

Denied validation of his self-image, Max retreats into reminiscence of his days at Epsom, a world that, while outside the family, allowed him to exercise the power of "fascination," one of the ideological characteristics of the father listed by Barthes. This "fascination" takes the form of the "masculine" gaze. Max performs "a kind of hypnotism" (p. 26) on the horses—specifically the fillies—that allows him to penetrate "the immediate forms of the sensible" and discover the truth of their nature:

I had an instinctive understanding of animals. . . . And not only the colts but the fillies. Because the fillies are more highly strung than the colts, they're more unreliable. . . . But I was always able to tell a good filly by one particular trick. I'd look her in the eye . . . I'd stand in front of her and look her straight in the eye, it was a kind of hypnotism, and by the look deep down in her eye I could tell whether she was a stayer or not. (p. 26)

Even when Max takes refuge in a memory of power, however, he becomes reduced to a parody of the Father, a comically exaggerated figure who proves incapable of exercising the cultural power he would represent. The "women" he subordinates through specular capture are, after all, only fillies—from what we can gather about Max's marriage, he proved singularly incapable of exercising this hypnotic power over Jessie. Lenny further deflates Max's pretensions to "masculine" power and epistemological mastery by redefining this "instinctive understanding" in stereotypically feminine terms: "What the boys want, Dad, is . . . [t]he special understanding of food, you know, that you've got" (p. 33).

Lenny's mockery here follows Max's refusal to demonstrate his "understanding" with the question that resonates throughout the play: "Who do you think I am, your mother?" (p. 32). Yet again, Max's words foreground Jessie's absence, an absence that plays a determining role in the crisis of family structure. This crisis does not arise from Max's failure to conform to the dimensions of the "symbolic father," for, as Lacan observes, the actual father can never correspond to the "symbolic father": "Even when in fact it is represented by a single person, the paternal function concentrates in itself both imaginary and real relations, always more or less inadequate to the symbolic relations that essentially constitutes it."[19] At issue, then, is not Max's failure to "be" the "symbolic father," but a failure of the processes of symbolic identification that equate the father with the Father—a failure, in other words, of the mother, whose (mis)recognition of the Father's Word as Law effects this identification. The most alarming threat to patriarchal stability thus issues not from the lack of correspondence between actual father and "symbolic father," but from that between actual mother and "symbolic mother"; from Jessie's absence, during her marriage as well as after her death, from the space in which patriarchy would contain her.

Jessie's challenge to patriarchal power becomes reinscribed in Lenny's rejection of Max's enunciative authority. If Jessie's "indeterminacy" and Lenny's mockery undermine Max's claims to power, the sheer inflation of those claims also contributes to the downfall of this would-be patriarch. While no occupant of the paternal position, as Lacan observes, can ever "be" the "symbolic father," such grandiloquent assertions of power as the threat to "chop [Lenny's] spine off" not only comically reduce Max, but also expose the status of this Father as cultural myth. Thrown into exaggerated relief by the disjuncture between word (the language of paternal authority) and speaker (the "sexless" [p. 88] descendent of the traditional comic *sennex*), patriarchal discourse becomes the object of a parodic treatment that holds it up for inspection, inviting the audience to perceive the radically contingent nature of patriarchal power—a contingency that the "symbolic father's" Word mystifies.

The Homecoming emphasizes this contingency by dramatizing the effects of Jessie's failure to provide the ideological (mis)recognition that the "symbolic father" requires. Rather than owing their verbal extravagance to an assured sense of mastery, Max's assertions of authority testify to his fear that the boundaries delimiting paternal power may prove vulnerable to encroachment, a fear we can discern in his "obsess[ion] with order and clarity. He doesn't like mess" (p. 49). Max's dislike of "mess" suggests a fear of the impurity and contamination that transgress and destroy the boundaries articulated by "masculine" symbolic systems, and that, in turn, articulate "masculine" identity. Not surprisingly, then, Max's fear of defilement takes the form of a fear of woman expressed in the kind of violent language characterizing his initial reaction to Ruth:

> Who asked you to bring *dirty* tarts into this house? . . . We've had a *smelly* scrubber in my house all night. We've had a *stinking pox-ridden* slut in my house all my night. . . . I haven't seen the bitch for six years, he comes home without a word, he brings a *filthy* scrubber off the street. . . . They come back from America, they bring the *slopbucket* with them. They bring the *bedpan* with them. . . . Take that *disease* away from me. (pp. 57–58; emphasis added)

This invective initially recalls Harry's description of Bill as "a slum slug." As my reading of that passage emphasized, Harry asserts "masculine" power by associating Bill with the ultimately self-consuming "slime" of a defiling "feminine" nature. Max's language, however, because of its excess, cedes power to Ruth by betraying the fear that motivates that excess. The representation of woman as a "dirty . . . stinking pox-ridden . . . filthy . . . slopbucket," a "bedpan" contaminated by "disease," clearly reveals the paranoid anxiety that belies all Max's claims to power.

Max's attempts to ward off his fear of engulfment within the flux of "feminine" disease result in a paradoxical role reversal that ultimately disqualifies his attempts to "be" the Father, a reversal that announces itself in his claim to have "g[iven] birth to three grown men! All on my own bat. . . . Don't talk to me about the pain of childbirth—I suffered the pain, I've still got the pangs—when I give a little cough my back collapses" (pp. 56, 63). This identification with the female role (as defined by patriarchy), completing the trajectory of Max's movement from would-be representative of the Father's Law to embodiment of the woman as reproductive agent, may initially seem confusing. Why should even a parodic version of the Father identify himself in terms of femininity? The answer lies in the kind of paranoia Max displays. Alice Jardine identifies a form of male paranoia in which the subject overcomes his "fear of the loss . . . of all boundaries . . . only by transforming himself into a 'woman.'"[20] As a male paranoiac, Max thus masters his fear of pollution—his fear, in other words, of woman—by internalizing the image of that defilement's potential source.

While this identification with the mother may "ward off" Max's fear, it cannot neutralize the threat Jessie poses—even after her death—to patriarchy. If Max incorporates the mother's image in a final effort to banish all trace of Jessie from the family, "she" continues to resist such erasure. We discover her presence in Max's paranoia, Lenny's refusal to validate the monologic power of Max's language, and the Oedipal crisis that convulses the family.

While the play clearly manifests Oedipal tensions,[21] I would argue that these tensions indicate a scenario more Lacanian than Freudian. Lacan's conceptualization of the Oedipus complex emphasizes the family's status as a network of symbolic relations that must generate appropriate subjects to occupy the positions these relations designate, and thus provides an useful theoretical lens through which to view *The Homecoming*. The complexities of the Lacanian Oedipal scenario demand an excursus into the realm of theory that, while somewhat lengthy, will help clarify Jessie's role in the crisis of family structure Pinter dramatizes.

For Lacan, "father" and "mother" are signifying spaces, symbolic positions that function as linguistic categories, drawing their meaning from the play of difference that defines their relationship within the closed signifying system formed by the family. The mother's recognition of the father's word promotes the elaboration of difference within the family. Recognizing the father's discursive power, the mother proclaims her own inadequacy—her "lack" thus defines his "potency," as his "potency" constitutes both her necessary "lack" and her desire for the plenitude that will complete it.

If patriarchy thus revolves around the axis of maternal desire, it also produces that desire. In my discussion of *The Birthday Party,* I argued that desire finds its locus in the symbolic order of a particular culture, since the encoding of values within language—within the symbolic—teaches the subject how and what to desire. As Lacan argues, "It must be posited that, produced as it is by an animal at the mercy of language, man's desire is the desire of the Other."[22] The mother's desire, then, is never "her" desire, but a desire produced within the patriarchal Other. Allowed only a negative relationship to those culturally privileged attributes of the Father, the mother will take them as her object to desire, will desire the "phallus"—the master signifer of "power, fascination, instituting authority, terror, power to castrate."

The mother's desire for the phallus resembles but is not identical to the Freudian concept of penis envy. The difference centers around the status of each term: as a purely anatomical appendage, the penis belongs to the "real," while, as a signifier, the phallus finds its locus in the symbolic. Indeed, the relation of phallus to penis replicates that of the "symbolic father" to the actual father. Just as no father can ever "be" the Father, no father can ever possess the phallus. The mother's desire for the phallus—her (mis)-recognition of the father as he who possesses the phallus—reveals the extent of her subjection to the Other and its ensemble of "attitudes and perceptual structures."

The ideological association of the father with the phallus plays a crucial role in the reproduction of the dominant culture. If the mother recognizes the father's word as law, if she associates the phallus with the father, then the child will displace its desire for the mother's desire onto the father, become liberated from the Desire-of-the-Mother and subject to the Name-of-the-Father, and enter the signifying network, the symbolic order of language that constitutes subjectivity. If, on the other hand, the mother withholds recognition of the father's utterance, if she identifies her child as the phallic object of desire, then the child will remain within the Oedipal matrix, subjected to the mother's desire, unable to gain access to the symbolic order, and deprived of subjectivity.

While this overview admittedly does not do full justice to all the complexities of Lacan's argument, it emphasizes those aspects of his Oedipal scenario that bear most directly on *The Homecoming.* Max's fear of the defiling woman, and his narrative representations

of Jessie as a "whore" and "slutbitch of a wife," indicates that
Jessie refused to recognize his word as Law, a refusal that poses
a threat to the hegemony of the phallus. From a Lacanian perspective, we can read this refusal as a failure of desire that puts in
question the entire patriarchal enterprise and the field of the Other
that becomes the agent for that enterprise. Since "man's desire is
the desire of the Other," we must refer "Jessie's" failure of desire
back to the Other, the symbolic order that manufactures the subject's desire. Jessie's refusal to play her part in the Oedipal scenario effectually transfers the site of lack from the female body to
the ideological structure that has failed to transform the woman
into a receptacle for (its) desire.

As the Lacanian version of the Oedipal drama suggests, Max's
attempts to conceal this gap in the structure by obliterating Jessie
foredooms itself. "Her" failure of desire reinscribes itself in her
sons' problematic relationship to the symbolic, their inability either
to firmly establish a purchase on their subjectivity or to appropriate
the signifying power of the word.

With the pauses, silences, and ellipses in his speech indicating
a depleted linguistic reserve, Joey represents the most extreme
example of the brothers' inability to situate themselves within the
symbolic. If language allows us to identify ourselves as subjects
through the fundamental act of saying "I," then Joey's first words in
the play, "Feel a bit hungry" (p. 32), lacking the "I," the elementary
signifier of self, indicate his failure to achieve subjectivity.

Having failed to emerge in the symbolic, Joey remains trapped
within what Lacan terms the imaginary, the order in which the
subject's relationships are characterized by identification and duality, the order in which the subject experiences both the mirror
stage and the symbiotic union with the mother that the resolution
of the Oedipus complex works to disrupt. Joey's exercises provides
a vivid dramatization of mirror-stage misrecognition: *"Joey in front
of the mirror. He is doing some slow limbering-up exercises. He
stops, combs his hair, carefully. He then shadowboxes, heavily,
watching himself in the mirror"* (p. 53). Pinter captures here the
fundamentally ambivalent relationship between the subject and the
image with which it identifies. Translating the image's physical
coherence into a sign of the self's ontological coherence, fasci-
nated by the reflection he "carefully" monitors, Joey defines himself entirely in terms of this spectacular image that remains in
tension with his own reality. Max points to this tension when he
evaluates Joey's prowess as a boxer: "That's your only trouble as
a boxer. You don't know how to defend yourself, and you don't

know how to attack" (p. 33). The irreducible disequivalence between the reflected image and Joey's actual performance as a boxer
indicates the subject's inevitable failure to bridge the spatial and
ontological gap dividing it from its ideal reflection.

This failure to become the image with which we identify leads
Lacan to define self-apprehension as a form of self-alienation, and
to posit the subject's oscillation between love for and aggressivity
towards the image—love because the image serves as an ideal representation, aggressivity because the externality of the image resists assimilation. Such fluctuating movement between
identification and aggressivity characterizes Joey's relationships
with women and further attests to his entrapment within the Oedipal matrix. When the mother refuses to associate the phallus with
the father, she herself becomes the quintessential object of the
child's desire, the object with whom it identifies.

With Jessie absent, however, Joey finds his desire for identification "frustrated" (p. 85); his aggressivity serves as a kind of barom-
eter measuring the depths of this frustration. Aggression defines
his professional life—"I'm a boxer in the evenings, after work. I'm
in demolition in the daytime" (p. 67)—as it defines his sexuality.
The one account of Joey's sexual adventures that we hear centers
around rape, brutality, dominance (pp. 82–83). As Joey's encounter
with Ruth indicates, however, such sexual violence only displaces
his frustrated desire for identification with the mother. His failure
to "go the whole hog" (p. 82) with Ruth enables a different kind
of consumation: "I've been the whole hog plenty of times. Sometimes . . . you can be happy . . . and not go the whole hog. Now
and again . . . you can be happy . . . without going any hog" (p. 84).

The final image of Joey and Ruth vividly captures the sense of
complete identification between self and (m)other: *"Joey walks
slowly across the room. He kneels at [Ruth's] chair. She touches
his head, lightly. He puts his head in her lap. . . . She continues to
touch Joey's head, lightly"* (pp. 96–98). The absence of speech here,
however, serves as a reminder that such identification can only
sustain itself within the imaginary, *i.e.*, at the cost of Joey's necessary exclusion from the symbolic. At the play's conclusion, then,
Joey remains barred from meaning; from access to the word as
symbolic substitute for the self; from the circuit of linguistic exchange that integrates the subject within the social. More a mark
of his subjection to the (m)other than a transcendent moment of
unity between self and (m)other, Joey's reverent prostration before
Ruth confirms his static entrapment within the Oedipal phase.

Lenny's verbal facility, his penchant for elaborate narrative and ability to wield words as weapons, suggests an higher degree of integration within the linguistic field than Joey enjoys; yet, if more articulate than his brother, Lenny nevertheless bears a similar Oedipal burden that problematizes his relation to the symbolic. Like Joey, Lenny does not possess full membership in the symbolic; unlike Joey, who exists in the no-man's-land between the symbolic and the imaginary, Lenny occupies a position on the border between the symbolic and the real. For Lacan, the subject's emergence in the symbolic upon the successful resolution of the Oedpius complex precipitates a rupture with the real—the realm of unmediated, unsymbolized experience—as well as with the imaginary. To emerge from the Oedipal stage is to live within the symbolic order that both alienates us from the immediacy of our experience, while conferring upon that experience linguistic presence. To live within the real (as do the psychotic and the child denied liberation from its Oedipal thralldom), on the other hand, entails entrapment within an horrifying immediacy in which language fails to play its mediating role, in which one remains caught in experience, unable to generate a signifier capable of registering and distancing that experience.

What does it mean, then, to assert that Lenny inhabits a border region between the symbolic and the real? In such a region the real constantly threatens to outstrip the symbolic, not because of any lack of signifiers, but rather because the signifiers no longer provide an epistemological framework guaranteeing the certainty of the world they attempt to symbolize. This sense of the radically attenuated nature of language's ability to mediate experience manifests itself in Lenny's attempt to trace the source of the ticking that repeatedly interrupts his sleep. Teddy's query, "Have you got a clock in your room" (p. 41), reveals a faith in the power of the word to encompass the contents of the real. Lenny's suspicion of language leads him to reject the logical but arbitrary link between sign ("clock") and referent (an object that ticks found in bedrooms): "I've been having a bit of a rough time with this clock. The tick's been keeping me up. The trouble is I'm not all that convinced it was the clock. I mean there are lots of things that tick in the night. . . . [T]his question of me saying it was the clock that woke me up, well, that could very easily prove something of a false hypothesis" (p. 44).

Informing this passage is a sense of the inevitable failure of the linguistic order of conceptual taxonomy to stabilize the world of things. Once the symbolizing power of the word falls into abeyance, perception threatens to slide into a kind of madness. When we "look at . . . objects in the day and they're just commonplace" (p. 44), we happily hit upon a moment in which they coincide with their linguistic definitions, and signifiers, signifieds, and referents appear indissolubly joined, but such a moment reveals the workings of chance rather than nature or necessity. At other times, however, these same objects undergo transformations and metamorphoses that violently unmoor them from their linguistic anchorage and plunge the spectator into the immediacy of the real without the protective distance of language's mediating power.

As vision becomes disjunct from the order of words that provide its structure, language proves incapable of symbolizing or representing anything other than itself. Lenny thus conceptualizes language in terms of self-reflexivity rather than in terms of unequivocal reference, a position endorsed by Teddy, Max, and Joey:

> *Lenny.* Take a table. Philosophically speaking. What is it?
> *Teddy.* A table.
> *Lenny.* Ah. You mean it's nothing else but a table. Well, some people would envy your certainty. . . . All right . . . *take* it, *take* a table, but once you've taken it, what you going to do with it? Once you've got hold of it, where you going to take it?
> *Max.* You'd probably sell it. . . .
> *Joey.* Chop it up for firewood. (p. 68)

Teddy, Max, and Joey move effortlessly from the linguistic sign "table" to the object that convention and usage designate by that sign, while Lenny's questions reveal a profound suspicion of this correspondence theory of language. How can one take a table (not to mention selling or chopping it up for firewood), when "table" is, quite literally, a word, and when no internal relationship exists to link this word to the idea of "table"? If Lenny's question remains unanswered, it also remains unanswerable: to define the "being" of a table through recourse to any conceptual category would only produce a proliferating array of signifiers whose relationship to their signifieds demonstrates as little necessity as the relationship between the sign "table" and the object we call "table."

That more is at stake in this representational crisis than the limits of ontological stability or epistemological certainty becomes apparent when Ruth offers her own "answer" to Lenny's questions:

> Look at me. I . . . move my leg. That's all it is. But I wear . . . underwear . . . which moves with me . . . it . . . captures your attention. Perhaps you misinterpret. The action is simple. It's a leg . . . moving.

My lips move. Why don't you restrict . . . your observations to that?
Perhaps the fact that they move is more significant . . . than the words
which come through them. (pp. 68–69)

Ruth's comments foreground the female body's capacity to escape
the (masculine) systems of representation that attempt to produce
an appropriate—*i.e.,* unthreatening—femininity. That men may
"misinterpret" women; that women may not correspond to the
passive "nice feminine girl[s] with proper credentials" (p. 65) of
ideal masculine representations; that the cultural order may lack
the power to make women live its representations of female sexuality—these are precisely the fears patriarchy can never completely
allay in either *The Collection* or *The Homecoming*.

Ruth does not so much change as extend the terms of the debate
on the nature of representation by placing in question the stability
of the representational practices that produce sexual difference
and actively contribute to the patriarchal configuration of power
relations. As Ruth's comments implicitly ask, if the status of tables
and clocks remains unstable, and if the world constantly threatens
to slip its representational moorings, how can patriarchy hope to
carry out its project of managing female otherness by encouraging,
if not coercing, women into identifying with the subject positions
of the feminine it represents in its ideological fictions?

At issue here is less the power of representation—the sign's ability to ensure the being of the object it presumes to designate—
than the power necessary to enforce representation, the power to
suppress knowledge of the kinds of slippages and disjunctures re-
vealed by Lenny's suspicion of the symbolic. When Ruth suggests
that men "misinterpret" the female body, she emphasizes that the
representational refashioning and coding of the body remains quite
distinct from the body's "actual" existence, even as the author(iz-
er)s of such codings attempt to deny the distinction by forcing the
body to live out its representation in a socially palpable form.
The claim that representation can *mis*interpret suggests the parallel
claim that representation can *only* interpret; that no inner relationship binds the particular representation to the object it purports
to represent.

Ruth adopts the same kind of skepticism Lenny manifests in
his discussion of the cock and the table, turning it against both
patriarchal representations of women—representations that
threaten to lose all force by betraying their status as misinterpreta-
tions—and against Lenny himself. Ruth's comments provide a response not only to Lenny's question concerning the ontology of

tables, but also to the two narratives that he recounts earlier in the play to establish his power over her. That Lenny utilizes narrative, in Pinter's words, to "keep the other in its place"[23] presents something of a paradox given his keen sense of the ineluctable disjuncture between word and world. Lenny's dependence upon narrative, his refusal to relinquish principles of representation that he himself has placed in question, suggests the central role played by representational practices in the production of masculine power.

The narratives detail acts of violence that allow Lenny to dominate women who attempt to transgress the boundaries defining the marginal space patriarchy assigns them. Both narratives figure this transgression in terms of the woman's usurpation of the linguistic authority that patriarchy appropriates as an ideological component of masculinity: "I was standing alone under an arch . . . when a certain lady came up to me and made me a certain proposal" (p. 46); "while I was having my mid-morning cup of tea in a neighbouring cafe . . . an old lady approached me and asked me if I would give her a hand with her iron mangle" (p. 48). Lenny meets the verbal aggression prompting these "unreasonable demands" (p. 48) with a display of brutal "masculine" aggression that restores the "natural" balance of power favoring the male at the expense of the female.

Perhaps the most striking feature of these accounts is the manner in which their content and the context in which Lenny narrates them mirror each other: not only do they relate the acts of violence Lenny directs against women, but the narration itself constitutes an act of violence against Ruth. While Lenny's narratives depict a kind of sadism, they also enact a kind of sadism, seeking to effect through language the same domination of Ruth that he achieves through physical brutality over the prostitute and the old lady. Ruth resists his sadism, however, by challenging his ability to exercise narrative power. Employing the conventionally negative representations of woman as whore and woman as polluted, Lenny declares that he might have considered accepting the prostitute's proposal, except that "she was falling apart with the pox" (p. 46). His fear of the pox, a fear of being submerged in female disease, prompts his savage attack on the woman. When Ruth asks Lenny, "How did you know she was diseased?" he replies, "How did I know? *(Pause.)* I decided she was" (p. 47).

Impressive as this response may sound, it evades the implications of Ruth's question and contradicts Lenny's keen sense of the limits of representational power manifested in his comments about the clock and the table. With his equation of narrative power and epistemological mastery—his assertion that as narrator he "knows" the prostitute was diseased because he can decide to represent her as diseased—Lenny now endorses the same view of the arbitrary bond between signifier and signified that at other moments in the play engenders his profound distrust of language. At issue here is the question, does power inhere in representation, or does power create a "base" for the "superstructure" of representation? Ruth's maneuvering Lenny into asserting omnipotence as a narrator addresses his question by forcing him to expose the tenuousness of his claims to mastery. Lenny's "I decided she was" transfers the source of power from language to the speaker, thus tacitly admitting that this power ultimately resides outside and functions as a necessary support for verbal authority. I am not suggesting that Pinter's plays categorically dissociate language and power, but rather that they repeatedly link linguistic power to more "material" forms of power, a link dramatized most vividly by Goldberg's dependence upon McCann's violence and Nicholas's dependence for his power as an interrogator upon state-supported violence. (One for the Road).

That Lenny lacks such "material" power becomes apparent as Ruth begins to mimic the image of woman he produces in his narrative. Echoing the prostitute's "proposal," her threat to "take" Lenny (p. 50), less the manifestation of a devouring female sexuality than an enactment of the masculine *construction* of that sexuality, confronts him with his own representation come to life. In effect, Ruth undermines Lenny's power as narrator by *staging* rather than submitting to her interpellation within the narrative, *performing* rather than undergoing the act of recognition through which an auditor, audience, or reader comes to identify with a subject position inside a particular narrative. While Lenny contains the threatening feminine other within his narrative through a kind of representational violence—both the attack on the prostitute and the more insidious violence perpetrated against women by imaging "the feminine" as a syphilitic whore—he lacks the ability to translate the discursive mechanisms of control into a tangible form of power capable of dominating Ruth.

Like Stella's final silence, Ruth's question and her subsequent mimetic rendering of the sexually threatening woman expose the gap betwen linguistic and "material" forms of power—a gap that parallels the disjuncture Lenny discovers between the sign and the world. If language lacks the incantatory efficacy to stabilize a world for which it can provide an epistemological guarantee, neither can it create the kind of extra-linguistic power that transforms mere words into the Word, utterance into law, and representation into reality. Trapped between Oedipal estrangement from the symbolic and dependence upon a language lacking in the inherent capacity to empower its speaker, Lenny inevitably fails to distance himself from the horrifying immediacy of the real, the realm of menacing clocks, tables, and women, fails to declare his mastery through a saving act of nomination.

Where Lenny fails, Teddy claims success; unlike his brother, Teddy declares he can "operate on things and not in things":

> It's a way of being able to look at the world. It's a question of how far you can operate on things and not in things. I mean it's a question of your capacity to ally the two, to relate the two, to balance the two. To see, to be able to *see*! . . . You're just objects. You just . . . move about. . . . But you're lost in it. You won't get me being . . . I won't be lost in it. (pp. 77–78)

This defense of what Teddy calls "intellectual equilibrium" (p. 78) affirms his freedom from Oedipal bondage and his full participation in the symbolic, the order allowing the subject to "operate on things" through the processes of linguistic representation. Teddy's comments here display the same sense of an univocal correspondence between language and the constituents of the real that he reveals earlier when he asserts that, "philosophically speaking," a table is a table. The primacy granted the visual by his privileging the ability "to see" reinforces this correspondence theory since visual mastery entails a linguistically ordered epistemological mastery—*i.e.,* we know what we see because the objects in our field of vision conform to the words with which we label them.

Teddy's own language, however, repeatedly undercuts these assertions of mastery over the real. Telling his father and brothers that "I can see what you do. It's the same as I do. But you're lost in it. You won't get me being . . . I won't be lost in it" (p. 78), Teddy betrays the anxiety masked by his claims to "intellectual equilibrium." Less the articulation of a philosophical stance than a defensive strategy projecting his inner fears onto an external object, the contrast Teddy draws between his family's lack of self-hood ("You're lost in it") and his own empowering ability "to see" fails to address the implications of his realization that "what you do . . . [i]s the *same* as I do." Attempting to displace his feared loss of self onto the family, he becomes the victim of his own language, which reinscribes this loss within Teddy: "You won't get me being . . . I won't be lost in it." Teddy stands condemned by the existential pun contained in "you won't get me being"; to escape "be[ing] lost in it," he retreats from "being," but this refusal of subjectivity reveals the extent to which Teddy has already become lost, a point ironically underscored by the blackout (in which he becomes lost to our vision) following immediately upon his words.

Teddy's flight from subjectivity belies the implicit assertion of linguistic authority suggested by his declared ability to "operate on things and not in things." His repeated attempts to withdraw from philosophical argument with Lenny; his comically ineffectual theft of Lenny's cheese-roll as a substitute for direct verbal or physical confrontation; his virtual refusal to intervene in the family's "assimilation" of Ruth—all of these examples, suggesting a kind of linguistic paralysis, serve to remind us that, like his brothers, Teddy remains trapped in an Oedipal crisis that disqualifies him from fully acceeding to the symbolic. Of all the brothers, Teddy apparently possessed the most intense Oedipal relationship to Jessie, as evidenced by Sam's comment, "You were always your mother's favourite. She told me. . . . You were always the . . . you were always the main object of her love" (p. 79).

Like Joey's violent aggressivity, of which it provides an inverse example, Teddy's paralytic detachment results from the deprivation he experiences owing to Jessie's absence. If Ruth embodies the longed-for return of the mother for Joey, she fulfills a similar function for Teddy. For Teddy, marriage provides the occasion for the male to negate his own sense of lack by regaining the maternal object in the figure of the wife. As this object, the missing component of Teddy's self, Ruth transforms absence into presence, a presence that Teddy attempts to manipulate. Throughout their first scene together, Teddy repeatedly attempts to position Ruth, placing verbal restrictions on her movements, at one point switching from entreaty ("Why don't you go to bed?" [p. 38]) to command ("Go to bed" [p. 38]). Such positioning obviously constitutes a bid for power and mastery, but it also points to Teddy's fear of repeating his loss of the "mother"—a fear Ruth both exposes and exploits as an instrument of resistance:

> Ruth. I think I'll have a breath of air.
> Teddy. Air? (Pause.) What do you mean? . . . But what am I going to do? (Pause.) The last thing I want is a breath of air. Why do you want a breath of air? . . . I'm not going to bed without you. . . .
> Ruth I won't be long. (She goes out of the front door. Teddy goes to

the window, peers out after her, half turns from the window, stands, suddenly chews his knuckles.) (pp. 39–40)

With the image of Teddy nervously chewing his knuckles, Pinter captures the barely repressed anxiety and insecurity of a man whose "intellectual equilibrium" fails to compensate for his paralyzing sense of loss and self-division. Perhaps nowhere else in the play does his lack of "being" reveal itself more clearly than in his panicked attempts to prevent Ruth from leaving the house, as if her spatial absence entailed the abolition of his self. Ruth's threat to produce her own absence adds an ironic twist to Teddy's pride in his capacity to "operate on things." Rather than implying a combined epistemological/linguistic/visual mastery, his ability "to see" here suggests his dependence upon the presence and visual image of Ruth, an image capable of inducing the same kind of identification that binds the child to the mother, an image that leaves Teddy "lost" in the imaginary.

As Joey remains trapped by the contradiction between aggressivity towards and identification with the image of the woman, and Lenny remains trapped between his distrust of language and his reliance upon narrative as a site for the production of power, so Teddy remains trapped between a dependence upon Ruth and the paralytic detachment that prevents his achieving "being" through any kind of decisive and empowering action. His ineffectual attempt to woo Ruth away from the family with the promise that "[y]ou can help me with my lectures when we get back. I'd love that" (p. 71) encapsulates this lack of "being." Hardly an attractive proposition from Ruth's perspective, Teddy's offer denies her status as an independent entity, while assimilating her as a constitutive element of his self. Paradoxically, however, Teddy's denial of Ruth's human (as opposed to sexual) difference grants her considerable power by defining her as the agent who will transform his lack into plenitude.

Like Stella, then, Ruth both embodies the identity of the husband and places that identity in jeopardy. Her decision to remain with the family "castrates" Teddy, depriving him of the repository of his being without granting him the compensations offered by the symbolic order. Her refusal to return with Teddy condemns him to repeat the rupture—occasioned by Jessie's death—of his union with the mother, thus banishing him from the confines of the imaginary. Ruth converts Teddy's homecoming into a kind of permanent exile: while at the play's conclusion Joey retreats into the imaginary and Lenny remains suspended between the symbolic and the real, Teddy remains barred from taking up a position in any of these registers. His lack of "being" ultimately consigns him to absence—his physical absence during the play's final tableau, and the ontological absence of the American "waste land" to which he returns. Ruth describes America as "all rock. And sand. It stretches . . . so far . . . everywhere you look. And there's lots of insects there" (p. 69)—a dessicated and infertile land that becomes the fitting site of Teddy's only possible homecoming.

Throughout this chapter, I have argued that we can trace the "dysfunctional" nature of Max's family to the cataclysmic effects of Jessie's failure of desire, her failure to recognize Max as the bearer of the Word and the phallus. If, however, desire emanates from the Other, articulated through the codes that constitute the language of cultural power, then Jessie's failure reveals the larger failure of the patriarchal order to ensure its own ideological reproduction. At stake here are both the family's role as site of this reproduction and the cultural privilege attached to the role of the "symbolic father." Max may tell his sons to "find yourselves a mother," but the real task facing the family is finding itself a Father, a figure who can inhabit the space of the "symbolic father," thus restoring the balance of patriarchal power relations.

As I suggested at the beginning of this chapter, it is *Ruth* who comes to occupy this position, providing the play with its ambiguous resolution. Ruth may resist the various forms of "masculine" power—violence (Joey), discursive capture (Lenny), control of the female body (Teddy)—directed against her, but her resistance depends upon her ability to mime the "fascination . . . instituting authority . . . power to castrate" that Barthes identifies as the ideological characteristics assigned to the "symbolic father." In the ensuing discussion, I want to focus on whether this mimicry dismantles or reconstitutes the field of patriarchal power.

Ruth's capacity for resistance depends upon her ability to manipulate the threat of a castration locating in the male that lack which patriarchy defines as an ideological component of femininity. Her ability to play the role of Joey's maternal object, suggesting that she gains mastery by protecting him against castration, seemingly contradicts what I have just asserted. Viewed from the perspective of the social universe structured by the symbolic order, however, Joey's identification with his new "mother" produces its own form of castration, since "the child, identifying with the [mother] . . . passively submissive and subjugated, is not a 'subject,' but a lack, a nothing . . . a blank."[24] Joey's silent prostration before Ruth during the play's final moments affirms his castration, his status as "a lack, a nothing," lacking even the basic ability to say "I."

I have already discussed how Ruth resists Teddy's bid for power—his attempt to fix her within spatial boundaries by placing restrictions on her movements—by ultimately refusing to serve as his maternal object, thus forcing hm to repeat the traumatic division, the traumatic *castration,* occasioned by Jessie's death. Similarly, Ruth's refusal to submit to Lenny's discursive manipulations "castrates" him by undermining his performance as narrator. By effectively challenging Lenny's verbal attempts at domination, Ruth not only rejects the passive role he would impose on her, but actively becomes the agent of castration, refusing to recognize his narrative as an expression of phall(ogocentr)ic power.

Ruth not only appropriates the power to castrate, but also turns "fascination" (one of the symbolic father's attributes identified by Barthes) against the patriarchal order that claims this power as it prerogative. To fascinate and exercise hypnotic power implies the coercive mastery of the gaze that dominates and transfixes the objects in its field of vision. In my discussion of *The Collection,* I argued that the gaze, with its ability to penetrate and demystify, functions as one of the most conspicuous manifestations of patriarchal power. Laura Mulvey summarizes how the visual transactions of the patriarchal scopic regime effect the subordination of women: "The determining male gaze projects its phantasy on to the female figure which is . . . simultaneously looked at and displayed, with [its] appearance coded for strong visual and erotic impact so that [it] can be said to connote *to-be-looked-at-ness.*"[25]

We might expect Ruth to exercise fascination by inverting the hierarchical ordering of the scopophilic drive, by appropriating the power of the gaze in order to transform men into the embodiment of "to-be-looked-at-ness." Rather than adopting this strategy, however, Ruth resorts to mimetic performance, a deliberate assumption of the role of women as spectacle that allows her to align exhibitionism with activity rather than passivity. She both actively solicits the male gaze and promotes the specular objectification of her body that the gaze effects, not as a mark of her subjection to patriarchy, but in order to create a site of resistance to and within the system that defines women in terms of lack. Ruth manipulates the dominant scopic economy, revealing that power can inhere in display as well as in spectatorship.

To explore how the scopic exchange, the alignment of male gaze with female image, provides the agency whereby Ruth assumes power, let me return to her "answer" to Lenny's question concerning the ontology of tables:

> Look at me. I . . . move my leg. That's all it is. But I wear . . . underwear . . . which moves with me . . . it . . . captures your attention. Perhaps you misinterpret. The action is simple. It's a leg . . . moving. My lips move. Why don't you restrict . . . your observations to that? Perhaps the fact that they move is more significant . . . than the words which come through them.

This passage enacts a complex strategy combining mimicry, fascination, and the threat of castration, less to undermine than to redefine the scopic regime. Ruth's self-display, a voluntary act rather than orchestrated by the male gaze, not only actively invites that gaze ("Look at me"), but also promotes the gaze's transformation of certain privileged zones of her body into fetishized objects. Initially, Ruth's courting of the fetishistic scopophilia producing the viewing subject's overvaluation of her legs and lips seems to replicate patriarchy's division of the sexes into men who look and women at whom they look. Similarly, her comment, "Perhaps the fact that [the lips] move is more significant . . . than the words which come through them," not only imprisons her within the field of the male gaze, but also endorses patriarchy's efforts to marginalize women by denying them a position of centrality and power within the symbolic order.

Far from a source of empowerment, Ruth's implicit sugestion that women are to be seen and not heard initially appears to validate the power wielded by the scopophilic lens. Her language, however, inaugurates a shift that both transfers power from the specular subject to the specular object and locates agency on the side of the object and passivity on the side of the subject. Her command to "look at me" suggests that the object structures and limits the gaze rather than the gaze transfixing the object. Her repeated use of "move" when discussing the fetishized zones of the body ("I . . . move my leg . . . It's a leg moving . . . My lips move") places the body beyond spatial constraint while leaving the spectator frozen in the act of looking. Finally, Ruth redefines the ocular transaction supporting the visual economy by denying that the gaze can effect a specular capture of the object; instead, the object "captures your attention," turning the gaze against its source, transforming the viewing subject into the victim of its own scopic desire.

What precisely is the nature of this desire that impels men not only to direct their gaze at women, but to fetishize and iconicize them? The answer to this question turns on a paradox: men *must* see women in order to deny their knowledge that women have nothing to see, must ensure women's visible presence in order to disavow their knowledge of women's anatomical absence. To phrase this another way, the fetishistic privileging of the woman's body (or any portion of that body) represents the male subject's defense against castration anxiety. In order to guard against his own fear of castration, the male rejects his primal "discovery" of the female's lack—the deficiency he locates in the woman's genital region—by "build[ing] up the physical beauty of the object, trans-forming it into something satisfying in itself."[26]

In "Fetishism," Freud provides the classical account of how fe-tishism provides the male with an avenue of escape from his castra-tion anxiety, his fear that he might find himself subject to the same castration that constitutes woman as his sexual other. While the essay attempts to preserve the Freudian paradigm of woman-lack/man-sufficiency (albeit a sufficiency susceptible to the threat of lack), Freud's text self-deconstructs when he describes the male's discovery of female "castration" as an "uncanny"[27] experience. In an essay devoted to conceptualizing the "uncanny," Freud defines this term as "that class of the frightening which leads back to what is known of old and long familiar."[28] The male's "uncanny" vision of the vagina (which, for Freud, entails the "horror" of not seeing the penis), then, does not so much constitute a discovery of the female's castration as it does a (re)discovery of his *own* castration, his own lack. That fetishism thus stems less from disavowal (the male subject's denial of the castration that marks woman as irreme-diably other) than from projection (the male subject's displacement of an internal insufficiency onto the exterior form of the female body) suggests its fragility as a defense mechanism. Because the "castration" fetishism works to negate is "uncanny," a *fait accom-pli* rather than a looming danger, the fetish always threatens to evoke the anxiety it must dispel.

I offer these observations to help clarify my assertion that Ruth's entrance into the dominant scopic economy as a fetishized object disrupts the organization of that economy and allows her to resist the encroachment of patriarchal power. Even when transformed into a fetish, the woman threatens to transgress the boundaries established by the scopic regime by confronting the male specular subject with an "uncanny" reflection of his own lack. Such a threat implicitly speaks through Ruth's meditation on the "meaning" of her lips: "My lips move. Why don't you restrict . . . your observa-

tions to that? Perhaps the fact that they move is more significant
. . . than the words which come through them." These lines reveal
the indissoluble link between castration and fetishism: as Ruth
suggests, the erotic overvaluing of her lips entails the social under-
valuing of her speech, entails a kind of castration that denies
women access to the phallic potency with which patriarchal ideology invests the Word.

Yet Ruth's comments raise the specter of another, more alarming
(from the perspective of the male specular subject) castration. Incapable of enunciating anything that patriarchy regards as meaningful or powerful speech, Ruth's lips frame a gaping hole, an
absence, a nothing-to-see that, through a metaphoric substitution,
simultaneously stands in for and evokes the "castrated" female
genitalia—stands in for because of the external displacement from
one zone of the body to another, and evokes because of the inevitable associations that form part of the word "lips'" semiotic baggage. Fetishism works precisely to exclude the "lips" from the
man's field of vision, but Ruth disrupts this operation by foregrounding her status as fetish and, therefore, as absence. Flaunting
her "lack" by drawing attention to the lips that men reduce to
silence, she cannot help but evoke the image of those other lips
that do not speak, the lips that the fetish must mask, the lips that
confront the male with the "uncanny" revelation of his own castration.

What would be the content of such a revelation? To answer this
question, let me emphasize that, as Lacan's account of the Oedipal
crisis suggests, the concept of male castration takes a symbolic
rather than anatomical reference: at issue here is the status of the
phallus rather than the penis. As the signifer of male privilege, the
phallus exceeds the penis in the same manner that the "symbolic
father" exceeds the actual father. As I observed in my discussion
of the play's Oedipal scenario, patriarchy demands that the wife
recognize the "symbolic father" by desiring "his" phallus. Such
desire assumes her subjection to the patriarchal ideology that collapses the symbolic into the real, promoting her (mis)recognition
of the penis as the phallus. Without the wife's desire not only would
the gap between phallus and penis reveal itself, but the phallus
itself would be exposed as an imposture, an ideological fiction
rather than an essential attribute of masculinity.

The lack at the heart of male castration, then, is a lack of the
phallus and not the penis. Indeed, as Lacan suggests in his remark
that "virile display itself appears as feminine,"[29] the display of the
penis that, taken in itself, possesses no privileged status, confirms

this lack by revealing the gap between the real (the penis as anatomical appendage) and the symbolic (the phallus as signifier of
cultural power). Sexual desire threatens to subvert the phallic order since it can only actualize itself in what Lacan terms "the real
of sexual copulation,"[30] the act that, by engaging the penis in all
its anatomical reality, deconstructs the myth of the phallus.

I have argued that Ruth's mimicry of the woman-as-fetish threatens to confront the men with their castration, their lack of the
phallus. She not only fascinates in her role as object of erotic
contemplation, but structures that contemplation, arousing and
manipulating the sexual desire that exposes the fraudulent status
of the phallus. The play gives vivid dramatic expression to the gap
between phallus and penis in Max's final ludicrous attempts to
subordinate Ruth to his desire:

> I'm too old, I suppose. She thinks I'm an old man. *(Pause.)* I'm not
> such an old man. *(Pause.)* . . . You think I'm too old for you? *(Pause.)*
> Listen. You think you're just going to get that big slag all the time?
> . . . *(He begins to groan, clutches his stick, falls on to his knees by
> the side of her chair. His body sags. The groaning stops. His body
> straightens. He looks at her, still kneeling.)* I'm not an old man.
> *(Pause.)* Do you hear me? *(He raises his face to her.)* Kiss me. (pp.
> 96–98)

With his groaning and physical debility, Max appears as the embodiment of impotence rather than "virile display." Judged from
the perspective of the phallus, however, *any* manifestation of sexual desire, *any* suggestion that the male possesses a real sexual
organ rather than the ultimate signifier, will reveal the male's insufficiency. Having aroused Max's desire, Ruth forces him to display
the castration and "femininity" (defined as lack of the phallus) that
mark male sexuality. She exposes the fraudulent nature of the cultural privilege granted the phallus by revealing, to phrase it bluntly,
that Max is a prick. As Jane Gallop writes, "Since the phallic order
demands that the law rather than desire issue from the paternal
position, an exposure of the father as desiring, a view of the father
as prick . . . feminizes him."[31]

Like *The Collection, The Homecoming* explores the cracks and
fissures in the structure of patriarchy by dramatizing the dissolution of the patriarchal family, an ideological support that helps
ensure the reproduction of that structure. *The Homecoming,* however, proceeds even further in this exploration than does the earlier
play: Ruth not only disables the family as an institution of "mascu-

line" power, but also reconstitutes the family as an unit in which power passes from the feminized father (Max) to the mother (Ruth). As Esslin observes, Ruth's victory "is the 'homecoming' of the title. It is not Teddy who has come back home . . . but the mother who has returned."[32] We can extend Esslin's remarks even further and say that the new configuration of family relations at the play's conclusion represents the homecoming not only of the mother but of matriarchy itself. Viewed from this perspective, Ruth's victory over Max enacts the return of the repressed to a position of dominant centrality.

Yet we must draw a distinction between structures of power and the *forms* of power that those structures seek to embody. Ruth effectively disables and reconstitutes one of those structures—the patriarchal family—but, in what amounts to the play's supreme irony, she can only achieve her victory through the exercise of phallic power: the power to castrate and the power to fascinate. In Ruth's victory, we can discern the ambiguity to which Diamond and Quigley respond: her empowerment disrupts the patriarchal ideology that equates the "masculine" and the phallus, while, at the same time, her own mimicry and appropriation of the Father's "hallucinatory attributes" secure the status of the phallus as the master signifier of cultural power. Rather than a victory over phallic power, the reconfiguration of the family as a matriarchal unit provides a new and stronger channel for that power than did the attenuated patriarchal unit over which Max presided. Indeed, at the risk of oversimplification, we can say that Ruth gains mastery because she is more phallic than Max, able to exercise the power to which Max can only lay verbal claim. To put this another way: it is not the mother, but the "symbolic father" who makes the homecoming that gives the play its title.

Ruth's relationship to phallic power illustrates Foucault's thesis that subjects do not so much possess power as they articulate the power that constitutes them: "The individual is an effect of power, and at the same time, or precisely to the extent to which it is that effect, it is the element of its articulation. The individual which power has constituted is at the same time its vehicle."[33] Like language (with which Foucault makes an implicit comparison when he identifies power as an object of articulation), power finds its locus of origin in a space beyond the subject who will attain subjectivity by its ability to internalize and become the "vehicle" of that power.

We should not mistake this conceptualizing of the subject as an "effect" of language and power for an expression of crude deter-

minism by either Foucault or—to the extent that his plays dramatize a similar view of the subject's relationship to power—Pinter.
Much of the power of Pinter's work stems from his ability to dramatize the tension between the subject's position as an "effect" of
power and the subject's ability to manipulate that power as the
"vehicle" of its "articulation," and it is this tension that produces
The Homecoming's ambiguity. As the "vehicle" of phallic power,
Ruth can utilize that power to undermine the structure of the patriarchal family; as the "effect" of phallic power (and *The Homecoming* always identifies power in terms of the phallus, no matter who
serves as the agent of that power), Ruth reifies the phallus through
"her" empowerment.

Despite their seeming differences, then, *The Homecoming* confronts its audience with the same vision of cultural power we saw
in *The Birthday Party:* a power capable of resisting resistance, of
colonizing and reconstituting itself in the very site of difference
from which opposition arises. Certainly the patriarchal cultural
order that *The Homecoming* interrogates finds itself beset by the
kinds of contradictions and crises absent from the world of *The
Birthday Party.* What links these works (and I would also include
The Collection here, since we see a version of the dominant paradigm of sexual difference reasserting itself as the "masculine"
Harry reduces Bill to the proper state of "feminine" passivity), is
the perception that the dominant cultural order remains in place
by controlling the codes that set the terms for and determine what
counts as power. That Ruth should both expose the fiction of the
phallus *and* come to embody the phallus suggests that patriarchy
will remain the dominant form of social organization as long as the
challenges to its hegemony conform to its grammar of power. To
return to an observation of Irigaray that I quoted earlier, the belief
that "one need only be a woman to remain outside phallic power"
can never produce a fundamental alteration in the play of patriarchal power relations. The "outside" of phallic power could only
take the form of a new economy of power, one which divorces
itself from the threat of castration, the hypnotic spell of fascination,
or any other ideological component of the Father's power. Whether
or not such an "outside" is possible (in Pinter's dramatic universe)
is a question I will consider in the following discussion of *Old
Times.*

5

"I'll Be Watching You": *Old Times* and the Field of Vision

I have argued that both *The Collection* and *The Homecoming* chart the cracks and fissures in the structure of patriarchy by focusing on those points of tension that threaten the dominant gender ideology and the subject positions, *i.e.,* the social identities, articulated through that ideology. At the same time, however, we have seen that this ideology possesses remarkable recuperative powers, locating itself within Harry and Bill's homosexual relationship and Ruth's "matriarchy." In both instances, *loci* of difference become sites of the same, preserving a paradigm of sexual difference that empowers the "masculine" while devaluing the "feminine." To challenge the patriarchal economy of power, as I suggested at the close of the preceding chapter, would entail adopting a strategy not contaminated by the kinds of assumptions upon which patriarchy rests. Such a strategy, for example, would not (as Ruth did) seek to transfer power from the male gaze to the female body on display, but would actively seek to invalidate all associations between specularity and power.

Whether such a strategy can ever succeed in locating a space outside the dominant specular economy is a question posed by *Old Times,* a play exploring the ideological uses of two prominent modes of vision in our culture—the voyeuristic gaze that demystifies and objectifies, and the narcissistic gaze serving as the vehicle for identification. While the play examines the importance of the gaze for the elaboration of patriarchal power relations, it also deconstructs the scopic division of labor that casts man as the active bearer of the look and woman as passive object of the look. Drawing upon both Sartre's concept of the "look-looked-at" and Lacan's theory of the disjuncture between the eye and the gaze, I will argue that the play reveals an instability inscribed within the very structure of the gaze—an instability that seemingly allows women to

108

occupy a space (or, more to the point, to disperse themselves across a number of spaces) outside the field of the gaze. I say "seemingly" because, like *The Homecoming, Old Times* concludes with a tableau that threatens to undo everything we have just witnessed, a tableau confronting us with a form of power that, phoenix-like, can arise at the very site of its defeat.

Like *The Collection* and *The Homecoming,* the action of *Old Times* centers around the battle for possession of a woman, a battle in which Anna and Deeley vie for control of Kate, Deeley's wife. I want to begin my discussion by examining a passage that italicizes the central role played by the gaze in this battle:

> *Deeley.* [Kate] likes taking long walks. All that. You know. Raincoat on. Off down the lane, hands deep in pockets. All that sort of thing. *(Anna turns to look at Kate.) . . . Sometimes I take her face in my hands and look at it. . . . Yes, I look at it, holding it in my hands.* Then I kind of let it go, take my hands away, leaving it floating.
> *Kate.* My head is quite fixed. I have it on.
> *Deeley. (To Anna.)* It just floats away.
> *Anna.* She was always a dreamer. *(Anna sits.)* Sometimes, walking, in the park, I'd say to her, you're dreaming, you're dreaming, wake up, what are you dreaming? *and she'd look round at me, flicking her hair, and look at me as if I were part of her dream.*[1]

This exchange exemplifies what G. G. Cima terms "the syntax of cinema"[2] running throughout the play. Like a camera moving in for a close-up, Deeley's language freezes Kate within a "shot," translating her into a cinematic image structured around the determining absence of the camera itself. Barthes offers the following as his "definition of the image, of any image: that from which I am excluded."[3] In the case of the cinematic image, this split between the subject and the object of representation—the presence of one term necessitating the absence of the other—guarantees the power of the cinematic apparatus, and specifically the camera producing, but absent from, the image. Subjecting Kate to its monitoring gaze, Deeley's language grants him the power of the camera to transcend the images it produces, to view from a different order from that to which the image belongs. His identification with the camera is at its most pronounced when he describes her walking with "raincoat on. Off down the lane, hands deep in pockets." Where is Deeley in relation to Kate as she walks? While the "lens" of his language insistently tracks her, never allowing her freedom from the cinematic space, Deeley himself remains invisible, transformed into the disembodied eye of the camera, framing her from a vantage exterior to his "Film's" diegesis. Detached from the spectacle, unrepresentable, Deeley asserts the power of the gaze divorced from the eye, a de-materialized gaze that frees him from the destiny of the body: to possess a body means that one can be filmed, can become an object of representation trapped in a specular prison; to possess the monolithic, unmediated gaze of the camera, the ultimate subject of representation, means that one stands invulnerable because invisible, the architect of the spectacular prison in which the image remains confined.

Deeley's scopic desire—a desire to gaze without fear of becoming an object of the gaze, a desire to disappear within and become transformed into the cinematic apparatus—manifests itself in such a ludicrously exaggerated assertion of power as "I had a great crew in Sicily. A marvellous cameraman. Irving Shultz. Best in the business. . . . I wrote the film and directed it. My name is Orson Welles" (p. 38). That Deeley can only claim authority by quoting Welles may undercut that claim, but it also reveals the extent to which he identifies himself with the sovereign power of cinematic technology.

As Brunmuller points out,[4] Deeley's "I wrote the film and directed it. My name is Orson Welles" approximates the final lines of two of Welles's films: *The Trial* ("I . . . wrote and directed this film. My name is Orson Welles") and *The Magnificent Ambersons* ("I wrote the script and directed it. My name is Orson Welles"). In neither film does Welles deliver these lines on camera; rather, he "appears" as a disembodied voice whose powerful "body" is nothing less than the cinematic apparatus itself. As he speaks the final line of *The Trial,* the camera focuses on the brilliant light cast by a slide projector; similarly, at the conclusion of *The Magnificent Ambersons,* the camera focuses on a microphone that recedes into darkness after Welles delivers the final line.

I will return to the ambiguity of Deeley's identification with Welles later; for the moment, I cite his quotation of the director in order to indicate the kind of absolute, monocular power—the power of the disincarnate "eye" of the camera—with which he attempts to subject Kate to scopic domination. His seemingly innocuous description of her appearance as she walks to the beach simultaneously positions her as object of the cinematic gaze and constrains her to remain objectified by abolishing all "off-screen" space.

Deeley aspires to the unblinking, fixated gaze that "arrests the flux of phenomena . . . in an eternal moment of disclosed pres-

ence,"[5] that transcends the troubling confusion between surface
and depth, appearance and being: "Sometimes I take her face in
my hands and look at it. . . . Yes, I look at it, holding it in my
hands." Remove the frame, fade out the "shot," and Kate dissolves
into the void beyond the camera, the no-man's-land ruthlessly excluded from cinematic "reality": "Then I kind of let [her face] go,
take my hands away, leave it floating."

Seemingly granting Deeley uncontested mastery of Kate, his
"syntax of cinema" can neither escape its primarily defensive function nor efface the anxiety of which it is a product. Such anxiety
manifests itself in his description of Kate's "floating," although we
may only realize this retrospectively, after Anna takes up the same
image in her description of Kate's emergence from the bath: "[A]
kind of floating. . . . She floats from the bath. Like a dream. Unaware of anyone standing, with her towel, waiting for her, waiting
to wrap it round her. Quite absorbed" (p. 50). While both Anna
and Deeley describe Kate in terms of "floating," the connotative
value of the word changes drastically from speaker to speaker.
Deeley's words do not so much define "floating" as one of Kate's
characteristics as they image "floating" as an effect of his sovereign
cinematic gaze, or, to be more precise, the *withdrawal* of that gaze:
"Sometimes I take her face in my hands *and look at it. . . . Then
I let it go . . . leave it floating."* According to Deeley, once the
monocular gaze of the director-as-camera turns away from the image it "creates" and upon which it bestows objectivity, that image
floats away into a kind of nothingness.

I would emphasize "according to Deeley" in the previous sentence. Keeping in mind Ruth's equation of representation with interpretation (thus allowing for the possibility of *mis*interpretation),
Deeley's words raise an important question: not so much why he
images Kate in terms of floating, but why he represents/interprets
this floating as a sign of powerlessness and contingency. Does his
"filming" of Kate, in other words, constitute an assertion of decisive male control or an expression of patriarchal anxiety?

Anna suggests a possible answer to these questions in her memory of Kate's appearance after a bath. Here, Kate's "floating" no
longer suggests the dissolution of subjectivity, but a radically mer-
ucrial subjectivity conceptualized in terms of flux, mulitplicity, and
slippage, a subjectivity that floats across the discursive categories
designed to entrap it. As Kate eludes Anna, "waiting to wrap [the
towel] round her," so she eludes Anna and Deeley's efforts
to"wrap" their representations and their gazes around her. Not
only does Kate's "floating," her resistance to definitional contain-

ment, allow her to escape the immobilizing force of Deeley (and Anna's) cinematic gaze, but she appropriates that gaze, transforming herself from passive spectacle to threateningly active spectator. Anna responds to Deeley's comment concerning Kate's floating with a memory of this dream-like floating that acknowledges Kate's power: "Sometimes, walking, in the park, I'd say to her, you're dreaming, you're dreaming, wake up, what are you dreaming? and she'd look round at me, flicking her hair, and look at me as if I were part of her dream."

Anna here employs the same "syntax of cinema" that marks Deeley's language, framing Kate in a verbal close-up, but, rather than granting her visual mastery over Kate, this shot betrays the radical instability of the cinematic scopic economy. Like the projector's light upon which the camera focuses at the conclusion of *The Trial,* Kate's look transformes her "audience" into a cinematic image, a projection of the specular object who now assumes the role of specular subject. As Jacqueline Rose observes, "The subject of representation is not only the subject of that geometrical perspective whereby it reproduces objects as images . . . it is also represent*ed* in that process . . . and thereby registered simultaneously as *object* of representation."[6] Kate's gaze exceeds and "floats" beyond the discursive perimeters Anna establishes, perimeters designed to guarantee that the specular object will yield itself to the surveillance and manipulation of a dominating specular subject.

I have paused at such length over this exchange between Anna and Deeley in order to illustrate how the play rejects an unproblematic specular model in which the subject institutes itself as subject and the other as object, adopting in its place a structure of specularity that sees subject and object as infinitely reversible positions. Indeed, since Anna, like Deeley, turns her gaze upon Kate in order to "arrest the flux of phenomena," transforming Kate's gaze from an object into an image, she paradoxically grants it the status and power lacked by her own cinematic look. De-real-izing Anna, "look[ing] at me as if I were part of her dream," the image of Kate's gaze transforms Anna from viewing point to vanishing point, from the still point of visual plentitude to a tangent within the other's visual field. Anna thus finds herself in the position Sartre explores when he asks what it means to possess a "look-looked-at":

Someone is looking at me! What does this mean? It means that I am suddenly affected in my being and that essential modifications appear in my structure. . . . Beyond any knowledge which I can have, I am this self which another knows. And this self which I am—this I am in a world which the Other has made alien to me . . . my own look . . . is stripped of its transcendence by the very fact that it is a *look-looked-at*. . . . In looking . . . I measure my power. But if the Other . . . sees me, then my look loses its power. . . . Thus being-seen constitutes me as a defenseless being. . . . I am in danger. This danger is not an accident but the permanent structure of my being-for-others. . . . Through the Other's look I live myself as fixed in the midst of the world, as in danger, as irremediable. But I know neither what I am nor what is my place in the world, not what face this world in which I am turns toward the Other.[7]

Like *Being and Nothingness* (from which I take the preceding passage) and *No Exit* (in which Pinter acted the role of Garcin for the BBC in 1965), *Old Times* explores "the permanent structure of my being-for-others," a structure determined by the "look-looked-at." Pinter, however, takes this concept even further than does Sartre, suggesting that the very process of looking—the structure of the gaze itself—becomes the source of our "looked-at-ness." As the passage quoted above suggests, for Sartre the experience of being watched seemingly entails the existence of a watcher, a figure whose inquisitorial gaze threatens to annihilate the existential integrity of the for-itself. At other points in *Being and Nothingness*, however, Sartre divorces the "look-looked-at" from an actual person, the most famous example being the discussion of the voyeur looking through a keyhole, who suddenly feels himself the object of a gaze even though no other is present at the scopic scene. The gaze, then, can manifest itself as a phenomenological, as well as physical, presence, and it is this phenomenological dimension upon which Lacan focuses in his discussion of Sartre:

In the scopic field, the gaze is outside, I am looked at, that is to say, I am a picture. . . . What determines me, at the most profound level, is the visible, is the gaze that is outside. It is through the gaze that I enter light and it is from the gaze that I receive its effects. Hence it comes about that the gaze is the instrument through which light is embodied and through which . . . I am *photo-graphed*.[8]

What exactly does Lacan mean when he refers to the gaze as "the instrument through which light is embodied," and how does this relate to the Sartrean concept of the "look-looked-at?" To answer this question, I want to consider the following anecdote Lacan relates. As a young man, Lacan took an holiday in a port town, where he would go out with the fishermen each day. On one of these trips, a fisherman pointed to a sardine can floating on the waves and remarked that while Lacan could see the can, the can could not see Lacan. Wondering why he felt unease at so trivial a comment, Lacan remarks:

> To begin with, if what [the fisherman] said to me, namely, that the can did not see me, had any meaning, it was because in a sense, it was looking at me, all the same. It was looking at me at the level of the point of light, the point at which everything that looks at me is situated—and I am not speaking metaphorically.[9]

Lacan recounts the story of the can to illustrate his thesis that the externality of the gaze points to a split between the eye and the gaze. Lacking an eye, the sardine can obviously cannot see Lacan, but, situated at the converging point of the light that it directs back to the spectator (like the image of the projector that concludes *The Trial*), it "photo-graphs" and institutes him in the order of the visible. As that anecdote suggests, then, every look is necessarily a "look-looked-at," since any object upon which our eyes fasten finds its locus "at the level of the point of light, the point at which everything that looks at me [and at which I look] is situated."

I have detoured through Sartre and Lacan because they help clarify the operations through which *Old Times* relentlessly interrogates the kind of transcendental scopic power to which its characters variously lay claim. Both Lacan and Pinter suggest, even more radically than Sartre, that the very structure of specularity deconstructs the self/other dichotomy that privileges the gaze of the specular subject while attempting to ensure the capture of the specular object. Pinter stages a parallel to the radical Lacanian structure of the "look-looked-at" in the opening sequence of the play through the relationship he establishes between the audience and the disposition of the three characters within the theatrical space.

The play begins in silence, the stage a "pure" visual field: *"Deeley slumped in armchair, still. Kate curled on a sofa, still. Anna standing at the window, looking out. Silence. Lights up on Deeley and Kate, smoking cigarettes. Anna's figure remains still in dim light at the window"* (p. 3). As Anna "remains still in dim light" throughout the opening dialogue between Deeley and Kate, Pinter creates a similar effect to that achieved by his use of the split stage in *The Collection*. Like the presentation of simultaneous scenes in James's flat and Harry's house, Pinter again produces a sensory bifurcation in his audience. Once the lights fade up on Deeley and Kate, we find our gaze irresistibly drawn to the shadowy and mysterious space inhabited by Anna even as the equally enigmatic dialogue draws our ears towards Deeley and Kate. At first, we expect a fit between word and image: the dialogue, centering around Deeley's attempts to gain information about Anna, extends the promise of casting its own light on her that would grant both Deeley and us epistemological possession of the dimly lit figure.

As the elusiveness of Kate's answers compounds rather than illuminates Anna's mystery, we find our eyes fastening ever more intently on Anna, as we attempt to submit her to a demystifying gaze predicated upon our position at the center of a perceptual horizon. Not only, however, does Anna's opacity frustrate our impulse to see, but, like Lacan's sardine can, she operates on and with light, borrowing the light cast by our gaze which she then emits back to us. As the audience viewing Welles's *The Trial* finds itself cast in the role of specular image trapped in the visual domain of the projector, so we in Pinter's audience find ourselves victimized by our scopic desire, by a gaze that, as it were, rebounds off Anna's enigmatic figure, returning to and securing us within "her" visual field. Because Anna stands *behind* the brightly lit area in which Deeley and Kate converse, she appears to *emit* the light that both surrounds and extends beyond them to "photo-graph" us and annex our subjectivity.

There is more at stake here than a question of frustrated audience desire: Pinter does not so much undermine the privileged ocular position we occupy in the theater—the position from which we see not only the objects of the characters' gaze, but also the characters in the very act of gazing—as he places in question any visual economy that conceptualizes the specular subject in terms of a privileged visual plenitude. The reciprocal scopic exchange Pinter establishes between spectator and spectacle thus articulates a paradigmatic structure of the gaze that, as Sartre and Lacan assert, necessarily possesses the status of a "look-looked-at." Once we become the objects of Anna's "look," instituted within her visual domain, we can no longer claim the unassailability of a privileged scopic position, but must acknowledge the futility of any attempt to ground power in the illusory promise of perceptual mastery. The play's opening sequence thus demystifies the "demystifying" gaze—the gaze to which Deeley lays claim at the very moment that Pinter challenges its hegemony:

Deeley. I shall be very interested.
Kate. In what?
Deeley. In you. I'll be watching you.
Kate. Me? Why?
Deeley. To see if she's the same person. (pp. 7–8)

Spoken during the opening dialogue, in which Deeley and Kate engage simultaneously with our attempts to submit Anna to specular capture, Deeley's lines possess an irony that only we can fully appreciate. The paradigm of scopic organization to which he appeals is the same paradigm on which we depend for a guarantee of the privileged vision that defines our identity as an audience. Indeed, Deeley implicitly equates perceptual mastery with the position occupied by the audience, as he transforms Anna and Kate's reunion into a dramatic performance at which he will assume the role of spectator. As he does through the play, Deeley here associates the subject of representation's necessary absence from the image it produces in the visual field with domination of that field. At the same time that he defines the audience as the locus of visual mastery, however, we are discovering the limits of that "mastery," discovering that while we may remain excluded from entrapment within the scene we observe, we cannot escape our subjection to the ontology of the gaze as a "look-looked-at."

I have argued that, through its dramatized parallels to the Sartrean and, even more significantly, Lacanian versions of the "look-looked-at," *Old Times* explores how the specular subject's capture and objectification are inscribed in the very act of looking; how the "reality" (for lack of a better term) of the visual field deconstructs the scopic economy both supporting and finding its support in patriarchal power relations. Pinter undermines this economy through staging the conflict between ocularcentrism and a "floating" image that resists reduction to a stable visual essence. Anna and Deeley attempt to assert the hegemony of the panoptic gaze that would allow them to achieve a transcendental vantage-point from which to position, limit, and contain the spectacle of Kate's body. As a kind of deterritorialized flux, a "floating," diffuse subjectivity, Kate incarnates a kind of visual opacity, the loose thread that ultimately unravels the various narratives of scopic triumph Deeley and Anna offer throughout the play. These narratives never transcend a troubling instability, most noticeable when they represent Kate's "floating" as a function of the withdrawal of the male gaze (Deeley) or as a sign of fawn-like shyness and timidity (Anna);

in other words, the narratives attempt to "domesticate" Kate's "floating," constructing it as an image of powerlessness.

This instability threatens to disrupt the narrative of Deeley and Kate's courtship. Deeley concludes his account of their first meeting and first sexual encounter by relating how he pondered the question of marriage:

[S]hould I . . . saddle myself with a slip of a girl not long out of her swaddling clothes whose only claim to virtue was silence but who lacked any sense of fixedness, any sense of decisiveness, but was compliant only to the shifting winds, with which she went, but not *the* winds, and certainly not my winds, such as they are, but I suppose winds that only she understood. . . . A classic female figure, I said to myself, or is it a classic female posture. (pp. 31–32)

Deeley predicates his reduction of Kate to a "classic . . . figure" or "posture" upon the assumed stability of a gaze that can transform objects into static images. Yet, even as he asserts the power of the gaze to "keep the other in its place," his narrative registers a note of anxiety as Kate's "floating" elusiveness—her "lack[ing] any sense of fixedness" and "complian[ce] only to the shifting winds"—frustrates his attempts at specular capture by resisting her reduction to a coherent visible essence.

I am less interested in how Deeley's narrative ultimately undercuts the kind of power it means to assert, however, than I am in how it attempts to deny its own implications by appealing to the dominant ideological coding of sexual difference. His account of Kate's "floating," her unreadable opacity, attempts to foreclose any association of these categories with empowerment. Thus, Deeley images her "floating" not in terms of affirmation and assertion, but in terms of absence and lack: she "*lacked* any sense of fixedness, any sense of decisiveness." He transforms Kate's resistance to representation into the *basis* for representation. The lack permeating the space of ontological "fixedness," the absence supplanting essence, here signify a specifically gendered essence: Kate is, in Deeley's words, "a classic *female* figure . . . or . . . a classic *female* posture."

For Deeley, then, Kate's indecipherability defines rather than masks her gendered subjectivity. If she evades his attempts to contain her within the perimeters of his narrative and scopic fields, producing his failure to represent the unrepresentable, then he will represent her *as* unrepresentable, as that which is necessarily excluded from representation. Such exclusion confirms her status as "a classic female figure," for those who exist beyond representation cannot achieve the subjectivity produced through self-representation. Her "only claim to virtue was silence"; not, according to Deeley, the silence that voices a kind of power, but the silence of the disempowered woman who necessarily occupies the margins of the linguistic field that elaborates and shapes the social.

Like James's assault on Stella's voice, Deeley's equation of silence with female "virtue" depends upon the ideological solidarity between male/language/power and female/silence/powerlessness. Yet it is precisely this patriarchal ideology that Deeley's narrative places in question. Like *The Collection* and *The Homecoming, Old Times* explores the stress points that render the conventions promoting "masculine" power less a fixed norm than a radically unstable ensemble of practices that calls for a repeated (re)negotiation of patriarchal control. Deeley's narrative undertakes to effect this negotiation, enacting a fundamentally defensive strategy that seeks to position Kate by offering a reading of her silence and elusiveness that can accommodate them to the patriarchal discourse of sexual difference—a discourse that constructs difference as the otherness that validates the consignment of women to the margins of the logosphere and the social field with which it is coextensive.

Conceptualizing representation as a site for the production or construction, rather than the expression or communication, of subjectivity, Teresa de Lauretis writes, "The representation of gender *is* its construction . . . [but] gender, like the real, is not only the effect of representation but also its excess, what remains outside discourse as a potential trauma which can rupture or destabilize, if not contained, any representation."[10] As these comments suggest, de Lauretis rejects the antithesis between the subject and object of representation, since the former is as much a discursive construction—an *effect* of representation—as the latter. De Lauretis's observations remind us that at stake in Deeley's urgent need to construct Kate as an acceptable, *i.e.,* unthreatening, "female figure" is the (re)inscription within discourse of the dominant patriarchal myth: the autonomous male subject, endowed with mastery of otherness, language, and cultural power, yet—and here we confront the "reality" that the myth would deny—dependent upon its differential relation to the "female figure" for its privileged status. Should Kate exceed her construction as the "classic female figure," then she would not only "rupture or destabilize" Deeley's representational project, but also the subject position Deeley attempts to fashion for himself through that project.

Deeley's reference to Kate as "a *classic* female figure" suggests that more is at issue here, however, than the impending collapse of the subjectivity inscribed and produced in his narrative. The description of Kate as a "classic" example of The Female, with its implicit invocation of the ensemble of codes, discourses, and values that constitute the symbolic order of patriarchy, reminds us that, like Goldberg, Deeley serves as a "mouthpiece" for these codes, that he is both an effect of and a vehicle for a power that he can never possess. I have previously referred to Anthony Wilden's assertion that "the Other . . . is the only place from which it is possible to say 'I am who I am.'" As the locus of language, hence also of subjectivity, the Other's discursive field constitutes the site of origin for Deeley's narratives: like James, Max, and Lenny, he speaks the Other's language, desires the Other's desire encoded in that language, enacts the scenario in which the Other's symbolic code inscribes the opposition between the sovereign male subject and the subjected female object, the antithesis obviously most central to the organization of patriarchal culture.

At stake in the play, then, is not simply "Deeley's" narrative, but the master narrative of patriarchy; not simply Deeley's subjectivity, but the masculine subject position articulated through and empowered by patriarchal ideology. Should Kate undermine "his" representation, she would effectually undermine the symbolic and cultural codes of patriarchy itself—the "voice" of the cultural Other speaking through Deeley as its "mouthpiece."

In *Old Times,* Pinter underscores the cultural appropriation of Deeley's subjectivity, his enclosure within the Other's discursive field, through intertextual allusion. Welles's *The Trial* and *The Magnificent Ambersons,* Carol Reed's *Odd Man Out,* and the popular songs quoted by Anna and Deeley (*e.g.,* "Blue Moon," "They Can't Take That Away from Me," etc.), all play a similar role in *Old Times,* a role determined by their status as texts that encode and reproduce the dominant values of their culture. These intertexts function as pre-texts for Deeley's subjectivity. I do not mean simply that the "plot" of Deeley's narratives, or of *Old Times* itself, offers a variation on *Odd Man Out* or dramatizes the erotic scenario of the songs. Rather, because he utilizes these intertexts to examine how Otherness installs itself in that space we designate as the "self," Pinter explores how Deeley identifies and constructs himself as a social subject through the mediation of these films and songs.

Since the power of representations in the formation of subjectivity occurs within the broader context of cultural coding, *Old Times* explores how such "innocuous" sources of entertainment as film and popular music become pressed into ideological service, how they do not simply elaborate but, through the subject positions they articulate, actively construct a specifically patriarchal ideology of sexual difference. Although neither *The Trial* nor *Odd Man Out* specifically concern themselves with questions of gender or sexuality, they both image the power of the gaze in terms that allow for its assimilation to structures of "masculine" power. The song lyrics are more overt and, at the same time, more insidious in their construction of a gendered subjectivity: more overt because they quite explicitly position the "classic female figure" as the object of an adoring, though no less inquisitorial, male gaze; more insidious because they mystify the power relationship that assigns the male subject mastery over the female object by deploying a sentimental rhetoric of love.

I have already noted the importance of the Welles films for Deeley's identification with the cinematic apparatus. What I want to emphasize here is the ambiguous nature of this identification. Like Max's ludicrous assertions of paternal authority, Deeley's exaggerated identification with Welles, expressed through his self-identification *as* Welles, undercuts the very power it is meant to assert. Deeley's "quotation" of Welles—"I wrote the film and directed it. My name is Orson Welles"—though undeniably comic, nevertheless provides an example of how the formation of subjectivity is elaborately mediated by representations and signifying practices issuing from the field of the Other.

To understand the nature of this mediation, we need to remember that Deeley does not merely quote Orson Welles; he quotes a line that Welles delivers in a complex moment of self-representation (Welles "as" microphone in *The Magnificent Ambersons;* Welles "as" projector in *The Trial*) enclosed within the larger representation of the film itself. Reality merges with image as Welles represents his subjectivity merging with the cinematic apparatus, and as Deeley, viewing the films and introjecting the images with which he will identify, merges his subjectivity with the apparatus, or, to be more precise, becomes the recipient of a subjectivity forged through the process of cinematic identification.

While Deeley's quoting Welles evokes the concluding shots of both *The Magnificent Ambersons* and *The Trial,* the latter—Welles delivering his line as a voice-over while the camera moves in for a close-up of a projector emitting a dazzling light that holds the audience in its "gaze"—provides a particularly apt image for Pinter's exploration of subjectivity as a representational effect. *A propos* of "conventional" Hollywood films (as opposed to the more meta-cinematic experiments of Welles), Kaja Silverman writes, "Many cinematic texts attribute to a fictional character faculties which actually belong to the apparatuses of enunciation, such as coercive vision. . . . While watching [such films] we fend to forget that the real source of its images is the camera."[11] The classic cinematic text performs its ideological work by effacing the technological apparatus that foregrounds its status as representation, thus creating the illusion that the (primarily male) protagonist both possesses and serves as point of origin of the gaze. Such a film encourages the kind of forgetfulness to which Silverman refers—the forgetfulness that allows the male spectator to identify with the male protagonist, and the female spectator to identify with an "appropriate" female image, the cinematic "classic female figure" positioned as the object of the gaze.

As Silverman's comments suggest, the ultimate object of our cinematic desire is nothing less than identification with the gaze itself. In the final shot of *The Trial,* Welles both promotes and demystifies the process of identification, allowing us to see the apparatus that realistic cinema conceals, encouraging our identification with that apparatus, while at the same time refusing to naturalize the gaze. Welles foregrounds the status both of the gaze and of our subjectivity as representational products rather than stable essences—the very effect that classic cinema seeks to escape through the forgetfulness it inculcates in its audience. Through this shot of the projector fixing us in the light emitted from its "eye" (a shot exhibiting the structure of the "look-looked-at"), Welles places in question any distinction between the representational "reality" of the images produced by the camera and the extra-discursive "reality" we claim to possess. Like the characters who "live" within the film, the audience depends upon the cinematic apparatus for the construction of its subjectivity, a point Pinter underscores by the Otherness that speaks through Deeley at the moment of self-designation: "My name is Orson Welles."

As a product of signifying practices, the audience's subjectivity becomes reinforced through an endless series of discursive re-inscriptions. It is hardly surprising, then, that when Deeley shifts from identifying with the camera to identifying with a character, he chooses a figure granted scopic mastery within a film. The film in question is Carol Reed's *Odd Man Out,* and the character is the artist Lukey (Robert Newton). If we look beyond the title's ironic commentary on Deeley, we can see why *Odd Man Out* provides a suitable intertext for *Old Times*. The film focuses on Lukey's desire to capture on canvas "the image of death-in-life"[12] embodied by the dying IRA chief Johnny McQueen (James Mason). At one point in the film, Lukey drags the mortally wounded McQueen out of hiding, placing him on a dais to pose him for a portrait. The scene grants Lukey's gaze the same annihilating force as the bullet lodged in McQueen.

Not only does Deeley claim to have first met Kate at a screening of *Odd Man Out,* but he filters the account of their meeting and developing relationship through his identification with Lukey/Newton:

> I . . . watched Odd Man Out and thought Robert Newton was fantastic. And I still think he was fantastic. And I would commit murder for him, even now. . . . And I left when the film was over . . . and then this girl came out and I think looked about her and I said wasn't Robert Newton fantatic . . . and I thought . . . this is a trueblue pickup, and when we had sat down in the café with tea she . . . told me she thought Robert Newton was remarkable. So it was Robert Newton who brought us together and it is only Robert Newton who can tear us apart. . . . [t]he next time we met we held hands. I held her cool hand . . . and I thought she was even more fantastic than Robert Newton. *(Pause)* And then at a slightly later stage our naked bodies met, hers cool, warm, highly agreeable, and I wondered what Robert Newton would think of this. What would he think of this I wondered as I touched her profoundly all over. (pp. 25–27)

If the repeated references to Robert Newton indicate how deeply intertwined Deeley's subjectivity has become with the figure of Lukey/Newton, they also reveal both the fragility of that identification and the extent to which film mystifies that fragility. As the viewing subject constituted through cinematic signifying practices, Deeley "forgets" that his identity and sense of visual power derive from subjection to the transcendent gaze of the cinematic apparatus. Such is the structure of the viewer's subjectivity that speaks through Deeley's various references to Robert Newton. We might also notice that if Deeley "forgets" his own status as an effect of cinematic signifying processes, he also "forgets" the ontological gap between Newton and Lukey. Deeley repeatedly refers to "Robert Newton" even when Lukey is clearly the object of his identification. Deeley's confusion of self and role—a confusion actively promoted by the cinematic apparatus—informs his own narrative strategy in the play. His need to master Kate through an enforced representation stems from the kind of reversal that characterizes his response to *Odd Man Out,* a reversal in which, rather than the actor disappearing in his role, the role disappears into the actor. Thus, Deeley can "forget" that Kate's role as "classic female figure" *is* a role, a product of representation rather than an index of her being, just as he "forgets" that Robert Newton is playing a role within the film.

Deeley's initial response to *Odd Man Out* involves a strong identification with Lukey/Newton that nevertheless seeks to preserve an ontological space between the reality of the viewing I/eye and the fiction of the cinematic text: "I . . . thought Robert Newton was fantastic. And I still think he was fantastic." The next sentence, however, inaugurates a subtle shift according the cinematic image a reality and power that places his own status in question: "And I would commit murder for him, even now."

The implications of this comment become even clearer as further references to Newton reveal that identification *with* entails subjection *to* the cinematic Other in whose field the viewer's subjectivity emerges: "So it is Robert Newton who brought us together and it is only Robert Newton who can tear us apart." Although these words constitute a strategic gambit on Deeley's part, an effort to outmaneuver Anna in the battle for Kate by denying her the power to "tear us apart," they also undermine that gambit by emphasizing the radical contingency marking not only Deeley's subjectivity, but the gendered subject positions in terms of which he views his marriage. Deeley's own words demystify the scopic power to which he lays claim—the power to eroticize Kate, transforming her from a woman who "was Brontë in secrecy if not in passion" (p. 62) into "a trueblue pickup"—proclaiming its status as a fiction embedded in representation, a fiction from which *his* as well as Kate's subjectivity derives: "Robert Newton . . . brought *us* together and . . . only Robert Newton . . . can tear *us* apart."

Deeley's claim that Newton "brought *us* together" collapses the dichotomy between the powerful male specular subject and the submissive female specular object that his narrative attempts to reify. Inadvertently, Deeley acknowledges that he shares with Kate the condition of subjection to a gaze that he can never appropriate, that exceeds him by virtue of its ability to bring *him* together, to endow him with an (illusory) sense of coherence and stability. Pinter here reveals the disequivalence between Deeley's gaze and the Gaze of the cinematic Other through which the viewing subject is "photo-graphed," the disequivalence that Lacan discusses in terms of a split between the eye and the gaze. Since "what determines me," as Lacan writes, "is the gaze that is outside," that traps me in the Other's visual field, "th[is] gaze is specified as unapprehensible."[13]

This sense of the gaze as transcendent, as the scopic *beyond* that transforms identification into a form of subject-ion, manifests itself in the ambiguity of Deeley's final reference to Newton. Recounting his first sexual encounter with Kate, Deeley elevates Newton to the level of an omnipotent cultural eye, the origin of all meaning and value, remembering that "I wondered what Robert Newton would think of this. What would he think of this I wondered as I touched her profoundly all over." The ambiguity centers around the problem of assigning a referent to "this," a problem that raises the question of where Deeley stands in relation to Newton's imagined gaze.

Since the reference to Newton immediately follows Deeley's description of Kate's "cool, warm, highly agreeable" body, we might assume that "this" refers to Kate. Such a reading translates Kate's body from an object into an image that necessarily situates Deeley, as the viewing subject, outside its confines. Deeley would thus find himself aligned with Newton, participating in the active power of the gaze that affords him mastery over the "classic female figure" displayed for his enjoyment. If "this" does indeed refer to Kate, then Deeley's narrative reinforces what Laura Mulvey terms the "active/passive heterosexual division of labor" that constructs "woman as image, [and] man as bearer of the look."[14] The spectacle of Kate lying naked, eroticized by Newton/Deeley's gaze, illustrates the power of cinematic representation to shape experience, as Kate conforms to the exhibitionist role assigned to women in mainstream film—a role in which "women are simultaneously looked at and displayed, with their appearance coded for strong visual and erotic impact so that they can be said to connote *to-be-looked-at-ness*."[15]

The slipperiness of "this," however, allows for a different reading, one that challenges rather than supports the ideology articulating the patriarchal scopic regime. "This's" referent suddenly shifts when Deeley asks for the second time what Newton would think: "What would he think of this I wondered *as I touched her profoundly all over*." Here, "this" includes in its referential scope both Kate *and* Deeley's sexualized bodies, thus objectifying Deeley and effecting a scopic inversion that transforms him into a cinematic image, existing only within the visual field of Newton, now positioned in the space of the audience (and the camera) as viewing subject. Again, Pinter emphasizes that what Sartre calls the condition of "being-seen" does not recognize gendered dichotomies; that cinematic identification subordinates the viewer *to* rather than equating it *with* the gaze of the male protagonist/camera; that every look is a "look-looked at." Pinter emphasizes, in other words, precisely what classic cinema needs its audience to "forget" in order to carry out its ideological work.

Mulvey argues, "According to the principles of the ruling ideology and the physical structures that back it up, the male figure cannot bear the burden of . . . objectification."[16] As the preceding discussion suggests, the cultural imperative that Deeley "forget" his own status as "being-seen" reminds us that at stake here are the structures of representation through which those ideological principles articulate the subject positions constituting the patriarchal version of sexual difference, *i.e.,* difference encoded in terms of who looks and who is looked at. The slightest suggestion that scopic mastery does not inhere in masculinity or that men prove as susceptible as women to the objectifying gaze would suffice to reveal the gap between sexuality and gender, exposing the latter as a cultural myth that, no matter how powerful, remains a myth— a fiction constructed through other fictions. This gap raises the question of power that the plays I have discussed all take up in various ways: from whence issues the power to enforce representation as reality, to foreclose the possibility of resistance, to prevent any assertion of the autonomy of lived experience not from representation *per se* (for *Old Times* never imagines a retrievable extradiscursive reality), but from representations encoding the principles of the dominant ideology?

When power becomes subsumed in an infinite series of representations, as it does in *Old Times,* then various structures of representation must provide the necessary support for each other. Thus, Deeley's ability to "forget" that the gendered subject position he inhabits is discursively constituted rather than natural is facilitated not only by the manner in which the film works to efface the presence of the cinematic apparatus, but also by other kinds of texts that reinforce and validate the identity he derives from film.

The Gershwin-Kern-Porter lyrics that Anna and Deeley sing in their musical duel provide the kind of textual and ideological reinforcement I am discussing. Like classic cinema they position men as active controllers of the gaze, and women as the objects displayed for erotic contemplation. Again like cinema, they can only perform their ideological function by inducing a state of forgetfulness, *i.e.,* by deploying a rhetoric of love that mystifies the power relations providing the fundamental content of the lyrics. Thus,

Deeley's musical celebration of Kate as his beloved masks a covert attempt to reduce her to the iconographic "classic female figure" of patriarchal fantasy.

First establishing a link between sexual mastery and the demystifying gaze ("You're lovely to look at, delightful to know" [p. 23]), he goes on to assert the gaze's power to arrest the object, thus isolating it from the surrounding flux and transforming it into an image that exists in a static visual field rather than in a mutable reality: "Blue moon, I see you standing alone" (p. 23). If any doubt remains that the lyrics mask a sadistic scopic violence that annuls women's particularity in order to create them as commodities to be possessed, we need only examine the kind of desire informing Deeley's certitude that "someday I'll know that moment divine, / When all the things you are, are mine!" (p. 23) Even when the lyrics do not overtly concern themselves with the act of looking—e.g., Gershwin's "They Can't Take That Away from Me"—they position the woman through a series of photographic images that reveal an urge to look:

> Deeley. (Singing.) The way you wear your hat . . .
> Anna. (Singing, softly.) The way you sip your tea . . .
> Deeley (Singing.) The memory of all that . . .
> Anna (Singing.) No, no, they can't take that away from me . . . The way your smile just beams . . . The way you haunt my dreams . . .
> Deeley (Singing.) No, no, they can't take that away from me. (pp. 53–54)

Scopic desire, however, does not necessarily translate into the efficacy of scopic power. If Gershwin's lyrics give voice to an urgent desire to see, they also point to the inevitable frustration of that desire: the beloved is, after all, neither woman-as-entity nor woman-as-object, but a "memory" that "haunt[s] my dreams." The reiterated affirmations of presence—"no, no, they can't take that away from me"—cannot conceal the absence of the beloved, an absence from which the song's "I"/eye must avert its gaze by constructing an alternative world of memory within which to dwell. Nor does Gershwin equate the memory of the beloved with her presence: employing the present tense in its first two lines ("The way you *wear* your hat / The way you *sip* your tea"), the song initially appears to describe a contemporaneous moment of visual plenitude, before the devastating irony of the third line ("The *memory* of all that") reveals that the "I" inhabits a present lacking in presence.

If the lyrics undercut the "I's" assertions of scopic mastery, they also undercut Anna and Deeley's attempts both to submit Kate to this mastery and to outmaneuver each other, a point Pinter underscores by setting word and "action" at odds. After Anna and Deeley sing the first verse, "*Kate turns from the window to look at them . . . walks down towards them and stands, smiling*" (p. 54). Again, Pinter dramatizes the subversive potential of the "look-looked-at" to deconstruct the gender-marked antithesis of man as specular subject/woman as specular object. While Anna and Deeley sing of the desire to enfold the beloved in their gaze, it is *they* who have become the spectacle, playing to Kate's gaze—a gaze all the more threatening for its challenge to "masculine" authority.

Anna and Deeley's exchange immediately following the song indicates that they recognize the nature of this threat:

Anna (To Deeley). Doesn't she look beautiful?
Deeley. Doesn't she? (p. 55)

As Mary Ann Doane writes, "Western culture has a quite specific notion of what it is to be a woman and what it is to be a woman looking. When a woman looks, the verb 'looks' is generally intransitive (she *looks* beautiful)."[17] Anna and Deeley attempt to reassert the integrity of this cultural construction by invoking the patriarchal version of the "look-looked-at," in which the woman looks beautiful for an approving male gaze. Kate may indeed "look beautiful," but she also looks *at* Anna and Deeley, and, with that look, challenges the ideological organization of the visual field.

Through his treatment of film and popular song, Pinter both explores how these forms of popular culture participate in the construction of the patriarchal ideology of sexual difference, and, by foregrounding what they demand their respective audiences "forget," suggests limits to their ability to structure experience. These limits do not assume a conflict in which the social construction of reality engages with and ultimately yields place to an unconstructed, unmediated reality. The conflict upon which Pinter focuses is, rather, a conflict of competing representations, each contesting the other's ability to legislate reality.

While Anna and Deeley's conflicting memories provide the play's most prominent example of competing representations, for the purposes of my discussion I am more concerned with two opposing modes of representing women's place in the scopic economy, one shared by Anna and Deeley, the other advanced in Kate's self-representation. That Kate repeatedly eludes Anna and Deeley's efforts at discursive capture neither constitutes the triumph of reality over representation nor inscribes her in the play as unrepresentable. Kate resists Anna and Deeley, not representation itself, for she ensures her victory in the play's power struggle through a representation that refuses her enforced silencing; indeed, that speaks through her silence.

Before concluding my discussion by examining the source of Kate's power, I want to clarify my apparently paradoxical claim that both Deeley *and* Anna accept a scopic regime that denies women access to the gaze. Certainly, Anna rejects any attempts to subject *her* to scrutiny by the male gaze. I have already discussed how the structure of the "look-looked-at" in the play's opening sequence effectually removes Anna from our visual field, frustrating our scopic desire. This frustration resonates throughout the play, most obviously in Deeley's memory of the party at which Anna "sat on a very low sofa, [and] I sat opposite and looked up your skirt. . . . simply sat sipping my light ale and gazed . . . up your skirt. You didn't object, you found my gaze perfectly acceptable" (p. 47).

This voyeuristic episode rehearses the same scopic production of the "classic female figure" celebrated in the song lyrics. In order to preserve the integrity of the scopic "division of labor," Deeley characterizes Anna not merely as subjected to his visual mastery, but as *desiring* that subjection: "You didn't object, you found my gaze perfectly acceptable." Anna's sardonic response, "I was aware of your gaze, was I?")p. 47)—a question Deeley ignores—suggests that, whether or not this incident actually occurred, the true source of the narrative lies in the image-repertoire of male fantasy, from which the song lyrics and mainstream cinema also derive. As Deeley's narrative illustrates, this image-repertoire both mystifies the "brutish" (p. 67) violence of scopic power by representing women as courting their objectification and sanctions a form of feminine desire that reinforces rather than challenges patriarchal power relations: the desire *to be* desired.

If Deeley's narrative shapes with the song lyrics an articulation of sexual difference around a scopic axis, it also resembles them by undermining the ocular mastery it sets out to affirm. Ultimately, Deeley's account of the party narrates the loss of the visual plenitude that confirms the power of the male gaze. Embroiled in an argument, he temporarily loses his scopic vantage-point. Returning to the couch, he discovered that "there was no one on it. I gazed at the indentation of four buttocks. Two of which were yours" (p. 48), two of which belonged to "a girl friend" (p. 47) of Anna's. Whether or not Kate is the "friend," the narrative registers Deeley's anxiety concerning her and Anna's relationship, an anxiety that translates into specular loss.

Like Gershwin's lover, Deeley must accept "the memory of all that" as compensation for the loss of woman-as-spectacle. Where his gaze previously enfolded Anna's erotic presence—"Your black stocking were very black because your thighs were so white" (p. 47)—it now encompasses the presence of absence: "I gazed at the indentation of four buttocks." That indentation, the site at which sight vanishes, confronts Deeley with the failure of the male gaze to position the female body according to the specifications of its desire. Not only, then, does Deeley's narrative rehearse the same movement from affirmation to loss that lies at the heart of "They Can't Take That Away from Me," it also follows the same trajectory that Pinter's selection and arrangement of *all* the lyrics map out— from the assertion of scopic master ("You're lovely to look at, delightful to know"), to anxiety concerning that mastery's instability ("When a lovely flame dies / Smoke gets in your eyes" [p. 24], to the ultimate frustration of scopic desire ("Oh, how the ghost of you clings" [p. 25]; "No, no, they can't take that away from me").

If, as Deeley fears, Anna refuses to inhabit the place patriarchy assigns women in the scopic economy, she nevertheless attempts to dominate Kate through the same exercise of visual mastery to which Deeley subjects her. That she and Deeley should adopt similar strategic maneuvers in relation to Kate is hardly surprising, for when the lover competes with a rival, the conflict plays itself out between two mirror images. Pinter complicates the classic erotic triangle, however, since the challenge to Deeley's authority issues not only from Anna-as-rival, but from lesbianism as a rival form of sexuality that threatens to undermine the patriarchal sexual economy structured around the woman as guarantee of the husband's authority.

Even more than Stella's suspected adultery or Ruth's imminent prostitution, Anna and Kate's lesbianism possesses the subversive potential to place in question an economy of desire in which value is the prerogative of the phallus, to undermine the institutional and representational structures that reify the phallus. The threat lesbianism poses to the phallic economy in *Old Times,* however, appears to contradict the point I want to argue: namely, that, like Deeley, Anna accepts the division of the scopic regime into male spectators and female spectacles. To resolve this contradiction, we need to ask if the play's representation of lesbianism allows for or attempts to avert its gaze from the potential subversiveness of desire between women, if lesbianism emerges as a site of cultural and erotic difference or as another instance of the same.

To clarify what is at issue here, I suggest that we regard the play's construction of lesbian desire as part of a pattern that recurs in *The Collection, The Homecoming,* and *Old Times.* I have discussed how all three of these plays attempt to demystify patriarchal ideology and dramatize challenges to the hegemony of that ideology. At the same time, however, they make a curiously ambiguous gesture towards recuperating the patriarchal construction of sexual difference that priviliges the former term in the masculine/feminine dichotomy.

As I argued in the preceding chapter, this ambiguity is particularly noticeable in *The Homecoming.* While the play traces the dissolution of the patriarchal family and its replacement by a matriarchal family unit, Ruth can effect this displacement of the patriarch only because she is more phallic than Max, possessing the attributes of the "symbolic father" to a degree that the play's actual father never does. Ruth may initiate the return of matriarchy, but it is a matriarchy clad in the vestments and armed with the weapons of patriarchal power. While *The Collection* exposes the homosexual structure of a patriarchal culture in which the manifest display of desire between men remains as "inadmissible" as its female counterpart, Harry and Bill's relationship grants the "masculine" figure dominance over the "feminine." If the cultural valorization of masculinity informs the power dynamics of an homosexual relationship, then difference becomes erased and that relationship will testify to the resilience and power of patriarchal ideology.

I would argue that Pinter's treatment of Anna's desire for Kate parallels this attempted recuperation of Harry and Bill. After one of Anna's rhapsodic reminiscences of her life with Kate, Deeley responds, "Sounds a perfect marriage" (p. 62). Deeley may speak the line ironically, but, at a certain level, the play encourages us to view Anna and Kate's relationship as another version of what patriarchy would define as "a perfect marriage," *i.e.,* a marriage that vests authority in the husband (or the lesbian who identifies with "masculine" power) and casts the wife as the guarantee of that authority. As Irigaray observes, in a discussion of the construction of lesbianism within patriarchal discourse,

The object choice of a *female* homosexual can only be determined by a particularly strong masculinity complex. . . . The essential thing, in any case, is to show that the object choice of the homosexual woman is determined by a *masculine* desire and tropism . . . [to show that t]he instincts that lead the homosexual woman to choose an object for her satisfaction are, necessarily, "male" instincts.[18]

I draw these comments from the section of *Speculum of the Other Woman* that Irigaray devotes to a critique of Freud's essay "The Psychogenesis of a Case of Homosexuality in a Woman." While the case history Freud analyzes differs in many respects from the relationship between Anna and Kate, his approach to the representation of female homosexuality throws into relief the recuperation of cultural power we see in *Old Times*.

Freud's essay details the case history of a young girl who sexually desires a woman ten years older than herself. His discussion of the etiology of this desire provides an exemplary instance of the erasure of difference through the inscription of the dominant ideology in the very site of difference. Freud claims "that in her behaviour towards her love-object [the girl] had throughout . . . developed a masculine attitude towards this object" and explains the development of this "attitude" by asserting that "the beloved lady was a substitute for—the mother. . . . [The patient] changed into a man and took her mother in place of her father as her love-object."[19]

Freud adduces yet another factor contributing to the patient's "homosexual" object-choice: "On account of her slender figure, regular beauty, and off-hand manner, the lady reminded [the patient] of her own brother, a little older than herself. . . . The girl's inversion . . . received its final reinforcement when she found in her 'Lady' an object which promised to satisfy . . . that part of her heterosexual libido still attached to her brother."[20] Such reinforcement leads Freud to conclude that his patient's object-choice "combined gratification of the homosexual tendency with that of the heterosexual one."[21]

Such a conclusion, however, remains problematic precisely because Freud's narrative elides the question of "the homosexual tendency," or, to be more precise, elides the category of female homosexuality, refusing to recognize the specificity of desire between women. On the one hand, the lady's correspondence with a masculine ideal (the brother) allows for the displacement of the patient's heterosexual libidinal attachment. On the other hand, the lady's correspondence with a feminine ideal (the mother) allows for the *same* displacement since, despite Freud's claim that this correspondence promises to gratify lesbian desire, he has stated that in order for the lady to act as a substitute for the mother, the patient had to "change into a man" and "develop a masculine attitude towards this" love-object. Whether the lady serves as substitute for the brother or the mother ultimately makes little difference: in both cases, Freud's analysis subsumes lesbianism within a structure that preserves the concept of sexual difference supporting the patriarchal economy of desire. Lesbianism *as* lesbianism remains as "inadmissible" within the discursive perimeters of the essay as it does within patriarchal culture itself. Freud's essay displays the workings of a cultural imaginary that cannot accomodate any play of desire that threatens the paradigm of sexual difference elaborated in his writings—a paradigm shaped by and shaping patriarchal ideology.

I would argue that we can discern the contours of a similar cultural imaginary in *Old Times*'s construction of female homosexuality. Whether this means Pinter stands as an apologist for patriarchal ideology or whether it is a logical extension of Pinter's conceptualization of cultural power is a question to which I will return in the conclusion. For now, I want to note that while *Old Times*, like *The Collection* and *The Homecoming*, explores the contradictions and points of tension within patriarchal culture, at the same time these plays represent potential sites of resistance as informed by the dominant paradigm of sexual difference and the valorization of the "masculine" within that paradigm, elaborated through patriarchal ideology.

Thus, like Freud's patient, Anna "change[s] into a man," both desiring a feminine love-object—an object that, drawing upon the same image-repertoire of *male* fantasy to which Deeley appeals, she describes as fawn-like, "Bronte in secrecy," "like a dream [u]naware of anyone"—and "develop[ing] a masculine attitude towards this object." *Old Times* defines this "attitude" in terms of the scopic desire that the text repeatedly links to masculinity. Although the play reveals, through the treatment of cinema and popular song, this desire as constructed rather than natural, Anna's identification with the gaze reinforces rather than challenges that construct.

To illustrate this last point, let me turn again to Anna and Deeley's musical combat. While the singing sequences provide the occasion for a kind of duel between Anna and Deeley, we can also regard them as a duet, or, rather, a kind of sung monologue in which two voices divide a single "I," a single *gendered* subject position, between them. I have already discussed how these lyrics participate in the scopic objectification of the woman's body. What I did not remark earlier is the thoroughly arbitrary manner in which Pinter divides the lyrics between Anna and Deeley; the scene would not have been altered had he given Anna's lyrics to Deeley or Deeley's to Anna. Regardless of which character sings which line, the lyrics voice an impulse to see that is specifically "masculine" in its construction of the "feminine" as spectacle and erotic display. By foregrounding the extent to which Anna and Deeley, as amorous subject and rival, mirror each other in their identification with the "masculine" subject position, the two musical sequences annul a threatening difference (the difference of a female desire that refuses to reify the phallus) in order to preserve a valorized difference (the patriarchal model of sexual difference that privileges the ideological solidarity between the masculine/the gaze/power at the expense of the equally ideological solidarity between the feminine/spectacle/powerlessness).

The musical duels/duets provide the clearest example of how the play's representation of lesbianism is governed by an inexorable logic of the same that transforms it into a mirror of patriarchal power relations. Since the play interrogates and brings enormous pressure to bear upon these relations, specifically as they are organized through the dominant scopic economy, the point I am arguing may appear academic. The erasure of difference, however, raises the question of how Pinter conceptualizes the power of cultural centrality—as a monolithic force that converts any possible challenge to its hegemony into an extension of that hegemony, or as an unstable field that cannot suppress alternative forms of power.

To answer this question, let me turn to Kate, the missing term in this discussion. Unlike Anna and Deeley, who associate power with a culturally privileged identity and implicitly appeal to the various forms of gendered dichotomies elaborated within patriarchy, Kate embraces the dissolution of boundaries both social and ontological. If Anna and Deeley need to nail identity in place, Kate, as the following passage illustrates, places the concept of identity in play:

> I feel fresh. The water's very soft here. Much softer than London. I always find the water very hard in London. That's one reason I like living in the country. Everything's softer. The water, the light, the shapes, the sounds. There aren't such edges here. And living close to the sea too. You can't say where it begins or ends. That appeals to me.

I don't care for harsh lines. I deplore that kind of urgency. I'd like to go to the East, or somewhere like that. . . . The only nice thing about a big city is that when it rains it blurs everything, and it blurs the lights from the cars, doesn't it, and blurs your eyes, and you have rain on your lashes. That's the only nice thing about a big city. (p. 55)

Kate's unprecedented outpouring of words, a flow of language mirroring the flow of subjectivity it describes, provides a sharp contrast both with her previous laconic utterances and with the narratives that constitute the major portion of Anna and Deeley's speeches. That Kate eschews the kind of reminiscing narrative in which Anna and Deeley engage implicitly acknowledges that once the self is represented as appropriable, it can all too easily become the property of the Other, as Anna and Deeley's "revisions" of each other's narratives repeatedly demolish the self each attempts to establish. It is hardly surprising that, in a play where the violence of scopic domination functions as the chief instrument of such appropriation, Kate should conceptualize subjectivity as an excess, transgressing the borders of the visual field—a state of perpetual flux, like the sea of which "you can't say [or see] where it begins and ends." While Anna and Deeley voice an urgent desire to see, Kate embraces the failure of vision: the "softness" of a world in which "the water, the light, the shapes" all lack "edges" and "harsh lines"; in which rain "blurs your eyes"; in which the subject confronts an endlessly shifting and mobile reality that mirrors the slippages structuring its own subjectivity.

Paradoxically, however, Kate's representation of a "floating" subjectivity does articulate a vision of a "self" that exists by virtue of being ungraspable and inaccessible. Like Stella, Kate possesses the kind of unassailability Freud associates with the narcissistic woman (see Chapter Three). In his discussion of narcissism, Freud reverses his customary paradigm of sexual difference, aligning women with psychic plenitude and men with absence. Rather than powered by the dynamic of feminine desire (the penis-envy that validates the cultural reification of the phallus), this paradigm depends upon the expression of a masculine desire—the desire to recapture narcissistic self-sufficiency—that always betrays its genesis in a profound sense of the lack that patriarchal ideology dictates must never receive discursive expression.

These comments suggest both the kind of desire at stake in the efforts of the play's two "masculine" figures to subject Kate to scopic mastery and why Anna and Deeley cannot articulate this desire. I have argued that both Anna and Deeley construct Kate's "floating" as a sign of weakness and "feminine" vulnerability, but such comments betray their own sense of Kate's narcissistic self-sufficiency: "She floats from the bath. Like a dream. Unaware of anyone standing, with her towel, waiting for her, waiting to wrap it round her. Quite absorbed." Rather than exuding fawn-like timidity, the woman Anna describes here has managed to preserve an enigmatic reserve and inaccessibility that removes her from the field of the others "waiting to wrap" her in their towels, their gazes, their narratives.

When Kate does emerge from her bath, *"she smiles at Deeley and Anna,"* exclaiming *"(with pleasure.)* Aaahh" (p. 53). Like Stella alone with her cat, Kate incarnates a sexuality that both fascinates and threatens the "masculine" lover—fascinates because the narcissistic woman retains the independence that, according to Freud, the man has rejected in order to pursue objectal love; threatens because such erotic self-sufficiency situates the narcissistic woman outside the place to which patriarchy would consign her.

Kate's final speech constitutes the most devestating assertion of the narcissistic "self" that "floats" beyond the representational enclosures in which Anna and Deeley would confine it. If Anna uses language to objectify Kate, "talk[ing] of me as if I were dead" (p. 30), Kate will employ language to literalize this simile: *"(To Anna.)* But I remember you. I remember you dead. *(Pause)* I remember you lying dead" (p. 67). For the first time in the play, Kate lays claim to that authority of memory that Anna and Deeley have attempted to appropriate. If this particular memory is obviously a fiction, it nevertheless grants Kate a decisive victory over Anna and Deeley since they accept the equivalence between memory and absolute power informing this narrative.

If Anna has represented Kate as an enigmatic text requiring a violent scopic demystification, Kate represents Anna as a self-deconstructing text, dissolving into the free-play of signifiers: "Your face was dirty. You lay dead, your face scrawled with dirt, all kinds of *earnest inscriptions, but unblotted, so that they had run,* all over your face, down to your throat" (pp. 67–68; emphasis added). If Anna would subject Kate to her inquisitorial gaze, Kate will appropriate the power of that gaze, forcing Anna to submit to the menace of "being-seen": "You didn't know I was watching you. I leaned over you. . . . When you woke my eyes were above you, staring down at you. . . . Your pupils weren't in your eyes. Your bones were breaking through your face. . . . I had quite a lengthy bath, got out, walked about the room, glistening, drew up a chair, sat naked beside you and watched you" (pp. 67–68).

Kate's triumph here lies in a kind of dialectical synthesis of the two positions within the specular economy: subject ("I . . . *watched* you") and object (" . . . sat *naked*"). It would perhaps be more correct to say that she assumes the role of object in order to stretch the category to its breaking point. Having "killed" Anna through the combined power of memory and vision, Kate has annihilated the gaze that sexualizes the "classic female figure," transforming it into a signifier of masculine desire. Without this gaze, Kate's nudity remains free from objectification, signifying a self-contained sexuality rather than the receptacle of an imposed eroticism.

When the narrative shifts its focus from Anna to Deeley, Kate inverts the paradigm of sexual difference governing the dominant scopic economy, arrogating to herself the power of the gaze while forcing Deeley to bear the burden of objectification. While Deeley masks the dynamics of scopic domination with the rhetoric of romance, *e.g.* the song lyrics, Kate's narrative foregrounds the sadism of the gaze:

> He lay there in . . . bed. . . . He thought I was going to be sexually forthcoming, that I was about to take a long promised initiative. I dug about in the windowbox, . . . scooped, filled the bowl, and plastered his face with dirt. He was bemused, aghast, resisted. . . . He suggested a wedding instead, and a change of environment. *(Slight pause)* Neither mattered. (pp. 68–69)

In an interpretive move that mirrors Anna and Deeley's attempts to construct Kate's self-sufficiency as a sign of weakness and lack, Esslin writes that her indifference to the marriage, coupled with her refusal "to be sexually forthcoming," grant her "the superiority of the frigid wife for whom sensuality has no meaning."[22] The claim that "sensuality has no meaning" for Kate seems rather dubious when we consider the obvious sensual if not erotic pleasure she derives from her bathing ritual: "When [Kate] gets in the bath . . . [she e]njoys it. Takes a long time over it. . . . A hell of a long time. Luxuriates in it. Gives herself a great soaping all over. . . . Really soaps herself all over, and then washes the soap off, sud by sud. Meticulously. She's both thorough and . . . sensuous" (p. 49).

I refer to Esslin less because I am interested in showing that the text does not support his analysis than because the terms of his analysis speak directly to what is at issue in the play. If, ultimately, Freud and Pinter do not/cannot imagine a female homosexual desire that threatens patriarchal power relationships, Esslin does not/

cannot conceptualize a woman's refusal "to be sexually forthcoming" *as* refusal: appealing to the notion of frigidity, he transforms active resistance into passive retreat. It is Esslin himself, however, who retreats from interrogating the concept of frigidity, from considering frigidity as a discursive construction rather than a natural psychic condition. Irigaray suggests that before labelling women as frigid, we both

> need to find out what the term "frigid" means in masculine discourse, and . . . need to examine the relationship between this "frigidity" and the aggressiveness that devolves upon the male in the sexual function, an aggressiveness that is exerted "independent of her consent." Perhaps female sexuality does not find its needs met by the violence, this rape, that "biology" supposedly demands of the male to ensure reproduction?[23]

That Esslin does not, and either cannot or will not, consider the implications of his use of frigidity as an unexamined category reveals his share in the dominant, *i.e.*, patriarchal, version of the cultural imaginary—an imaginary that excludes consideration of either the specificity of desire between women or the "needs" of female sexuality. As Irigaray's question suggests, the discursive deployment of frigidity may tell us more about male denial and anxiety than about female "lack." The phenomenon that "masculine discourse" must label frigidity in order to safeguard the integrity of the dominant sexual economy may in fact constitute a refusal of phallic violence in favor of an autoeroticism that, as Irigaray observes, differs markedly from the irremediably mediated form of male "auto"-eroticism:

> In order to touch himself, man needs an instrument: his hand, a woman's body, language. . . . And this self-caressing requires at least a minimum of activity. As for woman, she touches herself in and of herself without any need of mediation, and before there is any way to distinguish activity from passivity. Woman "touches herself" all the time, and moreover no one can forbid her to do so, for her genitals are formed of two lips in continuous contact. Thus, within herself, she is already two—but not divisible into one(s)—that caress each other.[24]

Irigaray's vision of an unmediated and literally self-gratifying female sexuality that refuses to accomodate itself to the imperatives of the phallic economy suggests what constructions of Kate as frigid (Esslin), "quite absorbed" in a dream-world (Anna), or the "classic female figure" (Deeley), all attempt to deny. "Thorough[ly]

and sensuous[ly] . . . soap[ing] herself all over"; emerging from
the bath exclaiming "with pleasure"; imagining herself walking
around the room after a bath, her body "glistening," on display
only for *her* gaze, responsive only to *her* touch: as these images
accrue to Kate, she comes to embody the kind of sexuality Irigaray
discusses, not only autoerotic—which, as the example of male au-
toerotism illustrates, does not necessarily preclude some form of
mediation—but "monologic" in its ability to dispense entirely with
the other.

The sexuality finds its representational correlative in Kate's final
speech, a declaration of independence from Anna and Deeley's
desires, gazes, and narrative constructions. I do not mean to imply
that the subject position she claims for herself is any less constructed or less dependent upon representation than the identities
Anna and Deeley would impose on her. Representational power,
however, does not mean only the power to construct a subject
position with which the addressee of the particular mode of representation will identify, but also the power to suppress alternative
representations—the kind of self-representation that emerges from
Kate's two major speeches. Her victory over Anna and Deeley
constitutes neither the triumph of truth over fiction nor of reality
over construction, but of one representation over others: the representation of a subjectivity "floating" beyond reach of the Other's
objectifying gaze.

The play does not conclude with Kate's speech, however, but
with an ambiguous tableau that reintroduces the question of scopic
domination, providing a broader, more problematic context in
which to view Kate's victory over Anna and Deeley: *"Lights up
full sharply. Very bright. Deeley in armchair. Anna lying on divan.
Kate sitting on divan"* (p. 71). Of this tableau David Savran writes,
"We see the configuration frozen in a blinding flash of light, just as
a flashbulb freezes its subject for an instant as the camera records
the image."[25] As Savran's simile suggests, the play concludes with
a representation of the very scopic power that it has subjected to
interrogation. What *Old Times* places in question, however, is less
the power of the gaze than the mystification of that power, the
kind of ideological forgetfulness that encourages the subject to
(mis)recognize the gaze as a function of the eye rather than as
produced by an ensemble of representational apparatus and reified
by a network of social institutions. While Sartre and Lacan con-
vincingly argue that the structure of the "look-looked-at" undermines a *specific subject's* assertions of ocularcentric power, they

also reveal the disjunction between the eye and the gaze that allows the latter to exceed the former.

Pinter's final tableau illustrates this excess: the sudden glare of the lights creates and directs the trajectory of, while transcending, our gaze. If, as Silverman notes, it is neither the audience nor the protagonist, but the camera and the cinematic apparatus, that function as the cinematic source of the gaze, then in theatre it is lighting that occupies the site of scopic origin. As the cinematic apparatus encourages the audience to forget its transcendence by remaining absent from the screen, so, depending on the nature of the theater in which we view *Old Times,* we may or may not see the stage lights, but we almost certainly will not see the light board operator. Finally, if the subject positions with which the film audience identifies are produced by the cinematic apparatus, effectually placing that audience under the apparatus's transcendent gaze, members of the theater audience find themselves in a similar position with regard to the formation of their subjectivity.

If the technical apparatus's gaze exceeds our own, it also exceeds that of the three frozen figures on the stage. Winner and losers in the game of desire and power that has played itself out on the stage, all find themselves arrested by a gaze, as Lacan argues, situated outside and beyond the subject, in the field of the Other. Anna and Deeley identify with but can never possess this gaze; Kate embraces a fluid subjectivity that appears to resist reduction to a visible essence, but, while her inaccessibility allows her to elude scopic capture by Anna and Deeley, the cultural gaze disperses itself across a vast network of social institutions and modes of representation, and can therefore survive the defeat of two of its vehicles.

The final tableau thus expresses the disjuncture between the subject and power that Pinter repeatedly dramatizes in his works: the capacity of a specific mode of cultural power both to exceed its "mouthpieces" (whether powerful like Goldberg or ultimately defeated like Deeley) and to remain beyond the reach of its opposition. It is hardly surprisingly, then, that even when Pinter attaches a name to the source of this power—Monty *(The Birthday Party),* Wilson *(The Dumb Waiter),* "the man who runs this country" *(One for the Road)*—it remains unrepresented and unrepresentable.

As these comments suggest, Pinter conceptualizes power as fundamentally irreducible to coherent visible form. We see Goldberg, but we do not see Monty; we see the light/gaze that fixes *Old Times's* characters in an eternal moment of display, but we do not see from whence or whom this gaze emanates. The paradoxical yet ultimate invisibility of this power—paradoxical because its "mouthpieces" are all too visible—suggests an alarming capacity to resist resistance. The final image in *Old Times* thus confronts us yet again with the troubling specter haunting all of the plays I have discussed: the specter of a form of cultural power so totalizing (if not totalitarian) that it admits of no outside, no position from which to decisively alter not simply the distribution of power, but the fundamental organization of the prevailing relations and definitions of power.

The very invincibility and ubiquity of this power accounts for that sense of menace that critics have repeatedly labelled "Pinteresque." What, after all, could be more menacing than the final tableau of *Old Times,* in which the panoptic gaze reasserts itself at the very moment when it has apparently been thoroughly deconstructed and disabled as a form of power? Our sense of menace at the final moment of the play, however, finds itself balanced by a troubling sense of the arbitrary nature of power in Pinter's works. I am pointing here to a certain gratuitousness in Pinter's *representation* of power rather than in the kind of power being represented. To clarify this comment, let me pose the following questions: Why *does Old Times* conclude with a symbolization of the form of power that the play has worked to demystify? Why are Anna's lesbian desire, Harry and Bill's homosexual relationship, and Ruth's status as matriarch all marked by the imprint of the dominant form of cultural power, a power that erases their potentially subversive difference? Why must Stanley passively accept his subjection as a "one-dimensional man"? Why does Goldberg fail to articulate a Jewish identity that would challenge the cultural coding of the Jew as "a true Christian"? These specific questions, in turn, raise a more fundamental question to which I will now turn in my conclusion: what are the consequences of the vision of cultural power elaborated in Pinter's plays?

6

Conclusion: "In the Light (or the Shadow) of Power"

In my discussion of *Old Times,* I proposed that we view the denial of difference informing Pinter's construction of lesbian desire as part of a recurring pattern in his works that also manifests itself in the representation of homosexuality in *The Collection* and the rise of matriarchy in *The Homecoming.* I call attention to this pattern because it foregrounds the question of how Pinter conceptualizes power. Even in plays that explore a crisis placing in jeopardy the power relations within the family, perhaps the central ideological apparatus of patriarchy, these relations are mirrored by and reconstituted within the various *loci* or cultural difference. It is almost as though, despite Stella, Ruth, and Kate's resistance to subjection, Pinter cannot imagine a form of mastery that departs from the dominant paradigm of cultural power.

At issue here, however, is less a "failure" of imagination than what I would call Pinter's "political" vision, a vision articulated through a cultural imaginary that reinscribes even as it critiques the operations of cultural power. We encounter the kind of pattern I am discussing not only in those plays dealing specifically with questions of gender and sexuality, but also in *The Birthday Party,* a play identifying cultural difference in terms of ethnicity. As I argued in my discussion of this play, Goldberg and McCann repeatedly identify themselves in terms of their difference, but a difference constructed by an ensemble of cultural codes that transform it into an index of socialization. Within the Other's discursive field, assimilation no longer entails denial of ethnicity; rather, declaring oneself a Jew or an Irish Catholic now becomes a sign of assimilation. When Goldberg ironically responds to McCann's expression of social validation, "You've always been a true Christian," with the understated "in a way," he falls victim to his own irony, since the play demonstrates that Goldberg can only play his role as the Other's "mouthpiece" by becoming "a true Christian," by identifying himself as a Jew in a culture that defines the Jew in the image of Christianity. Pinter encapsulates the status of the ethnic other within such a culture in Goldberg's account of his Uncle Barney, "an all-round man . . . a cosmopolitan" who, in terms of the play, is never more "Jewish" than in the cosmopolitanism that annuls his difference.

In *The Birthday Party,* then, Pinter represents the cultural order, and the forms of power that ensure its perpetuation, as unshakably homogeneous and monolithic. His vision of culture provides a dramatic parallel to that of Barthes in *"Pax Culturalis":* "Culture is not only what returns, it is also and especially what remains in place, like an imperishable corpse: it is a bizarre toy that *History never breaks* . . . in whose bosom everyone is gathered without apparent conflict."[1] A culture "in whose bosom everyone is gathered without apparent conflict"—such is the product of absolute power within the cultural sphere: not the power to contain or ruthlessly annihilate sites of resistance, but the power to foreclose the very possibility of resistance.

Goldberg and McCann cannot experience their difference *as* difference since the codes through which they "define" themselves exclude the concept of difference, with its suggestions of conflict between the margins and the center. Indeed, the cultural order for which these characters serve as "mouthpieces" consolidates its power by effectually transforming the margins into the center, gathering those who occupy sites of potential resistance to its "bosom," and allowing them to speak its encratic language—a language, as Barthes observes, "articulated . . . develop[ed] . . . marked in the light (or the shadow) of Power; of its many state, institutional, ideological machineries."[2]

Unlike *The Birthday Party, The Collection, The Homecoming,* and *Old Times* explore the possibility of resistance to the (specifically patriarchal) cultural order, its structures of representation and ideological apparatus. In these three plays, Pinter focuses on the potentially dislocating energies of such oppositional strategies as mimicry and the construction of a dispersed, "floating" subjectivity that would dislodge both the concept of an unitary individual or social subject and the cultural order that draws its ideological support from such a concept.

At the same time, however, these plays juxtapose the kind of resistance and intervention practiced by Stella, Ruth, and Kate against another version of the denial of difference dramatized in *The Birthday Party.* Like Goldberg and McCann, Harry, Ruth, and

Anna become "mouthpieces," articulating the cultural power that constitutes them, thus illustrating the Foucauldian dictum (and here Foucault sounds very much like Althusser and even a certain strain in Lacan) that I cited in connection with *The Homecoming:* "The individual is in effect of power, and at the same time, or precisely to the extent to which it is that effect, it is the element of its articulation."[3] Jew, Irish Catholic, homosexual, matriarch, lesbian—produced through the encratic language of Power, these de-differentiated *loci* of difference testify to the alarming capacity of a cultural order to resist resistance, to "remain in place" by reconstituting itself within the sites of "otherness."

To varying degrees, then, these four plays (and we can regard them as representative of Pinter's work as a whole in this respect) betray a profound sense of dis-ease and doubt; a sense that demystifying the nature of cultural power and revealing the contradictions within the ideology from which that power draws its support do not in themselves constitute a *decisive and final* dismantling of the institutional and discursive mechanisms through which the cultural order reproduces itself; a sense that, like the "gaze" that traps the characters in an eternal moment of impasse at the conclusion of *Old Times,* these mechanisms of power will remain operative even if those who seek to embody that power suffer defeat.

In "The Politics of Anxiety: Contemporary Socialist Theatre in England," C. W. E. Bigsby traces the growing sense of skepticism pervading the work of such politically committed dramatists as Edgar, Hare, and Poliakoff, comparing it to a similar sensibility in the work of such a "non-political" playwright as Pinter. While their early plays tend to dramatize an unshakable belief in both the efficacy of political action and the possibility of radically transforming the cultural order, Bigsby finds that, as this order continues to "remain in place" despite various attempts to undermine it, "instability has invaded the [later] work of these socialist writers— not merely a sense of disillusionment, but doubt about the nature and status of art and of simple models of social action."[4] Bigsby maintains that such doubt expreses itself in these dramatists' increasing concern with a form of alienation that does not so much resist as exceed political analysis—not the alienation of a single class denied control over both the means of production and the means of ideological reproduction, but an even more inclusive and fundamental ontological alienation:

> The unease which lay beneath the surface of much fifties drama [e.g., "Theatre of the Absurd"] now invades contemporary socialist theatre

in England, and to some degree the distinction between these plays and the work of Pinter, Beckett, or even (despite the political differences) Stoppard, begins to blur. The insecurity and alienation which this drama now explores can no longer be wished away with a simple transformation of the political system.[5]

If Edgar and Hare are beginning to explore the kind of ontological dislocation dramatized in Pinter's early plays—the so-called "comedies of menace"—it is also true that the sense of insecurity and anxiety marking Pinter's work manifests itself in a kind of cultural alarm. Esslin identifies the thematic core of the "absurdists" (among whose number he includes Pinter) as a "sense of metaphysical anguish at the absurdity of the human condition," an anguish that Pinter expresses through his focus on the efforts of "man trying to stake out a modest place for himself in the cold and darkness that envelops him."[6] Esslin argues that Pinter conveys this "darkness" through his penchant for dramatizing "the commonplace situation that is gradually invested with menace, dread," and a mystery that is nothing less than "the impenetrable mystery of the universe."[7]

There are two problems with Esslin's attempt to make Pinter conform to his definition of the "absurd": (1) a tendency to generalize the category of "metaphysical anguish," and (2) a privileging of the metaphysical at the expense of the social and the political. I would argue that appealing to a thematic concern with the "anguish," "dream," and "mystery of the universe" that Esslin views as central to the absurdist *zeitgeist* hardly constitutes an adequate response to the issues of cultural power Pinter's work explores. While renouncing the ideological and epistemological reassurance implicit in the realism of an Osborne or Wesker, Pinter's plays address themselves, as does the work of these two dramatists, to the vicissitudes of living within a specific cultural order rather than an incomprehensible universe.

Unlike Pinter himself, Esslin insists on placing social and political concerns within brackets, stating quite explicitly that in Pinter's plays, "we have always seen man stripped of the accidental circumstances of social position or . . . context."[8] At issue here is not whether Esslin is simply incorrect in his reading of the plays as offering a poetic image of a fundamental—*i.e.,* a-cultural and universal—existential anxiety, but how such a reading allows him to ignore the very real concern with the structures of domination and cultural power that, as I have argued throughout this study, play a central role in Pinter's work. Seizing upon the thematics of "metaphysical anguish," Esslin excludes a consideration of the all too infrequently remarked political dimension of these plays. While Pinter may indeed accept Ionesco's proposition that, "cut off from his religious, metaphysical, and transcendental roots, man is lost,"[9] the immediate problem facing Stanley, Stella, Ruth, and Kate is their inability either to cut themselves off from or to dismantle a cultural order that, as Barthes writes, "remains in place, like an imperishable corpse."

If political dramatists like Edgar and Hare increasingly concentrate on the kind of "insecurity and alienation" we associate with Pinter, we can also say that Pinter relates this sense of "insecurity" to the cultural construction of subjectivity, to the subject's status as "an effect of power, and . . . the element of its articulation." In other words, like the socialist playwrights examined by Bigsby, Pinter grounds his vision of "insecurity" in the meticulous operation of the social, Goldberg's "external force" that produces and installs itself within the subject's "interiority."

Given what I would call this political dimension of Pinter's *oeuvre*, the "new direction" of two one-act plays, *One for the Road* and *Mountain Language,* seems less a radical departure than a logical extension of his earlier writing. At the conclusion of my discussion of *The Birthday Party,* I remarked that Pinter's vision of the social homogeneity of capitalist culture represented an extension of the ideological universe of totalitarianism. *One for the Road* and *Mountain Language* directly engage this universe by focusing on the authoritarian state—a state remarkably similar in its operation to the "one-dimensional" cultural order of *The Birthday Party* and the patriarchal culture of *The Collection, The Homecoming,* and *Old Times.*

In both *One for the Road* and *Mountain Language,* the consolidation of state power produces the ultimate triumph of the Other's word. The victory of the encratic language of the state over the acratic language elaborated outside of, hence inherently in opposition to, the forms and structures of dominant power provides the thematic core of *Mountain Language.* In this play, Pinter dramatizes the conflict between center and margin, the (political) economy of the same and the resistance of difference, and the constraining monologic word and a subversive heteroglossia as a conflict between two languages: "the language of the capital" (the officially sanctioned language of the state) and the language of the mountain people (designated as "enemies of the state"). The play is set in a prison on the day when women from the mountains have been granted permission to visit their incarcerated husbands and sons. Before entering the prison, an officer informs them of the restrictions placed on their speech:

> Now hear this. You are mountain people. You hear me? Your language is dead. It is forbidden. It is not permitted to speak your mountain language in this place. You cannot speak your language to your men. It is not permitted. Do you understand? . . . It is outlawed. You may only speak the language of the capital. That is the only language permitted in this place. You will be badly punished if you attempt to speak your mountain language in this place. This is a military decree. It is the law. Your language is forbidden. It is dead. No one is allowed to speak your language. Your language no longer exists.[10]

As Goldberg and McCann exercise their power over Stanley by reducing him to the silence of an *infans,* waiting for the "gift" of the Other's language, so the state either literally reduces its opposition to silence (since the play indicates that the mountain women cannot speak the language of the capital) or forces it to speak a language that, by virtue of its official status, voices state power, a language that serves as an ideological instrument for the creation of docile political subjects. If *The Birthday Party* explores how the cultural codes erase difference by constituting the subject in the Other's image, *Mountain Language* and *One for the Road* demonstrate how the political version of these codes erases difference by constituting the subject in the image of the state. Once subordinated to the language of the capital, the mountain people will effectually lose the cultural alterity that separates them from the people of the capital.

Such a monologic word functions as the most powerful expression of the totalitarian impulse—the inexorable logic of the same— that transforms the state into an all-encompassing hall of mirrors in which the subject repeatedly (mis)recognizes itself in the image of the other members of what Nicolas, the interrogator in *One for the Road,* calls the "commonwealth of interest":

> I have never been more moved, in the whole of my life, as when . . . the man who runs this country announced to the country: We are all patriots, we are as one, we all share a common heritage . . . *(Pause.)* I feel a link, you see, a bond. I share a commonwealth of interest. I am not alone. I am not alone![11]

Nicolas's articulated sense of shared identity enacts at the level of voice the kind of abdication of "self" that it describes. As Nicolas responds to his leader's speech, recognizing "himself" in the image of the collective "one" with which his subjectivity merges, his voice dissolves into the monolithic Voice of state power. Nicolas's comments vividly illustrate the homogenizing energy of the monologic word: the "link" he "feels" does not arise from unmediated experience but is discursively produced, the defining characteristic of the subject position with which the speech encourages him to identify.

Once located within that position, Nicolas becomes a "mouthpiece" for a Power that always exceeds him: "I run the place. God speaks through me" (p. 36). A tension only partly resolved by Nicolas's position of authority within the state exists between the different claims of power advanced by these two statements. While literally true in terms of the unspecified detention center in which *One for the Road* is set, "I run the place" images Nicolas not only as possessed of absolute power but as the *originary site* of that power, a claim immediately contradicted by "God *speaks through* me." Through this contradiction, Pinter captures the very contingency and disappearance upon which entrance to the scene of power is predicated. Like Goldberg, McCann, and the officer in *Mountain Language* who functions as the voice of "the law," Nicolas is spoken through rather than speaking, subject-ed *to* as well as subject *of* a power with which he can never coincide.

I am not suggesting that Nicolas lacks power, but that Pinter carefully distinguishes between Power and the subjects it constitutes. As Foucault observes, the status of the subject as an "effect" of power implies a kind of ontological gap that precludes an absolute equation of the subject with power. The subject, in other words, may be dislodged from the position it occupies *without fundamentally altering the dominant forms and relations of power* (as Max can be feminized while the ideological status of the "symbolic father" remains unaffected). *One for the Road* and *Mountain Language,* then, dramatize the precarious purchase on power held even by those who occupy the subject positions of authority within the state.

In the second scene of *One for the Road,* Nicolas questions the young son (also named Nicolas) of the two dissidents he has arrested:

Nicolas. What is your name?
Nicky. Nicky.
Nicolas. Really? How odd. *(Pause.)* (p. 55)

The tense pause allows the audience as well as Nicolas to register the "oddness" of the situation, implicitly raising the question: does the doubling restrict itself to the level of the names, or will Nicolas himself become subjected to Nicky's fate? With the exception of the exchange I have quoted above, the play never directly addresses the possible implications of such doubling, but, with the understatement of "How odd," Pinter introduces a subtle note of unease that Nicolas's assertions of absolute power—a power that the subject can never possess—fail to allay.

Mountain Language contains a more explicit example of the anxiety arising when the victimizer senses the possibility that he will come to inhabit the place of the victim. When a prison guard hits one of the visiting women for speaking to her son in the mountain language, the prisoner attempts to intercede: "She's old. She doesn't understand" (p. 31). The guard responds, casting the prisoner in the role of the other, but the opposition between the two men collapses as soon as the guard sets it in place:

> *Guard.* Whose fault is that [if the mother doesn't understand the language of the capital]? *(He laughs.)* Not mine, I can tell you. And I'll tell you another thing. I've got a wife and three kids. And you're all a pile of shit. *(Silence.)*
> *Prisoner.* I've got a wife and three kids.
> *Guard.* You've what? *(Silence.)* You've got what? *(Silence.)* What did you say to me? You've got what? *(Silence.)* You've got *what? (He picks up the telephone and dials one digit.)* Sergeant? I'm in the Blue Room . . . yes . . . I thought I should report, Sergeant . . . I think I've got a joker in here. . . . *(The Sergeant comes in.)*
> *Sergeant.* What joker? *(Blackout)* (pp. 31–33)

When the lights go up on the scene again, the sergeant has exited, but remains all too visibly present as we see that: "[t]*he prisoner has blood on his face . . . [and] sits trembling*" (p. 43) The violent reprisal with which the guard responds to the prisoner's assertion of shared identity—the repeated phrase "I've got a wife and three kids"—suggests how desperately those who occupy positions of power need to differentiate themselves from the powerless, the only version of difference acceptable within an homogenous cultural or political order.

In both of these plays, then, Pinter raises the possibility that those who (are allowed to) identify with the subject positions through which Power articulates itself can never completely escape a certain instability, the threatening suggestion that when the despotic gaze of Power's "mouthpiece" looks into the eyes of the other, it sees reflected a version of itself. Like Deeley and Anna, Nicolas defines his authority in terms of a "demystifying" gaze that tran-scends the condition of the "look-looked-at": "The eyes of people who are brought to me here. They're so vulnerable. The soul shines through them" (p. 33). When the other bears the same name as or shares certain characteristics with the "mouthpiece," however, then the vulnerability of which Nicolas speaks seems to include the victimizer along with the victim, the powerful as well as the powerless.

Pinter, however, never equates this instability at the level of the subject with an instability at the level of state power itself. Nicolas and the guard may one day find themselves inhabiting the uninhabi-table space of Nicky and the prisoner, but Pinter suggests that the state itself, in Barthes's words, "is not only what returns, it is also and especially what remains in place." In Pinter's dramatic universe, what I would call, at the risk of tautology, the power of Power lies precisely in its nature as a *beyond,* that which is located elsewhere than in the subjects it produces.

Infinitely capable of reconstituting itself, Power can survive the sacrifice of its "mouthpiece" and can draw strength even from a reversal of its own decrees. *Mountain Language* concludes with the guard informing the prisoner that, in accordance with a new law, he will now be allowed to converse with his mother in their own language. Rather than a sign of defeat, however, such a "con-cession" only confirms the absolute authority of the state:

> *Prisoner.* Mother, you can speak. *(Pause.)* Mother, I'm speaking to you. You see? We can speak. You can speak to me in our own lan-guage. *(She is still)* . . . I am speaking to you in our own lan-guage. . . . It's our language. . . . *(She does not respond.)* Mother? . . . Mother? *(She does not respond. She sits still. The prisoner's trembling grows. He falls from the chair on to his knees, begins to gasp and shake violently. The sergeant walks into the room and studies the prisoner shaking on the floor.)*
> *Sergeant (To guard).* Look at this. You go out of your way to give them a helping hand and they fuck it up. *(Blackout)* (pp. 45–47)

Even if we regard the mother's silence as an act of resistance—a refusal to speak a language that, now granted official recognition, no longer "belongs" to the mountain people—the prisoner's col-lapse together with the mockery of the sergeant's comment, which is also the play's final line, suggest the ultimate futility of such resistance when directed against a field of power that articulates itself not only through the ideological coercion of language, but also through the more direct and naked coercion of the repressive state apparatus.

Pinter's focus in these plays on the repressive rather than the ideological state apparatus allows him to develop a thematic motif that runs through the plays I have discussed in this study: the relationship between linguistic and extra-linguistic power, *i.e.,* violence. In "Writing the Event," Barthes argues that violence is itself structured like a language: "However one decides to account for it, tactical or psychoanalytic, violence implies a language of violence, i.e., of signs (poerations or pulsions) repeated, combined into figures (actions or complexes), in short, a system"[12] or code. It is a mark of the unassailable position of the state in these plays that no contradiction exists between the "language of violence" and the violence of language.

One for the Road and *Mountain Language* give dramatic expression to Barthes's dictum that "violence implies a language of violence," as they increasingly blur the line that separates state violence from the language of the law that both sanctions and draws support from such violence. We can turn to the officer's proclamation outlawing the mountain language for an example of this "language of violence." What he says not only possesses the status of law, but is "a military decree," an utterance whose linguistic force (as a decree) is inseparable from the repressive violence it can command (as a *military* decree): "You will be badly punished if you attempt to speak your mountain language."

Perhaps the most disturbing example of this conflation of the language of state power and the articulation of that power through the "language" (in Barthes's sense of the word) of torture and murder occurs at the conclusion of *One for the Road*. Nicolas releases the dissident Victor, and when the latter asks if his son Nicky will also be granted his freedom, the interrogator replies, "Your son? Oh, don't worry about him. He was a little prick. *(Victor straightens and stares at Nicolas. Silence. Blackout)*" (pp. 79–80). Nicolas's line repeats, with one essential difference, his earlier remark to Nicky's mother Gila: "Your son is . . . a little prick" (p. 71). Because Pinter does not dramatize Nicky's murder, we have the sense that Nicolas's words possess the power to kill, that, when harnessed to the language of state power, the simple grammatical ability to shift from present tense to past tense transforms the speaking subject into an executioner. If, as Barthes writes, "violence implies a language of violence," then the "representation" of Nicky's murder provides an example of such language—a language in which sign and referent have spilled over into each other to such an extent that the monologic word appears coextensive with the murderous deed.

It is not my intention to minimize (or to claim that Pinter minimizes) the brutality these plays contain—Nicky's murder, Victor's torture, Gila's repeated rapes, the prisoner's beating—by discussing violence in terms of language; rather, I would argue that, by encouraging us to recognize a metaphorical equivalence between the two, Pinter reveals that the absolutist state can only ensure its monopoly on power if it controls both the discursive and repressive apparatus. In this sense Nicolas is not wrong when he tells Victor, "You probably think I'm part of a predictable, formal, long-established pattern, i.e. I chat away friendly, insouciant, I open the batting, as it were . . . while another waits in the wings, silent, introspective, coiled like a puma. No, no. It's not quite like that" (pp. 35–36). In terms of plot, of course, it is like that since Nicolas does not actually participate in the acts of violence detailed in the play; in terms of the dynamics of power, however, Nicolas is correct since the "silent" operations of violence locate themselves within the space created by the discourse of state power—an ideological discourse in which the state mystifies its own recourse to violence through the rhetoric of preserving the "commonwealth of interest," or else, as in the case of the officer's proclamation in *Mountain Language,* de-nominates torture and murder, choosing to speak of punishment as a legal category.

In an interview published in the American edition of *One for the Road,* Nicholas Hern asks Pinter if he feels that the play can in any way participate in the dismantling of the kind of totalitarian practices he both explores and demystifies. The playwright offers an unequivocally pessimistic response: "There's no point, it's hopeless. That's my view. . . Because reason is not going to do anything. Me writing *One for the Road,* documentaries, articles, lucid analyses, Averell Harriman writing in the *New York Times,* voices raised here and there, people walking down the road and demonstrating. Finally it's hopeless. There's nothing one can achieve" (p. 20).

These remarks reveal that Pinter harbors no illusions concerning the efficacy of reason and the liberal humanist ideology that assigns it a privileged position when confronted with a political system that can itself justify authoritarian practices by laying ideological claim to reason. With its recognition of limits it refuses to transgress and beyond which resides the otherness of the irrational, the discourse of reason implies a concept of law, of the allowable, of the code. Is an oppositional appeal to reason likely to dismantle a state such as that depicted in *Mountain Language*—a state that does not engage in torture but "severely punish[es]"; that clearly defines which actions it finds acceptable and which unacceptable, *i.e.,* irrational; that always operates within the limits of its law (even if that law merely sanctions a kind of totalitarian power); a state, in other words, erected (at least in the abstract) on the principle of reason?

If "reason is not going to do anything," we may ask why Pinter does not explore oppositional politics in these plays. Nowhere in these two works is any indication given that the prisoners or Victor and Gila are either involved in some organized resistance movement or contemplate the overthrow of the government; indeed, we scarcely perceive them as "political" in the most conventional sense of the word. As Pinter observes to Hern, this can partly be explained by the fact that, under certain conditions, independent thought suffices to transform one into an enemy of the state: "These people, generally speaking—. . . whether it's Czechoslovakia or whether it's Chile—ninety per cent of them have committed no offence. There's no such thing as an offence, apart from the fact that *everything* is. . . . Their very existence is an offence" (pp. 15–16).

Yet such remarks do not address the issue of why Pinter, in *One for the Road* and *Mountain Language,* does not (indeed, *cannot*) represent an oppositional set of political practices. This question, however, extends beyond these two plays to encompass Pinter's work as a whole. As I have argued throughout this study, Pinter's plays offer a dystopian vision of the invincibility of regnant forms of cultural and political power. In the tradition of such images as Weber's "iron cage," Adorno's "administered society," and Levi-Strauss's "monoculture," Pinter offers a dramatized "theory" of cultural power that conceptualizes that power as unalterable, not susceptible to fundamental change.

By offering such a vision, however, Pinter's works enter a strange and disturbing complicity with the object of their critique. I am not claiming that Pinter either supports totalitarianism, positions himself as a staunch defender of patriarchal power, or endorses the kind of cultural violence that shapes Stanley's subjectivity. I am arguing that by leaving little room for resistance or the elaboration of oppositional practices, the totalizing nature of his analysis of cultural power tends to reify that power. Despite the insistence with which they demystify the operations of power, these plays, as it were, are written from the "point of view" of that power, repeatedly reinscribing even as they work to dismantle it. In this context, the symbolic reappearance of the panoptic gaze that concludes *Old Times* becomes the quintessential image of power in Pinter's *oeuvre*—a power whose ability to "remain in place" depends more upon *how* it is conceptualized and represented than upon its actual operations.

To clarify this comment, we might consider a general similarity between Pinter and Althusser. In my discussion of *The Birthday Party*, I suggested that we regard Pinter's plays as examples of dramatic *Ideologiekritik* that conceptualize the ideological fashioning of subjectivity in Althusserian terms. In *Lenin and Philosophy*, Althusser articulates an extremely influential and no less controversial theory of ideology (see Chapter Two). Much of the controversy[13] centers around the totalizing nature of this theory: while Althusser traces the operations of ideology in minute detail, demystifying and deconstructing the categories of the "natural," the ineluctably given, and the epistemologically obvious that act as smokescreens for the dissemination of ideology, his critique leads to impasse since it proposes no way to resist subjection to ideological power. For Althusser, the subject always responds in an "appropriate" manner to the image with which it is encouraged to identify, always serves as a prop for the prevailing economy of power through (mis)recognizing itself in the mirror of the Other's cultural codes.

We see this Althusserian vision of Pinter's texts when Goldberg (mis)recognizes the Jew in the image of the "true Christian"; when Harry, Ruth, and Anna all in their different ways identify the ideological attributes of "masculine" power as the only *possible* form of power. On the one hand, Pinter's dramatizing of this kind of (mis)recognition forecloses our romanticizing those groups consigned to the margins of culture, *i.e.*, the naive, essentializing gesture that sees lesbianism, homosexuality, or female empowerment as *inherently* contestatory, *inherently* subversive of the status quo. Pinter reminds us how easily cultural alterity can be erased through the imposition of a totalizing logic of the same. The problem arises when Pinter's plays and Althusser's theory see this annihilation of difference as inevitable, as a consequence of how the mechanisms of cultural power function rather than as the logical extension of their vision of power. If it is naive to privilege the subversive capabilities of difference simply because of its status *as* difference, it is certainly equally problematic to posit the inescapable co-optation of difference, its disappearance within the Other.

To assume that ideological power always succeeds in producing subjects in its image is to assume that meaning is fixed rather than subject to the vicissitudes of *how* we receive and respond to the codes, messages, and representations that produce our subjectivity. There is always the chance that our response can lead to a refusal of the Other's meaning; that is, not a refusal of subjectivity, but an articulation of that subjectivity in terms that differ from its prevailing cultural coding. To cite an example: I argued against Baker and Tabachnik's reading of Goldberg as an assimilated Jew. The discourse of assimilation implicitly invokes the existential duality of "authentic existence" and "bad faith," here given a specifically ethnic inflection. Baker and Tabachnik, in other words, assume an original, ontologically complete identity called "Jewishness," from which one can be alienated through the process of assimilation, but also (and most importantly) to which one can authentically return.

As I observed above, Pinter's works reject such essentialism; identity neither exists "out there" in some utopian space beyond the limits of culture nor offers itself as an unmediated form of experience, but is always fashioned through representation. We might expect these structures of representation to serve as sites of ideological struggle, but *The Birthday Party* negates the very idea of such struggle. Goldberg's inability to contest the subject position his culture allows Jews to occupy—the position of the Jew as the "true Christian"—by "coding" Judaism in terms that would grant it some measure of cultural specificity suggests not only that we receive the message emitted from the Other, but that we understand and passively accept that message according to the Other's dictates. Goldberg's failure to complete the sentence "Because I believe that the world . . . ," his failure to reject the "I" imposed upon him, in terms of the play, is not *his* failure, but a sign of the inescapable subjection to cultural power that marks human subjectivity.

The Collection comes closest to moving beyond this impasse, to considering the possibility that the process through which the subject receives and processes the Other's call can lead to a rejection of that call. I have discussed Stella in terms of Irigaray's definition of the mimic, the woman who "assume[s] the feminine role deliberately," in order to undermine the ideological apparatus producing that role. The mimic, in other words, must be able to resist her interpellation within the dominant ideology; indeed, she must be able to recognize ideological representations *as* representations, roles, discursively constituted subject positions that, therefore, can be constituted differently.

Irigaray admits that mimicry can only form the "initial phase" of the feminist project of re-fashioning women's subjectivity in a field of relations that does not borrow its structure from the phallic economy of power. Mimicry demystifies the workings of that economy, but does not in itself articulate new subject positions for women to inhabit. While mimicry allows Stella to escape subjection to patriarchal power, *The Collection* allows us to see its limits if it is regarded as anything more than an "initial phase" in a larger project. Through mimicry, Stella effects a reversal in the prevailing ideological equation of language with "masculine" power and silence with "feminine" powerlessness. Casting herself as the silent woman at the very moment when patriarchy demands her voice, she transforms silence into a form of empowerment. This reversal, however, while destabilizing privileged ideological terms of patriarchal culture, *retains* the language/silence binary that enables the elaboration of those terms.

As a mimic, Stella provides a kind of immanent critique of patriarchy, a critique whose limits are set by its immanence. Like the other plays I have discussed, *The Collection* does not/cannot offer a vision of a transformed cultural order but shows cultural power reasserting itself. As I have argued, we see this reassertion when Harry and Bill's relationship—a "marriage" in which Bill's "feminine" powerlessness guarantees Harry's "masculine" identity as the figure of authority—recuperates and renders operable the representations governing the gendered balance of power within patriarchy. The question is, how do we read such recuperation? In part, ironically; given that the play reveals the economy of homosexual desire underwriting and underlying the heterosexual patriarchal order, it is perfectly consistent with the logic of demystification that an homosexual relationship should embody patriarchal power relations in their "pure" form. At the same time, however, Harry and Bill's relationship suggests that even those who inhabit the space of cultural difference are "marked in the light (or the shadow) of Power"; that ideological machinery can preserve the cultural order from the threat of such difference by producing alterity in the image of that order; that the operations of such machinery can prevent the articulation of alternative subject positions and modes of power.

To talk about ideological machinery is to assume a concrete specificity in the analysis of power that these plays certainly possess. *One for the Road* and *Mountain Language* explore the role of the repressive state apparatus in supporting the mystifying rhetoric of the totalitarian state. *The Birthday Party, The Collection,*

The Homecoming, and *Old Times* all focus on the family as a site for the transmission and reproduction of the dominant patriarchal ideology. With its focus on how such texts as films and songs participate in the construction of the "classic female figure," *Old Times* indicates at least one process—the dissemination of popular culture—through which the cultural coding of gender gains currency within patriarchy.

At the same time that Pinter's work exhibits this attention to specifics, there is a certain level of abstraction in the way these plays conceptualize power, a level at which power no longer remains bound within particular institutions or apparatus, but is hypostatized as a kind of anonymous, transcendent force. This sense of reified Power is particularly strong when we consider the relationship between language and cultural power in the plays. More than any other contemporary dramatist working in the English-language theater, Pinter has alerted audiences to how language, in its dimension as cultural code, functions as a vehicle for the transmission of cultural power; how language transforms speakers into the Other's "mouthpieces." Once again, however, Pinter's vision of the totalizing nature of power limits his critique. The plays make the leap from dramatizing how cultural codes function as ideological supports of the social order to suggesting that they are no longer up for grabs in the struggle to determine who controls cultural power. Pinter's characters often use these codes to gain ascendency in their struggle for power over others, but the terms that define both what counts as *cultural* power and what kind of social arrangements will become entrenched through the exercise of such power have always already been decided.

There is a sense, then, that if power embeds itself in the materiality of language, it also floats beyond language, that the cultural codes emanate from a quasi-Platonic "Idea" of Power present in the codes as an absent cause. To discuss language in terms of an intersection of presence and absence is implicitly to evoke the kind of insights provided by Lacan's linguistic theories. I have cited Lacan throughout these pages to elucidate specific moments in the plays, but there is a more general affinity between Pinter and Lacan (at least the "structuralist" Lacan) I want to indicate, an affinity suggested by the following passage from the *Discours de Rome:* "Symbols in fact envelop the life of man in a network . . . so total that they bring to his birth . . . the shape of his destiny; so total that they give the words that will make him faithful or renegade, the law of the acts that will follow him . . . even beyond his death."[14]

While Lacan attempts here to describe the emergence of subjectivity within the material network of language, his invocation of destiny transforms language into the tool of an abstract force to which the subject can never gain access. It is this force, this *power*, that imposes the words that mark the subject as "faithful or renegade," "mouthpiece" of the same or sign of otherness. This passage leaves no room for the subject to adapt, appropriate, or reject these codes; rather, the subject must undergo a continuous and inescapable subjection to the power of a destiny that works through, without being irreducible to, the symbolic order. It is precisely this Lacanian vision of language as the agent of destiny that we find in Pinter's plays. For Pinter, as for Lacan, the subject remains enveloped within a determining structure of cultural codes that maps the trajectory of its existence; that allows "its" empowerment only if such empowerment leaves the cultural order intact; that leaves it, like Sartre's characters, in a state of impasse from which there is no exit.

I have been arguing that Pinter's plays, like the theories of Althusser and Lacan (and certain elements in the writings of Barthes and Foucault), reinscribe the formations and relations of power they critique by placing that power beyond struggle, beyond a final and decisive act of oppositional intervention. While the plays fail to move from deconstructing to reconstructing the field of cultural power, it is certainly true that such reconstruction could not occur without the kind of demystifying scrutiny of the operations of power in which these plays engage. We may reject the sense of impasse and political quietism informing Pinter's judgment that "finally it's hopeless. There's nothing one can achieve," that the cultural order will always "remain in place," but to dismiss out of hand the plays' analysis of how power works would amount to ignoring the contribution they make towards a theorization of power.

In this context, I am thinking particularly of Pinter's refusal to equate the subject and power. Bigsby has attacked the reductionistic strategies of those political plays "which turns kings into simple betrayers, captains of slave-ships into cynical manipulators *only*, judges into conscious dealers in injustice *and nothing else*."[15] At least part of what Bigsby objects to in these plays is the implication that those in positions of authority "own" power; that they constitute a site of origin not only for the exercise, but also for the production of power; and that, therefore, simply removing these figures from their privileged positions will result in the decisive dismantling of the power they embody.

Pinter, on the other hand, conceptualizes the subject's relation to power in more Foucauldian terms: the subject remains an *effect* that emerges from the operations of a power that remains irreducible to the dimensions of that subject. Power does not display itself solely through the negative activity of oppression, but also—indeed, fundamentally—through the creation of the subject positions with which we identify and in which we install ourselves. Both those who "possess" and those who lack authority in Pinter's universe thus share a similar contingency and instability, a similar disappearance within the field of the Other.

If this sense of radical disjuncture between the subject and power—a disjuncture revealing the extent to which the latter exceeds the former—accounts at least in part for Pinter's pessimistic assessment of the chances for social transformation, it also testifies to the playwright's success in avoiding the trap of underestimating the power and sophistication of the cultural and political practices he explores. Refusing to locate power exclusively within the subject, Pinter's plays remain free of the kind of unexamined subversive gestures that equate the defeat of a partriarch with the collapse of patriarchy, or the dislodging of those who operate the repressive state apparatus with the dismantling of authoritarian power.

At the same time that Pinter's plays reject the simple equation of the subject with power, they also problematize the critique of *Ideologiekritik,* a critique I will term the "implosion theory" of ideology. I have argued that these plays share with Althusser a sense of the monolithic unassailability of ideology. One line of critique running throughout commentary on Althusser entails pointing out that subjectivity is always plural, since we inhabit multiple subject positions, that the possibility for tension and contradiction between these subject positions will inevitably create fissures within and undermine any "unified" ideology that attempts to effect our subjection. Such a critique—the "implosion theory"—projects the ultimate disintegration of an ideology unable to suppress the proliferating array of contradictions between our various subject positions in which it must anchor its "mouthpieces."

If the Althusserian account of ideology tends to reify the existing cultural order by rendering it immune to any fundamental change, the implosion theory errs by underestimating the resiliency of ideology. This implosion theory represents a transformation of the classical Marxist view that capitalism itself would ultimately fall victim to the crises of production that it had once initiated in order to achieve social and economic hegemony. Rather than complacently enacting its role in this scenario, capitalism has met the pressures of crisis through an evolution from a market through an imperialistic stage and, finally, to the current multinational, postmodern form analyzed in great detail in Fredric Jameson's recent work.[16] There is no reason to believe that ideology will fall where capitalism triumphed. Indeed, one need look no further than the triumph of the so-called New Right in England and the U.S. in order to see the relative ease with which the dominant ideology *can* colonize and neutralize potential sites of resistance, thus surviving its own imminent crises.

In *The Birthday Party,* the kind of ideological conflict upon which the implosion theory places its hopes never materializes, but *The Collection, The Homecoming,* and *Old Times* all explore the fundamental contradiction inscribed within patriarchy's construction of the "classic female figure": the contradiction between "wife" and "whore." While such contradiction threatens the stability of the system of ideological representations articulating patriarchal power relations, the plays suggest that this conflicting inscription of female subjectivity cannot, in and of itself, undermine patriarchy and produce a new social order. If we can ascribe the entrenchment of patriarchy in these plays to Pinter's view of cultural power as an unshakable totalizing network, we can also ascribe it to the plays' refusal to make the leap of faith required by the implosion theory. Indeed, the plays suggest that recognizing ideological contradictions will only yield oppositional practices if those practices are situated outside the terms of the contradiction.

To clarify this last point, let me turn again to the ambiguities surrounding Ruth in *The Homecoming*'s climactic contract scene. While Ruth's deliberate assumption of the role of "whore" foregrounds the tensions in the wife/whore opposition, and while her manipulation of the rhetoric of economics and legality foregrounds the exploitation of women within patriarchy, her mimicry only reinscribes her status as a commodity. Her apparent empowerment as a subject free to dispose of her body as she pleases, a whore who (in Pinter's words) "would not be a harlot in her own mind," masks the extent to which such "empowerment" proves recuperable by, rather than subversive of, patriarchal culture. Ruth fails because she attempts to challenge this culture by provoking a crisis of and from within its ideological images ("wife" and "whore") rather than attempting to fashion a subject position that does not refer (even through mimicry) to the terms and definition of patriarchy.

If *The Homecoming* fails to envision this alternative subject po-

sition, it does succeed in allowing *us* to see the habitual meanings
and values attached to the cultural construction of femininity. I
emphasize "us" because, at the risk of stating the obvious, the
effectivity of political drama ultimately depends on how we receive
it, what we take away from it. Some pages back, I referred to
Pinter's vision as dystopian; like all dystopian literature, his plays
provide cautionary examples that we should not ignore. While rejecting the conclusion to which his plays implicitly point, *i.e.,* the
vision of an oppressive cultural order or state as "what remains in
place, like an imperishable corpse," his plays do dramatize how
cultural power *needs* to work to ensure the reproduction of the
prevailing social arrangements. Indeed, his plays dramatize how
power *will* work without the elaboration of oppositional practices.
Through demystifying the operations in power, Pinter can compel
his audience directly to confront the question of how power participates in the formation of "appropriate" subjects—subjects who
remain subjected to the Other. While we should not equate *recognition of* this process with *resistance to* this process, the latter would
be impossible without the former. Halfway through his fourth dec-
ade as a playwright, then, we can look back over Pinter's work
and, despite differences in style and focus, regard it as constituting
one of the more interesting projects within the field of contemporary drama: a complex investigation of the subject's positioning
within the field of the Other, an intensive exploration of the manner
in which subjectivity emerges "in the light (or the shadow) of
Power."

Notes

Chapter 1. "The Pinter Problem" Re-Problematized

1. Cited in Martin Esslin, *Pinter the Playwright* (London: Methuen, 1984), p. 21.

2. James R. Hollis, *Harold Pinter: The Poetics of Silence* (Carbondale: Southern Illinois University Press, 1970), p. 13.

3. Adrian Brine, "Mac Davies Is No Clochard," *Drama* 56 (1961): p. 36.

4. Esslin, *Pinter the Playwright*, p. 238.

5. Harold Pinter, *Complete Works: One* (New York: Grove Press, 1977), p. 15.

6. Hollis, *Harold Pinter*, p. 13.

7. Austin E. Quigley, *The Pinter Problem* (Princeton: Princeton University Press, 1975), pp. 25–26.

8. Ibid., p. 27.

9. Ibid., p. 46.

10. Esslin, *Pinter the Playwright*, p. 238.

11. Quigley, *The Pinter Problem*, p. 52.

12. Ibid., pp. 53–54.

13. Cited in Tzvetan Todorov, *Mikhail Bakhtin: Dialogical Principle*, trans. by Wlad Godzich (Minneapolis: University of Minnesota Press, 1984), p. 62.

14. Ibid., p. 48.

15. Anthony Wilden, *System and Structure: Essays in Communication and Exchange* (London: Tavistock, 1972), pp. 22–23.

16. Harold Pinter, *The Birthday Party*, in *Complete Works: One*, pp. 27–28.

17. Roland Barthes, *S/Z*, trans. by Richard Miller (New York: Hill and Wang, 1974), p. 100.

18. Pinter, *The Birthday Party*, p. 88.

19. Harold Pinter, *Old Times*, in *Complete Works: Four* (New York: Grove Press, 1981), p. 31.

20. Martin Esslin, *The Theatre of the Absurd* (Harmondsworth, Middlesex: Penguin Books, 1980), p. 410.

21. Harold Pinter, *One for the Road* (New York: Grove Press, 1986), p. 7.

22. Esslin, *Pinter the Playwright*, p. 36.

23. Ibid.

24. Louis Althusser, *Lenin and Philosophy*, trans. by Ben Brewster (New York: Monthly Review Press, 1971), p. 211.

25. John Fuegi, "The Uncertainty Principle and Pinter's Modern Drama," in *Harold Pinter: Critical Approaches*, ed. by Steven H. Gale. (Rutherford, N.J.: Fairleigh Dickinson University Press, 1986).

26. Richard Gilman, "The Pinter Puzzle," *New York Times*, 22 Jan. 1967, sec. 2, p. 1.

27. Pinter, *Complete Works: One*, p. 13.

Chapter 2. "You'll Be Integrated": Subjectivity as Subjection in *The Birthday Party*

1. Althusser, *Lenin and Philosophy,* p. 182.

2. Harold Pinter, *The Birthday Party,* in *Complete Works: One,* p. 60.

3. Steven H. Gale, *Butter's Going Up: A Critical Analysis of Harold Pinter's Work* (Durham, N.C.: Duke University Press, 1977), p. 53.

4. Lois G. Gordon, *Strategems to Uncover Nakedness: The Dramas of Harold Pinter* (Columbia: University of Missouri Press, 1968), p. 8.

5. Kaja Silverman, *The Subject of Semiotics* (New York: Oxford University Press, 1983), p. 126.

6. See particularly Gale, *Butter's Going Up,* and Bernard F. Dukore, *Harold Pinter* (New York: Grove Press, 1982.)

7. Kristin Morrison, *Canters and Chronicles* (Chicago: The University of Chicago Press, 1983), p. 152.

8. Herbert Blau, *Take up the Bodies* (Urbana: University of Illinois Press, 1982), p. 133.

9. Jacques Lacan, *Écrits: A Selection,* trans. by Alan Sheridan (New York: W. W. Norton, 1977), p. 2.

10. Ibid., pp. 2, 6.

11. Ibid., p. 4.

12. Ibid.

13. Althusser, *Lenin and Philosophy,* p. 212.

14. Ibid.

15. Ibid., p. 210

16. Cited in Todorov, *Mikhail Bakhtin,* p. 96.

17. Lacan, *Écrits,* pp. 41–42.

18. Gale, *Butter's Going Up,* pp. 44–45.

19. Lacan, *Écrits,* p. 42.

20. Ibid.

21. Pinter, *Complete Works: One,* p. 13.

22. Jacques Lacan, *The Four Fundamental Concepts of Psycho-Analysis.* Trans. by Alan Sheridan (New York: W. W. Norton, 1978), p. 118.

23. Peter Handke, "Nauseated by Language," *The Drama Review* 49 (1970): p. 60.

24. Cited in Todorov, *Mikhail Bakhtin,* p. 96.

25. Lacan, *The Four Fundamental Concepts of Psycho-Analysis,* p. 235.

26. Anthony Wilden, *System and Structure: Essays in Communication and Exchange* (London: Tavistock, 1972), pp. 22–23.

27. Pinter, *Complete Works: One,* p. 14.

28. Roland Barthes, *S/Z,* p. 100.

29. William Baker and Stephen E. Tabachnik, *Harold Pinter* (Edinburgh: Oliver and Boyd, 1973), p. 54.

30. Barthes, *S/Z,* p. 100.

31. Jacques Derrida, *Of Grammatology,* trans. by G. C. Spivak (Baltimore: Johns Hopkins University Press, 1980), p. 305.

32. Juliet Flower MacCannell, *Figuring Lacan: Criticism and the Cultural Unconscious* (Lincoln: University of Nebraska Press, 1986), p. 131.

33. Lacan, *Écrits,* p. 305.

Chapter 3. "It's Part of Their Nature": Woman's Truth in *The Collection*

1. Harold Pinter, *The Collection,* in *Complete Works: Two* (New York: Grove Press, 1977), p. 151.

2. Ferdinand de Saussure, *Course in General Linguistics,* trans. by Wade Baskin (New York: McGraw-Hill, 1966), p. 121.

3. Stephen Heath, "Family Plots," in *Comparative Criticism,* ed. by E. S. Shaffer, Vol. 5 (Cambridge: Cambridge University Press, 1983), p. 321.

4. Ibid., p. 318.

5. Saussure, *Course in General Linguistics,* p. 67.

6. Elin Diamond, *Pinter's Comic Play* (Lewisburg, Pa.: Bucknell University Press, 1985), pp. 112–13.

7. Michel Foucault, *The Birth of the Clinic: An Archaeology of Medical Perception,* trans. by A. M. S. Smith (New York: Pantheon Books, 1973), pp. 165–66, 121.

8. Jean-Paul Sartre, *Being and Nothingness,* trans. by H. E. Barnes (New York: Philosophical Library, 1956), p. 708.

9. Anthony Wilden, *System and Structure: Essays in Communication and Exchange* (London: Tavistock, 1972), p. 294.

10. Sigmund Freud, "On Narcissism: An Introduction," in *The Standard Edition of the Complete Psychological Works,* trans. by James Trachey, Vol. 14 (London: Hogarth Press, 1953–74), p. 88.

11. Ibid.

12. Ibid., p. 49.

13. Luce Irigaray, *This Sex Which Is Not One,* trans. by Catherine Porter and Carolyn Burke (Ithaca: Cornell University Press, 1985), pp. 186, 185.

14. Ibid., p. 170.

15. Ibid., pp. 192–93.

16. Ibid., p. 171.

17. Ibid., p. 193.

18. Gale, *Butter's Going Up,* p. 123.

19. Michel Foucault, *The History of Sexuality,* trans. by Robert Hurley (New York: Vintage Books, 1980), p. 45.

20. Irigaray, *This Sex Which Is Not One,* p. 76.

21. Ibid.

22. Ibid.

23. Ibid.

24. Ibid., p. 85.

25. Ibid., p. 76.

Chapter 4. "The Structure Wasn't Affected": *The Homecoming* and the Crisis of Family Structure

1. Irigaray, *This Sex Which Is Not One,* p. 76.

2. Shoshana Felman, "The Critical Phallacy," *Diacritics* (Winter 1975): p. 3.

3. Toril Moi, *Sexual/Textual Politics* (London: Methuen, 1985), p. 143.

4. Quigley, *The Pinter Problem,* p. 225.

5. Elin Diamond, *Pinter's Comic Play* (Lewisburg, Pa.: Bucknell University Press, 1985), p. 157.

6. Roland Barthes, *S/Z*, p. 36.

7. Henry Hewes, "Probing Pinter's Play," *Saturday Review* 50 (1967): p. 57.

8. Irigaray, *This Sex Which Is Not One*, pp. 85, 84.

9. Ibid., p. 85.

10. Ibid., p. 191.

11. Harold Pinter, *The Homecoming*, in *Complete Works: Three* (New York: Grove Press, 1978), p. 93.

12. Irigaray, *This Sex Which Is Not One*, pp. 178–79.

13. Luce Irigaray, *Speculum of the Other Woman*, trans. by G. C. Gill (Ithaca: Cornell University Press, 1985), p. 122.

14. Ibid., p. 118.

15. Irigaray, *This Sex Which Is Not One*, p. 81.

16. Wally Secombe, "The Housewife and Her Labour under Capitalism," *New Left Review* 83 (1973): p. 15.

17. Diamond, *Pinter's Comic Play*, p. 141.

18. Cited in Anika Lemaire, *Jacques Lacan*, trans. by David Macey (London: Routledge and Kegan Paul, 1977), p. 83.

19. Jacques Lacan, *Écrits*, p. 67.

20. Alice A. Jardine, *Gynesis* (Ithaca: Cornell University Press, 1985), p. 98.

21. See Lucina P. Gabbard, *The Dream Structure of Pinter's Plays: A Psychoanalytic Approach* (Rutherford, N.J.: Fairleigh Dickinson University Press, 1976), pp. 183–208.

22. Lacan, *Écrits*, p. 264.

23. Harold Pinter, *Complete Works: One*, pp. 14–15.

24. Lemaire, *Jacques Lacan*, p. 82.

25. Laura Melvey, "Visual Pleasure and Narrative Cinema," in *Feminism and Film Theory*, ed. by Penley (New York: Routledge, 1988), p. 62.

26. Ibid., p. 64.

27. Sigmund Freud, *Sexuality and the Psychology of Love* (New York: Collier Books, 1963), p. 217.

28. Sigmund Freud, "The Uncanny," in *The Standard Edition of the Complete Psychological Works*, trans. by James Strachey. Vol. 17 (London: Hogarth Press, 1953–74), p. 220.

29. Jacques Lacan, *Feminine Sexuality*, ed. by Juliet Mitchell and Jacquelin Rose, trans. by Jacqueline Rose. (New York: W. W. Norton, 1985), p. 85.

30. Ibid., p. 82.

31. Jane Gallop, *The Daughter's Seduction: Feminism and Psychoanalysis.* (Ithaca: Cornell University Press, 1982), pp. 37–39.

32. Martin Esslin, *Pinter the Playwright*, p. 159.

33. Michel Foucault, *Power/Knowledge: Selected Interviews and Other Writings, 1972–1977* (New York: Pantheon Books, 1980), p. 98.

Chapter 5. "I'll Be Watching You": *Old Times* and the Field of Vision

1. Harold Pinter, *Old Times*, in *Complete Works: Four* (New York: Grove Press, 1981), pp. 20–21.

2. See Gary Gibson Cima, "Acting on the Cutting Edge: Pinter and the Syntax of Cinema," *Theatre Journal* 36, no. 1 (1984): pp. 43–56.

3. Roland Barthes, *A Lover's Discourse,* trans. by Richard Howard (New York: Farrar, Strauss and Giroux, 1978), p. 132.

4. See Albert R. Braunmuller, "A World of Words in Pinter's *Old Times,*" *Modern Language Quarterly* 40 (1979): pp. 53–74.

5. Norman Bryson, *Vision and Painting: The Logic of the Gaze* (New Haven: Yale University Press, 1983), p. 94.

6. Jacqueline Rose, *Sexuality in the Field of Vision* (London: Verso, 1986), pp. 190–91.

7. Jean-Paul Sartre, *Being and Nothingness,* trans. by H. E. Barnes (New York: Philosophical Library, 1956), pp. 260–68.

8. Jacques Lacan, *The Four Fundamental Concepts of Psycho-Analysis,* trans. by Alan Sheridan. (New York: W. W. Norton, 1978), p. 106.

9. Ibid., p. 95.

10. Teresa de Lauretis, *Technologies of Gender* (Bloomington: Indiana University Press, 1982), p. 3.

11. Silverman, *The Subject of Semiotics,* pp. 47–48.

12. Diamond, *Pinter's Comic Play,* p. 165.

13. Lacan, *The Four Fundamental Concepts of Psycho-Analysis,* p. 83.

14. Mulvey, "Visual Pleasure and Narrative Cinema," pp. 63, 62.

15. Ibid., p. 62.

16. Ibid., p. 63.

17. Mary Anne Doane, *The Desire to Desire* (Bloomington: Indiana University Press, 1987), p. 177.

18. Irigaray, *Speculum of the Other Woman,* pp. 98–99.

19. Freud, *Sexuality and the Psychology of Love,* pp. 141, 143–45.

20. Ibid., pp. 143, 147.

21. Ibid., p. 143.

22. Martin Esslin, *Pinter the Playwright,* p. 193.

23. Irigaray, *Speculum of the Other Woman,* p. 97.

24. Luce Irigaray, *This Sex Which Is Not One,* p. 24.

25. David Savran, "The Girardian Economy of Desire: *Old Times* Recaptured," *Theatre Journal* 34, no. 1 (1982): p. 52.

Chapter 6. Conclusion: "In the Light (or the Shadow) of Power"

1. Roland Barthes, *The Rustle of Language,* trans. by Richard Howard (Berkeley: University of California Press, 1986), pp. 100–101.

2. Ibid., p. 107.

3. Michel Foucault, *Power/Knowledge,* p. 98.

4. C. W. E. Bigsby, "The Politics of Anxiety: Contemporary Socialist Theatre in England," *Modern Drama* 24, no. 4 (1981): p. 400.

5. Ibid., p. 403.

6. Martin Esslin, *The Theatre of the Absurd,* 23–24, 401–2.

7. Ibid., pp. 401–2, 263.

8. Ibid., pp. 401.

9. Cited in Ibid., p. 23.

10. Harold Pinter, *Mountain Language* (New York: Grove Press, 1989), p. 21.

11. Harold Pinter, *One for the Road* (New York: Grove Press, 1986), pp. 50–51.

12. Barthes, *The Rustle of Language,* p. 153.

13. For a recent example of this kind of critique, see Terry Eagleton, *Ideology: An Introduction* (London: Verso, 1991).

14. Jacques Lacan, *Écrits,* p. 68.

15. Bigsby, "The Politics of Anxiety," p. 397.

16. See Fredric Jameson, *Postmodernism, or the Cultural Logic of Late Capitalism* (Durham, N.C.: Duke University Press, 1991).

Bibliography

Plays by Harold Pinter

Complete Works: One. New York: Grove Press, 1977.
Complete Works: Two. New York: Grove Press, 1977.
Complete Works: Three. New York: Grove Press, 1978.
Complete Works: Four. New York: Grove Press, 1981.
The Hothouse. New York: Grove Press, 1980.
Mountain Language. New York: Grove Press, 1989.
One for the Road. New York: Grove Press, 1986.
Other Places. New York: Grove Press, n.d.

Checklist of Pinter Criticism

Adler, Thomas P. "From Flux to Fixity: Death in Pinter's *No Man's Land.*" *Arizona Quarterly* 35 (1979).

———. "Notes towards the Archetypal Pinter Woman." *Theatre Journal* 33, no. 3 (1981).

———. "Pinter's *Night:* A Stroll down Memory Lane." *Modern Drama* 17 (1974).

Alexander, Nigel. "Past, Present, and Pinter." *Essays and Studies by Members of the English Association* 27 (1974).

Allison, Ralph, and Charles Wellborn. "Rhapsody in an Anechoic Chamber: Pinter's *Landscape.*" *Educational Theatre Journal* 25 (1973).

Almansi, Guido. "Harold Pinter's Idiom of Lies." In *Contemporary English Drama,* ed. C. W. E. Bigsby, New York: Holmes and Meier, 1981.

——— and Simon Henderson. *Harold Pinter.* London: Methuen, 1983.

Amend, Victor E. "Harold Pinter: Some Credits and Debits." *Modern Drama* 10 (1967).

Aylwin, Tony. "The Memory of All That: Pinter's *Old Times.*" *English* 22 (1973).

Back, Lillian. "The Double in Harold Pinter's *A Slight Ache.*" *Michigan Academician* 15, no. 3 (1983).

Baker, William, and Stephen E. Tabachnik. *Harold Pinter.* Edinburgh: Oliver and Boyd, 1973.

Beckerman, Bernard. "The Artifice of Reality in Chekhov and Pinter." *Modern Drama* 21 (1978).

Bensky, Lawrence M. "Harold Pinter." In *Writers at Work: The Paris Review Interviews,* ed. Alfred Kazin. New York: Viking, 1967.

Ben-Zvi, Linda. "Harold Pinter's *Betrayal:* The Patterns of Banality." *Modern Drama* 23 (1980).

Berkowitz, Gerald M. "Pinter's Revision of *The Caretaker.*" *Journal of Modern Literature* 5 (1976).

Bermel, Albert. *Contradictory Characters.* New York: E. P. Dutton, 1973.

Bernhard, F. J. "Beyond Realism: The Plays of Harold Pinter." *Modern Drama* 8 (1965).

Benstock, Shari. "Harold Pinter: Where the Road Ends." *Modern British Literature* 2 (1977).

Boulton, James T. "Harold Pinter's *The Caretaker* and Other Plays." *Modern Drama* 6 (1963).

Brater, Enoch. "Cinematic Fidelity and the Forms of Pinter's *Betrayal*" *Modern Drama* 24, no. 4 (1981).

———. "Pinter's *Homecoming* on Celluloid." *Modern Drama* 17 (1974).

———. "Time and Memory in Pinter's Proust Screenplay." *Comparative Drama* 13 (1979).

Braunmuller, Albert R. "A World of Words in Pinter's *Old Times.*" *Modern Language Quarterly* 40 (1979).

Body, Alan. "The Gift of Realism: Hitchcock and Pinter." *Journal of Modern Literature* 3 (1973).

Brooks, Mary E. "The British Theatre of Metaphysical Despair." *Literature and Ideology* 12 (1972).

Brown, John Russell. "Dialogue in Pinter and Others." *Critical Quarterly* 7 (1965).

———, ed. *Modern British Dramatists: A Collection.* Englewood Cliffs, N.J.: Prentice-Hall, 1968.

———. "Mr. Pinter's Shakespeare." *Critical Quarterly* 5 (1965).

———. *Theatre Language: A Study of Arden, Osborne, Pinter and Wesker.* London: Allen Lane, 1972.

———, ed. *Twentieth Century Views: Modern British Dramatists (New Perspectives).* Englewood Cliffs, N.J.: Prentice-Hall, 1984.

Burghardt, Lorraine Hall. "Game Playing in Three by Pinter." *Modern Drama* 17 (1974).

Burkman, Katharine H. *The Dramatic World of Harold Pinter: Its Basis in Ritual.* Columbus: Ohio State University Press, 1971.

———. "Earth and Water: The Question of Renewal in Harold Pinter's *Old Times* and *No Man's Land.*" *West Virginia University Philological Papers* 25 (1979).

———. "Harold Pinter's *Betrayal:* Life before Death—and After." *Theatre Journal* 34, no. 4 (1982).

———. "Hirst as Godot: Pinter in Beckett's Land." *Arizona Quarterly* 39, no. 1 (1983).

———. "Pinter's *A Slight Ache* as Ritual." *Modern Drama* 11 (1968).

Burton, Deidre. *Dialogue and Discourse.* London: Routledge and Kegan Paul, 1980.

———. "Making Conversation on Conversational Analysis, Stylistics, and Pinter." *Language and Style* 12 (1979).

Cardullo, Bert. "A Note on *The Homecoming.*" *Notes on Contemporary Literature* 14, no. 4 (1984).

———. "Pinter's *The Homecoming* and Albee's *A Delicate Balance.*" *Explicator* 42, no. 4 (1984).

———. "Pinter's *The Homecoming.*" *Explicator* 42, no. 3 (1984).

Carpenter, Charles A. "The Anonymity of Dread: Pinter's *The Dumb Waiter.*" *Modern Drama* 16 (1973).

———. "Quicksand in Pinterland: *The Caretaker.*" *Arizona Quarterly* 33 (1977).

———. "Victims of Duty? The Critics, Absurdity, and *The Homecoming.*" *Modern Drama* 25, no. 4 (1982).

———. "What Have I Seen, the Scum or the Essence?': Symbolic Fallout in Pinter's *Birthday Party.*" *Modern Drama* 17 (1974).

Cavander, Kenneth. "Interview with Harold Pinter." *In Focus on Film and Theatre,* ed. James Hurt. Englewood Cliffs, N.J.: Prentice-Hall, 1974.

Cima, Gary Gibson. "Acting on the Cutting Edge: Pinter and the Syntax of Cinema." *Theatre Journal* 36, no. 1 (1984).

Coe, Richard M. "Logic, Paradox and Pinter's *Homecoming.*" *Educational Theatre Journal* 27 (1975).

Cohen, Marshall, "Theater 67." *Partisan Review* 34 (1967).

Cohn, Ruby. "The Absurdly Absurd: Avatars of Godot." *Comparative Literature Studies* 2 (1965).

———. "Latter Day Pinter." *Drama Survey* 3 (1964).

———. "Words Working Overtime: *Endgame* and *No Man's Land.*" *Yearbook of English Studies* 9 (1979).

———. "The World of Harold Pinter." *Tulane Drama Review* 6, no. 3 (1962).

Cook, David, and Harold F. Brooks. "A Room with Three Views: Harold Pinter's *The Caretaker.*" *Komos* 1 (1967).

Davies, Russell. "Pinter Land." *The New York Review of Books* 25 January 1979.

Dawick, John. "Punctuation and Patterning in *The Homecoming.*" *Modern Drama* 14 (1971).

Deer, Harriet, and Irving Deer. "Pinter's *The Birthday Party:* The Film and the Play." *South Atlantic Bulletin* 45, no. 2 (1980).

Diamond, Elin. "Parody Play in Pinter." *Modern Drama* 25, no. 4 (1982).

———. "Pinter's *Betrayal* and the Comedy of Manners." *Modern Drama* 23 (1980).

Dick, Kay. "Mr. Pinter and the Fearful Matter." *Texas Quarterly* 4, no. 3 (1961).

Dukore, Bernard F. *Harold Pinter.* New York: Grove Press, 1982.

———. "The Pinter Collection." *Educational Theatre Journal* 7 (1974).

———. "Pinter's Staged *Mobologue.*" *Theatre Journal* 32 (1980).

———. "The Theatre of Harold Pinter." *Tulane Drama Review* 6, no. 3 (1962).

———. "What's in a Name? An Approach to *The Homecoming.*" *Theatre Journal* 33, no. 2 (1981).

———. *Where Laughter Stops: Pinter's Tragicomedy.* Columbia: University of Missouri Press, 1976.

———. "A Woman's Place." *Quarterly Journal of Speech* 52 (1966).

Durbach, Errol. "*The Caretaker:* Text and Subtext." *English Studies in Africa* 18 (1975).

Durrani, Osman. "Partners in Isolation: An Inquiry into Some Correspondences between Kafka's *Der Verschollene* and Pinter's *The Caretaker.*" *Forum for Modern Language Studies* 16 (1980).

Dutton, Richard. *Modern Tragicomedy and the British Tradition.* Norman: University of Oklahoma Press, 1986.

Eigo, James. "Pinter's *Landscape.*" *Modern Drama* 16 (1973).

English, Alan C. "Feeling Pinter's World." *Ball State University Forum* 14, no. 1 (1973).

Esslin, Martin. "Godot and His Children: The Theatre of Samuel Beckett and Harold Pinter." In *Experimental Drama,* ed. W. A. Armstrong. London: G. Bell, 1963.

———. "Letter to Peter Wood." *The Kenyon Review* 3, no. 3 (1981).

———. *The Peopled Wound: The Work of Harold Pinter.* Garden City, N.Y.: Doubleday, 1970.

———. *Pinter the Playwright.* London: Methuen, 1984.

———. "Pinter Translated." *Encounter* 30, no. 3 (1968).

———. *The Theatre of the Absurd.* Harmondsworth, Middlesex: Penguin Books, 1980.

Fischer, Andreas. "Poetry and Drama: Pinter's Play *The Birthday Party* in Light of His Poem 'A View of the Party.'" *English Studies* 60 (1979).

Fletcher, John. "A Psychology Based on Antagonism: Ionesco, Pinter, Albee, and Others." In *The Two Faces of Ionesco,* eds. Rosette C. Lamont and Melvin J. Friedman. Troy: Whitston, 1978.

Gabbard, Lucina P. "The Depths of *Betrayal.*" *Journal of Evolutionary Psychology* 4, nos. 3–4 (1983).

———. *The Dream Structure of Pinter's Plays: A Psychoanalytic Approach.* Rutherford, N.J.: Fairleigh Dickinson University Press, 1976.

———. "The Roots of Uncertainty in Pinter and Stoppard." *Forum H* 16, no. 3 (1978).

Gaggi, Silvio. "Pinter's *Betrayal:* Problems of Language or Grand Metatheatre?" *Theatre Journal* 33, no. 4 (1981).

Gale, Steven H. *Butter's Going Up: A Critical Analysis of Harold Pinter's Work.* Durham, N.C.: Duke University Press, 1977.

Gallagher, Kent G. "Harold Pinter's Dramaturgy." *Quarterly Journal of Speech* 52 (1966).

Ganz, Arthur. "A Clue to the Pinter Puzzle: The Triple Self in *The Homecoming.*" *Educational Theatre Journal* 21 (1969).

———, ed. *Pinter: A Collection of Critical Essays.* Englewood Cliffs, N.J.: Prentice-Hall, 1972.

———. *Realms of the Self.* New York: New York University Press, 1980.

Gillen, Francis. "'All These Bits and Pieces': Fragmentation and Choice in Pinter's Plays." *Modern Drama* 17 (1974).

———. "'. . . Apart from the Known and Unknown': The Unreconciled Worlds of Harold Pinter's Characters." *Arizona Quarterly* 26 (1970).

———. "'Nowhere to Go': Society and the Individual in Pinter's *The Hothouse.*" *Twentieth Century Literature* 29, no. 1 (1983).

Goodman, Florence Jeanne. "Pinter's *The Caretaker: The Lower Depths Descended*," *Midwest Quarterly* 5 (1963).

Gordon, Lois G. *Strategems to Uncover Nakedness: The Dramas of Harold Pinter.* Columbia: University of Missouri Press, 1968.

Hammond, Geralsine. "Something for the 'Nothings' of Beckett and Pinter." *CEA Critic* 39, no. 2 (1972).

Hayman, Ronald. *Harold Pinter.* New York: Ungar, 1973.

Hays, Peter L., and Stephanie Tucker. "No Sanctuary: Hemingway's 'The Killers' and Pinter's *The Birthday Party. Papers on Language and Literature* 21, no. 4 (1985).

Heilman, Robert B. "Demonic Strategies: *The Birthday Party* and *The Firebugs*." In *Sense and Sensibility in Twentieth Century Writing: A Gathering in Memory of William Van O'Connor,* ed. Brom Weber. Carbondale: South Illinois University Press, 1970.

Henkle, Roger B. "From Pooter to Pinter: Domestic Comedy and Vulnerability." *Critical Quarterly* 16 (1974).

Hinchliffe, Arnold P. *Harold Pinter,* rev. ed. Boston: Twayne, 1981.

———. "Mr. Pinter's Bellinda." *Modern Drama* 11 (1968).

Hidon, Michael. "To Verify a Proposition in *The Homecoming*." *Theatre Journal* 34, no. 1 (1982).

Hoefer, Jacqueline. "Pinter and Whiting: Two Attitudes towards the Alienated Artist." *Modern Drama* 4 (1962).

Hollis, James R. *Harold Pinter: The Poetics of Silence.* Carbondale: Southern Illinois University Press, 1970.

Hornby, Richard. *Script into Performance: A Structuralist View of Play Production.* Austin: University of Texas Press, 1977.

Hudgins, Christopher C. "Dance to a Cut-Throat Temper: Harold Pinter's Poetry as an Index to Intended Audience Response." *Comparative Drama* 12 (1978).

———. "Inside Out: Filmic Technique and the Theatrical Depiction of a Consciousness in Harold Pinter's *Old Times*." *Genre* 13 (1980).

———. "*The Basement:* Harold Pinter on BBC-TV." *Modern Drama* 28, no. 1 (1985).

Hughes, Alan. "'They Can't Take That Away from Me': Myth and Memory in Pinter's *Old Times*." *Modern Drama* 17 (1974).

Hughes, Kenneth James. *Signs of Literature: Language, Ideology and the Literary Text.* Vancouver: Talonbooks, 1986.

Hurrell, Barbara. "The Menace of the Commonplace: Pinter and Magritte." *The Centennial Review* 27, no. 2 (1983).

Imhof, Rudiger. "Pinter's *Silence:* The Impossibility of Communication." *Modern Drama* 17 (1974).

———. "Radioactive Pinter." In *Papers of the Radio Literature Conference, 1977,* ed. Peter Lewis. Durham, England: Department of English, University of Durham, 1978.

Jiji, Vera M. "Pinter's Four Dimensional Home: *The Homecoming*." *Modern Drama* 17 (1974).

Jones, John Bush. "Stasis as Structure in Pinter's *No Man's Land*." *Modern Drama* 19 (1976).

Kahon, Albert E. "The Artist as Con Man in *No Man's Land.*" *Modern Drama* 22 (1979).

Kaufman, Michael W. "Action That a Man Might Play: Pinter's *The Birthday Party.*" *Modern Drama* 16 (1973).

Kennedy, Andrew M. *Six Dramatists in Search of a Language: Studies in Dramatic Language.* London: Cambridge University Press, 1975.

Kerr, Walter. *Harold Pinter.* New York: Columbia University Press, 1967.

King, Noel. "Pinter's Progress." *Modern Drama* 23 (1980).

————. "Pinter's Screenplays: The Menace of the Past." *Southern Review* 14, no. 1 (1981).

Kirby, E. T. "The Paranoid Pseudo Community in Pinter's *The Birthday Party.*" *Educational Theatre Journal* 30 (1978).

Knowles, Ronald." *The Hothouse* and the Epiphany of Harold Pinter." *Journal of Beckett Studies* 10 (1985).

Kreps, Barbara. "Time and Harold Pinter's Possible Realities: Art as Life, and Vice Versa." *Modern Drama* 22 (1979).

Kunkel, Francis L. "The Dystopia of Harold Pinter." *Renascence* 21 (1968).

Lahr, John, ed. *Casebook on Harold Pinter's* The Homecoming. New York: Grove Presses, 1971.

————. "Pinter and Chekhov: The Bond of Naturalism." *Tulane Drama Review* 13, no. 3 (1968).

Lamont, Rosette C. "Pinter's *The Homecoming:* The Contest of the Gods." *Far-Western Forum* 1 (1974).

Leech, Clifford. "Two Romantics: Arnold Wesker and Harold Pinter." In *Contemporary Theatre,* eds. Brown and Bernard Harris. London: Edward Arnold, 1962.

Lesser, Simon O. "Reflections on Pinter's *The Birthday Party.*" *Contemporary Literature* 13 (1972).

Martineau, Stephen. "Pinter's *Old Times:* The Memory Game." *Modern Drama* 16 (1973).

Mast, Gerald. "Pinter's *Homecoming.*" *Drama Survey* 6 (1968).

Mayberry, Robert. "A Theatre of Discord: Some Plays of Beckett, Albee and Pinter." *Kansas Quarterly* 12, no. 4 (1980).

McAuley, Guy. "The Problem of Identity: Theme, Form and Theatrical Method in *Les Negres, Kaspar* and *Old Times.*" *Southern Review* 8 (1975).

McGuiness, Arthur E. "Memory and Betrayal: The Symbolic Landscape of *Old Times.*" In *Drama and Symbolism,* ed. James Redmond. Cambridge: Cambridge University Press, 1982.

Miller, Mary Jane. "Pinter as a Radio Dramatist." *Modern Drama* 17 (1974).

Morgan, Ricki. "The Multiple Nature of Reality in Pinter's *The Caretaker.*" *Quarterly Journal of Speech* 64 (1978).

————. "The Range of Emotional States in Pinter's *Collection.*" *Educational Theatre Journal* 30 (1978).

————. "What Max and Teddy Come Home to in *The Homecoming.*" *Educational Theatre Journal* 25 (1973).

Morrison, Kristin. *Canters and Chronicles.* Chicago: The University of Chicago Press, 1983.

————. "Pinter and the New Irony." *Quarterly Journal of Speech* 55 (1969).

Murphy, Robert P. "Non-Verbal Communication and the Overlooked Action in Pinter's *The Caretaker*." *Quarterly Journal of Speech* 58 (1972).

Nelson, Gerald. "Harold Pinter Goes to the Movies." *Chicago Review* 19, no. 1 (1966).

Ooi, Vicki C. H. "Edward Agonistes or Anagonistes? Theme and Structure of *A Slight Ache* by Harold Pinter." *Theatre Research International* 3 (1978).

————. "Pinter in Cantonese: Language, Stage and Meaning." *Sydney Studies in English* 2 (1976–77).

Osherow, Andrew R. "Mother and Whore: The Role of Woman in *The Homecoming*." *Modern Drama* 17 (1974).

Page, Malcolm. "The Cricket Allusion in Harold Pinter's *The Birthday Party*." *Notes and Queries* 27 (1980).

Palmer, David S. "A Harold Pinter Checklist." *Twentieth Century Literature* 16 (1970).

Pearce, Howard D. "Dimensions of Mimesis: Sophocles' *Philoctetes* and Pinter's *No Man's Land*." In *All the World Drama Past and Present Two*, ed. Karelisa V. Hartigan. Washington, D.C.: University Press of America, 1982.

Pesta, John. "Pinter's Usurpers." *Drama Survey* 6 (1967).

Postlewait, Thomas. "Pinter's *The Homecoming:* Displacing and Replacing Ibsen." *Comparative Drama* 15, no. 3 (1981).

Powlick, Leonard. "A Phenomenological Approach to Harold Pinter's *A Slight Ache*." *Quarterly Journal of Speech* 60 (1974).

————. "Temporality in Pinter's *The Dwarfs*." *Modern Drama* 20 (1977).

Prentice, Penelope. "Ruth: Pinter's *The Homecoming* Revisited." *Twentieth Century Literature* 26 (1980).

Quigley, Austin E. "*The Dumb Waiter:* Undermining the Tacit Dimension." *Modern Drama* 21 (1978).

————. "*The Dwarfs:* A Study of Linguistic Dwarfism." *Modern Drama* 17 (1974).

————. *The Modern Stage and Other Worlds*. New York: Methuen, 1985.

————. *The Pinter Problem*. Princeton: Princeton University Press, 1975.

Rao, N. M. "The Self-Commenting Drama of Our Time." *The Aligarh Journal of English Studies* 9, no. 2 (1984).

Rickert, Alfred D. "Perceiving Pinter." *English Record* 22, no. 2 (1971).

Rosador, Kurt T. "Pinter's Dramatic Method: *Kullus, The Examination, The Basement*," *Modern Drama* 14 (1971).

Rosen, Carol. *Plays of Impasse*. Princeton: Princeton University Press, 1983.

Sahai, Surendra. "Harold Pinter: Drama of the Troubled Psyche." *Literary Half Yearly* 23, no. 1 (1982).

Salmon, Eric. "Harold Pinter's Ear." *Modern Drama* 17 (1974).

Savran, David. "The Girardian Economy of Desire: *Old Times* Recaptured." *Theatre Journal* 34, no. 1 (1982).

Schechner, Richard. "Puzzling Pinter." *Tulane Drama Review* 11, no. 2 (1966).

Schiff, Ellen P. "Pancakes and Soap Suds: A Study of Childishness in Pinter's Plays." *Modern Drama* 16 (1973).

Schroll, Herman T. *Harold Pinter: A Study of His Reputation, 1958–1969.* Metuchen, N.J.: Scarecrow, 1971.

Skloot, Robert. "Putting out the Light: Staging the Theme of Pinter's *Old Times.*" *Quarterly Journal of Speech* 61 (1975).

Smith, Leslie. "Pinter the Player." *Modern Drama* 22 (1979).

Stamm, Rudolf. "*The Hothouse:* Harold Pinter's Tribute to Anger." *English Studies* 62, no. 3 (1981).

States, Bert O. "The Case for Plot in Modern Drama." *Hudson Review* 20 (1967).

———. "Pinter's *Homecoming:* The Shock of Nonrecognition." *Hudson Review* 21 (1968).

Storch, R. F. "Harold Pinter's Happy Families." *Massachusetts Review* 8 (1967).

Sykes, Alrene. *Harold Pinter.* New York: Humanities, 1970.

———. "Harold Pinter's *Dwarfs.*" *Komos* 1 (1967).

Taylor, John R. *Harold Pinter.* London: Longmans, 1969.

Tefs, Wayne. "Pinter and Psychoanalytic Criticism." *The Sphinx* 10 (1979).

Thomson, Peter. "Harold Pinter: A Retrospect." *Critical Quarterly* 20, no. 4 (1978).

Trussler, Simon. *The Plays of Harold Pinter: An Assessment.* London: Gollancz, 1973.

van Laan, Thomas F. "The Dumb Waiter: Pinter's Play with the Audience." *Modern Drama* 24, no. 4 (1981).

Walker, Augusta. "Messages from Pinter." *Modern Drama* 10 (1967).

Warner, John H. "The Epistemological Quest in Pinter's *The Homecoming.*" *Contemporary Literature* 11 (1970).

Weightman, John. "Another Play for Pinterites." *Encounter,* July 1975.

Weitz, Shoshana. "Reading for the Stage: The Role of the Reader-Director." *Assaph* 2, pt. C (1985).

Wells, Linda S. "A Discourse on Failed Love: Harold Pinter's *Betrayal.*" *Modern Language Studies* 13, no. 1 (1983).

Whitaker, Thomas R. "Playing Hell." *Yearbook of English Studies* 9 (1979).

Whittemore, Nena Thames. "Deja Vu: Pinter's 'Silence,' *Landscape,* and *Silence.*" *Centerpoint* 1, no. 3 (1975).

Zeifman, Hersh. "Ghost Trio: Pinter's *Family Voices.*" *Modern Drama* 27, no. 4 (1984).

Zinman, Toby Silverman. "Pinter's *Old Times.*" *Explicator* 43, no. 2 (1985).

Other Works Consulted and Cited

Althusser, Louis. *Lenin and Philosophy.* Translated by Ben Brewster. New York: Monthly Review Press, 1971.

Bakhtin, Mikhail. *The Dialogic Imagination.* Translated by Caryl Emerson and Michael Holquist. Austin: University of Texas Press, 1981.

———. *Problems of Dostoevsky's Poetics.* Translated by Caryl Emerson. Minneapolis: University of Minnesota Press, 1984.

Barthes, Roland. *A Lover's Discourse.* Translated by Richard Howard. New York: Farrar, Strauss and Giroux, 1978.

———. *The Rustle of Language.* Translated by Richard Howard. Berkeley: University of California Press, 1986.

———. *S/Z.* Translated by Richard Miller. New York: Hill and Wang, 1974.

Benveniste, Emile. *Problems in General Linguistics.* Translated by M. E. Meek. Coral Gables, Fla.: University of Miami Press, 1971.

Bigsby, C. W. E. "The Politics of Anxiety: Contemporary Socialist Theatre in England." *Modern Drama* 24, no. 4 (1981).

Blau, Herbert. *Blooded Thought.* New York: Performing Arts Journal Publications, 1982.

———. *The Eye of Prey.* Bloomington: Indiana University Press, 1987.

———. *Take up the Bodies.* Urbana: University of Illinois Press, 1982.

Bryson, Norman. *Vision and Painting: The Logic of the Gaze.* New Haven: Yale University Press, 1983.

Culler, Jonathan. *Ferdinand de Saussure.* New York: Penguin Books, 1977.

———. *On Deconstruction.* Ithaca: Cornell University Press, 1982.

De Lauretis, Teresa. Technologies of Gender. Bloomington: Indiana University Press, 1982.

Derrida, Jacques. *Of Grammatology.* Translated by G. C. Spivak. Baltimore: Johns Hopkins University Press, 1980.

Doane, Mary Anne. *The Desire to Desire.* Bloomington: Indiana University Press, 1987.

Elam, Keir. *The Semiotics of Theatre and Drama.* London: Methuen, 1980.

Engels, Friedrich. *The Origins of the Family, Private Property, and the State.* New York: International Publishers, 1972.

Felman, Shoshana. "The Critical Phallacy." *Diacritics,* Winter, 1975.

Foucault, Michel. *The Birth of the Clinic: An Archaeology of Medical Perception.* Translated by A. M. S. Smith. New York: Pantheon Books, 1973.

———. *Discipline and Punish.* Translated by Alan Sheridan. New York: Vintage Books, 1979.

———. *The History of Sexuality.* Translated by Robert Hurley. New York: Vintage Books, 1980.

———. *Power/Knowledge: Selected Interviews and Other Writings, 1972–1977.* New York: Pantheon Books, 1980.

Freud, Sigmund. *New Introductory Lectures on Psychoanalysis.* Translated by James Strachey. New York: W. W. Norton, 1965.

———. "On Narcissism: An Introduction." In *The Standard Edition of the Complete Psychological Works,* translated by James Strachey. Vol. 14. London: Hogarth Press, 1953–74.

———. *Sexuality and the Psychology of Love.* New York: Collier Books, 1963.

———. "The Uncanny." In *The Standard Edition of the Complete Psychological Works,* translated by James Strachey. Vol. 17. London: Hogarth Press, 1953–74.

Gallop, Jane. *The Daughter's Seduction: Feminism and Psychoanalysis.* Ithaca: Cornell University Press, 1982.

Handke, Peter. "Nauseated by Language." *The Drama Review* 5, no. 1 (1970).

Heath, Stephen. "Family Plots." In *Comparative Criticism,* ed. E. S. Shaffer. Vol. 5. Cambridge: Cambridge University Press, 1983.

Irigaray, Luce. *Speculum of the Other Woman.* Translated by G. C. Gill. Ithaca: Cornell University Press, 1985.

―――. *This Sex Which Is Not One.* Translated by Catherine Porter and Carolyn Burke. Ithaca: Cornell University Press, 1985.

Jardine, Alice A. *Gynesis.* Ithaca: Cornell University Press, 1985.

Kristeva, Julia. *The Kristeva Reader.* Edited by Toril Moi. New York: Columbia University Press, 1986.

―――. *Powers of Horror: An Essay on Abjection.* Translated by L. S. Roudiez. New York: Columbia University Press, 1982.

Lacan, Jacques. "Desire and the Interpretation of Desire in *Hamlet.*" Translated by James Hulbert. *Yale French Studies* 55–56 (1977).

―――. *Écrits: A Selection.* Translated by Alan Sheridan. New York: W. W. Norton, 1977.

―――. *Feminine Sexuality.* Edited by Juliet Mitchell and Jacqueline Rose. Translated by Jacqueline Rose. New York: W. W. Norton, 1985.

―――. *The Four Fundamental Concepts of Psycho-Analysis,* Translated by Alan Sheridan. New York: W. W. Norton, 1978.

―――. "Structure as an inmixing of an Otherness Prerequisite to Any Subject Whatsoever." In *The Structuralist Controversy,* ed. Richard Macksey and Eugenio Donato. Baltimore: Johns Hopkins University Press, 1970.

Lemaire, Anika. *Jacques Lacan.* Translated by David Macey. London: Routledge and Kegan Paul, 1977.

MacCannell, Juliet Flower. *Figuring Lacan: Criticism and the Cultural Unconscious.* Lincoln: University of Nebraska Press, 1986.

Merleau-Ponty, Maurice. *The Visible and the Invisible.* Translated by A. Lingis. Evanston, Ill.: Northwestern University Press, 1968.

Metz, Christian. *The Imaginary Signifier: Psychoanalysis and the Cinema.* Translated by Celia Britton, Annwyl Williams, Ben Brewster, and Alfred Guzetti. Bloomington: Indiana University Press, 1977.

Moi, Toril. *Sexual/Textual Politics.* London: Methuen, 1985.

Mulvey, Laura. "Visual Pleasure and Narrative Cinema." In *Feminism and Film Theory,* ed. Penley. New York: Routledge, 1988.

Rose, Jacqueline. *Sexuality in the Field of Vision.* London: Verso, 1986.

Sartre, Jean-Paul. *Being and Nothingness.* Translated by H. E. Barnes. New York: Philosophical Library, 1956.

―――. *The Psychology of Imagination.* Translated by Bernard Frechtman. New York: Washington Square Press, 1968.

―――. *Sartre on Theater.* Translated by Frank Jellinek. New York: Pantheon Books, 1976.

De Saussure, Ferdinand. *Course in General Linguistics.* Translated by Wade Baskin. New York: McGraw-Hill, 1966.

Secombe, Wally. "The Housewife and Her Labour under Capitalism." *New Left Review* 83 (1973).

Silverman, Kaja. *The Acoustic Mirror.* Bloomington: Indiana University Press, 1988.

―――. *The Subject of Semiotics.* New York: Oxford University Press, 1983.

Smith, Paul. *Discerning the Subject.* Minneapolis: University of Minnesota Press, 1988.

Todorov, Tzvetan. *Mikhail Bakhtin: Dialogical Principle.* Translated by Wlad Godzich. Minneapolis: University of Minnesota Press, 1984.

Voloshinov, V. N. *Marxism and the Philosophy of Language.* Translated by L. Matejka and I. R. Titunik. New York: Seminar Press, 1973.

Wilden, Anthony. *System and Structure: Essays in Communication and Exchange.* London: Tavistock, 1972.

Wittgenstein, Ludwig. *On Certainty.* Translated by Denis Paul and G. E. M. Anscombe. New York: Harper and Row, 1972.

———. *Philosophical Investigations.* Translated by G. E. M. Anscombe. New York: Macmillan, 1958.

Index

Absence, 126, 129, 156
Absurdist theatre, 22, 143–44
Adorno, Theodor, 47, 152
Adultery: homosexuality and, 65, 70; lesbianism and, 129; narcissism and, 62, 63; verbal, 55–56; wife/whore opposition and, 53–54, 82
Aggressivity, 91, 98, 137
Althusser, Louis: Foucault and, 143; on "husband-and-wife-being," 24; on ideology, 32, 33, 153, 158; Lacanian mirror stage and, 29–30; *Lenin and Philosophy,* 153; Marcuse and, 48; on subjectivity/subjection, 27; symbolic father and, 31; tragic scenario and, 28
Anna *(Old Times),* 116, 140; on Kate's "floating" subjectivity, 111; Kate's self-sufficiency and, 134–35, 136, 137, 138; male homosexuality and, 130; Newton and, 123; Nicolas and, 148; scopic regime and, 128, 129, 139; singing by, 126–27, 132–33; stage lighting of, 114, 115, 139; "syntax of cinema" and, 109, 112
Anxiety, 144, 148. *See also* Male anxiety
Assimilation, 141, 154
Audience gaze, 139; *The Collection,* 56–58, 59–60, 63; *Old Times,* 115, 116
Authority: linguistic, 45; state, 145–52, 158
Autoeroticism, 137
Autonomy, imaginary, 32, 78

Baker, William, 42, 154
Bakhtin, Mikhail, 19, 31, 36
Barney *(Birthday Party),* 41–42, 142
Barthes, Roland: on cultural codes, 21; on culture, 142, 145; on images, 109; on power, 157; on the state, 149; on

the symbolic father, 77, 85, 100, 101; on violence, 150
Beckett, Samuel, 22, 144
Being and Nothingness (Sartre), 113
"Being-seen" condition, 124, 125, 135
Bigsby, C. W. E., 143, 145, 157
Bill *(Collection),* 51, 52, 53, 54, 55; Anna/Kate relationship and, 130; "femininity" of, 71, 72, 107, 155; James and, 66–72; Ruth and, 87; stage lighting of, 59, 60; on Stella, 56, 57
Binary thought, 70, 71
Birthday Party, The, 26–49; *The Collection* and, 58–59, 67; critical reception of, 13; cultural codes in, 40, 41, 146; cultural power in, 154; desire in, 89; *The Homecoming* and, 80, 96, 107; monolithic cultural order and, 141–42; Stanley/Meg exchange in, 20–21, 34, 38; mentioned, 23, 139, 145, 153, 155
Blau, Herbert, 29
"Blue Moon," 119
Braunmuller, Albert R., 110
Brine, Adrian, 13, 14, 15, 16

Capitalism, 47–48, 145, 158–59
Castration complex, 62, 100–101, 103, 104, 106. *See also* Male anxiety
Catholicism, 45, 141
Cats, 61, 62, 63
Children, 92
Christianity, 44, 48, 141–42
Cima, G. G., 109
Cinema: audience of, 124–25; Deeley and, 109–12, 119, 122; female exhibitionism in, 124; patriarchal ideology and, 120, 127, 128, 156; Silverman on, 121; stage lighting and, 139
Class antagonism, 71
Clichés, 21–22, 40, 41, 42

178

Coercive language, 36. *See also* Violence, verbal

Collection, The, 50–75, 76, 108; family structure in, 80–81; *The Homecoming* and, 82, 83, 94, 101, 105, 107; mimicry in, 73–75, 76, 154–55; *Old Times* and, 109, 114–15, 118, 130, 132; power relations in, 23–24; mentioned, 26, 49, 141, 142, 155, 159

"Comedies of menace," 144

Commodification, female: in *The Homecoming,* 159; Irigaray on, 78; marriage and, 79, 82; prostitution as, 79–80; in song lyrics, 126

"Commodities among Themselves" (Irigaray), 64

Confession, 68–69, 74

Cosmopolitanism, 142

Cultural codes, 21, 40, 41, 146, 154

Cultural order-principle, 44

Cultural power: in *The Birthday Party,* 26, 38–39, 142; clichés and, 22; cultural codes and, 21; ideology as, 32, 48; language and, 156, 157; "mouthpieces" and, 139, 143; politics and, 141, 152; reassertion of, 155; subjectivity and, 22–23, 27–28, 160; unassailableness of, 47,1 40, 159. *See also* Law of culture; Other, the

Culture/Nature dichotomy, 71

Deeley *(Old Times):* audience identity and, 116; cinema and, 109–12; clichéd representations of, 22; Kate's indecipherability and, 117–18; Kate's self-sufficiency and, 134–35, 136, 137, 138; Lukey/Newton and, 122–24; Nicolas and, 148; patriarchal ideology and, 119; scopic regime and, 128–29; singing by, 125–27, 132–33; stage lighting of, 114, 115, 139; Welles and, 110, 120, 121

Defilement, 87

De Lauretis, Teresa, 118

"Demystifying gaze." *See* Audience gaze

Derrida, Jacques, 43

Desire, 20, 22, 36, 37, 88–89

Diamond, Elin, 56, 63, 77, 84, 106

Discours de Rome (Lacan), 156–57

Disease, 87–88, 95–96

Division of heterosexual labor, 124, 128

Doane, Mary Ann, 127

Dueling, 69–70, 71–72

Dukore, Bernard F., 28

Dumb Waiter, The, 23, 139

Economic transactions, 79

Edgar, David, 143, 144, 145

Egoism, 62

Empowerment: in *The Homecoming,* 106, 107, 159; in *Old Times,* 117; passivity as, 73, 155; prostitution and, 77–78, 79–80; subjectivity and, 157. *See also* Power

Esslin, Martin: on *The Homecoming,* 106; on metaphysical anguish, 144–45; on *Old Times,* 136–37; on Pinter's language, 13, 14, 15, 16, 17; on political problems, 23, 24

Etiquette, 21

Exhibitionism, 124

Existential anxiety, 144

Existentialism, 27

Expressive theory of language, 13, 14, 15, 16, 17

Failed language, 15–16, 92–93

Families, 76–107; female sexuality and, 53; patriarchal power and, 24; socialization in, 37–38, 81, 83, 156

Fascination, 100, 101, 106

Fascism, cultural, 47, 140

Fatherhood, 84–85, 86. *See also* Law, paternal; Patriarchy; Symbolic fathers

Feline self-sufficiency, 61, 62, 63

Female disease, 87–88, 95–96

Female sexuality, 50–75, 94, 96, 137–38. *See also* Lesbianism; Prostitution; Wife/whore opposition

"Feminity" (Freud), 62

Fetishism, 102, 103, 104

"Fetishism" (Freud), 103

"Floating" subjectivity, 111, 116–17, 133–34, 139

Forbidden language, 145–46, 149, 150

Forgetfulness, 125

Foucault, Michel: on confession, 68, 74; on gazing, 56, 57; on "invisible visibility," 60; on power, 106–7, 143, 147, 157, 158

Frankfurt School, 47

Freud, Sigmund, 62, 89, 136; "Femininity," 62; "On Narcissism," 61–62, 134,

135; "The Psychogenesis of a Case of Homosexuality in a Woman," 131–32
Frigidity, 136, 137
Fuegi, John, 24–25

Gale, Steven H., 24–25, 28, 32–33, 66
Gallop, Jane, 105
Garcin *(No Exit)*, 113
Gaze. *See* Audience gaze; Scopic transactions
Gender representation, 118, 125
Genet, Jean, 22
Gershwin, Ira, 125, 126
Gila *(One for the Road)*, 150
Gilman, Richard, 25
Goldberg *(Birthday Party)*, 33–47, 48; clichés of, 21–22, 40, 42; Deeley and, 119, 139; Jewishness of, 41–42, 44, 48, 141–42, 154; Nicolas and, 147; physical violence and, 96; Stella character and, 76; as symbolic father, 31, 80; verbal violence of, 20, 34, 146
Gordon, Lois G., 28

Handke, Peter, 35, 47
Hare, David, 143, 144, 145
Harold Pinter: Critical Approaches (Gale), 24–25
Harriman, Averell, 151
Harry *(Collection)*: Anna/Kate relationship and, 130; Bill and, 70–71, 72, 107, 155; Max and, 87; stage lighting of, 59; on Stella, 53, 55
Heath, Stephen, 52, 53, 54
Hern, Nicholas, 151, 152
Heterosexuality, 64–65, 69, 71, 124, 131
Hobson, Harold, 13
Hollis, J. R., 13, 14–15, 16
Homecoming, The, 76–107, 108; *Old Times* and, 109, 118, 130, 132; power relations in, 23–24; wife/whore opposition in, 79, 82–83, 159–60
Homosexuality: in Bill/Harry relationship, 70–71, 130; in Bill/James relationship, 66–67, 68; patriarchy and, 50, 64–66. *See also* Lesbianism
Hothouse, The, 23
Humanist ideology, 48, 151
Husband identity, 62–63, 73, 80–81

Ideologiekritik, 47, 153, 158

Ideology: cultural order and, 27; discourse and, 33; family transmission of, 81, 83; "implosion theory" of, 158–59; mirror stage and, 29, 30; totalizing impulse of, 48, 153
Imaginary autonomy, 32, 78
Imaginary order, 90
"Implosion theory," 158–59
Individualism, 28, 29
"Insecurity," 145
Insulting rhetoric, 70, 82
"Intellectual equilibrium," 97
Interrelational function of language, 18, 20, 22
Ionesco, Eugène, 22, 145
Irigaray, Luce: on female status, 80, 107; on frigidity, 137; on lesbianism, 130–31; on mimicry, 73, 74, 76, 154–55; on patriarchal homosexuality, 64–65, 66, 70, 71, 72; on prostitution, 78, 79; *Speculum of the Other Woman,* 131
Irish Catholicism, 45, 141
Irony: *The Birthday Party,* 48, 141–42; *The Collection,* 55; *The Homecoming,* 77, 106; *Old Times,* 116; "They Can't Take That Away from Me," 126

James *(Collection),* 51, 52, 53, 54, 55; Bill and, 65–72; Deeley and, 118; Max and, 82; staging of, 59, 60; Stella and, 57, 62, 64, 73–74
Jameson, Fredric, 159
Jardine, Alice, 88
Jessie *(Homecoming):* family dysfunction and, 88, 100; Max and, 81–82, 84, 86, 87, 89–90; Oedipal complex and, 89–90, 91, 98; Teddy and, 99
Joey *(Homecoming),* 90–91, 92, 93, 99, 100–101
Judaism, 41–42, 44, 48, 141–42, 154

Kaspar (Handke character). 35, 36
Kate *(Old Times),* 114–19; cliché representations of, 22; lesbianism of, 129, 131; *Odd Man Out* and, 122–24; power of, 127, 128; self-sufficiency of, 135–38; Stella and, 72; subjectivity of, 111, 116–17, 133–34, 139; "syntax of cinema" and, 109–12
Kern, Jerome, 125

Lacan, Jacques: on desire, 37; *Discours de Rome,* 156–57; Foucault and, 143; on ideology, 33; on "illusion of autonomy," 32; on mirror stage, 29–30; Oedipal complex and, 88–92, 104; on paternal law, 84; on scopic regime, 108, 113–14, 115, 123–24, 138–39; on sexuality, 105; on subjectivity, 33; on symbolic father, 31, 77, 86; mentioned, 24, 25, 27

Language: coercive, 36; cultural power and, 156, 157; expressive theory of, 13, 14, 15, 16, 17; failure of, 15–16, 92–93; forbidden, 145–46, 149, 150; interrelational function of, 18, 20, 22; subjectivity and, 19, 106–7, 156–57; violent, 20, 34, 46, 87, 150–51

Langue (codified language system), 18, 19, 20, 21, 37

Laryngitis, 43

Law: of culture, 26, 31; of desire, 20, 22, 37; of exchange, 78; paternal, 84, 88, 90

Lenin and Philosophy (Althusser), 153

Lenny *(Homecoming),* 92–94; maternal infidelity and, 82–83; Max and, 84, 85, 86–87; Ruth and, 78, 94–96, 101, 102; Teddy and, 98, 99; whore/wife opposition and, 79

Lesbianism, 129–32, 133, 136, 141

Lévi-Strauss, Claude, 152

Liberal humanist ideology, 48,151

Lighting, stage, 59, 115, 138–39

Lip symbolism, 103–4

"Look-looked-at" concept, 108, 112–13, 114, 115, 138–39; audiences and, 116, 124–25; in *One for the Road,* 149; subversive potential of, 127; *The Trial* and, 121

Lukey *(Odd Man Out),* 121–22, 123

Lulu *(Birthday Party),* 34, 35

Lyrics. *See* Popular songs

McCann *(Birthday Party)* 33–38, 41, 42, 45; on Goldberg's "Christianity," 44, 48, 141–42; physical violence of, 46; verbal violence of, 20, 34, 96, 146

MacCannell, J. F., 44

MacGregor *(Homecoming)* 85

McQueen, Johnny *(Odd Man Out),* 122

Madness, 35

Magnificent Ambersons, The (film), 110, 119, 120

Male anxiety, 54–55, 61, 87, 95, 99. *See also* Castration complex

Male fantasy, 128, 132

Male gaze: *The Collection,* 65, 101; *The Homecoming,* 85–86, 101–3; *Old Times,* 116, 128, 129; song lyrics, 120, 126–27

Male paranoia, 87–88

Male power. *See* Patriarchy

Male sexuality: autoeroticism and, 137, 138; phallic privilege and, 105; violence and, 91, 95; visual dimension of, 57. *See also* Penis

Manchester Guardian, 13, 14, 16

Marcuse, Herbert, 47

Marginal groups, 153

Marriage, 24, 53, 79, 98–99, 117

Marxist theory, 158

Mason, James, 122

Maternal desire, 88–89

Maternal role, 81, 83, 84, 86

Matriarchy, 77, 106, 108, 130, 141

Max *(Homecoming):* authority of, 86–87; Deeley and, 120; fatherhood concept and, 84–85; Jessie and, 81–82, 89–90; Lenny and, 84, 85, 93; paranoia of, 87–88; Ruth and, 105, 106, 130; whore/wife opposition and, 79, 82; mentioned, 147

Maxims, 21–22, 40, 41, 42

Meg *(Birthday Party)* 20–21, 22, 34, 38, 80

Memory, 135, 136

Metaphysical anguish, 144–45

Mimicry: *The Collection,* 51, 73–75, 76, 154–55; *The Homecoming,* 77, 78–79, 100, 101, 105, 106, 159

Mirror stage, 29–30, 31, 35, 58, 90

Moi, Toril, 76

Monty *(Birthday Party)* 35, 42, 43, 45, 139

Morrison, Kristin, 28

Mountain Language, 23, 26, 145–52, 155

"Mouthpieces": in *The Birthday Party,* 43, 142; in *The Collection,* 63; Handke on, 47; "implosion" theory and, 158; in *Old Times,* 119; power and, 44, 139, 143

Mulvey, Laura, 101, 124, 125

Names, 31
Narcissism, 61–62, 63, 108, 134, 135
Narrative power, 95–96, 101
Narrative self-definition, 32
New Right ideology, 159
Newton, Robert, 121, 122, 123, 124
Nicolas *(One for the Road)*, 96, 146–47, 149, 150, 151
Nicky *(One for the Road)*, 147–48, 150
No Exit (Sartre), 113, 157

Odd Man Out (film), 119, 121–23
Oedipal tensions, 88–92, 97, 104
Old Times, 108–40; clichéd representations in, 22; power in, 23–24, 153
One for the Road, 145–52, 155; *The Homecoming* and, 96; violence in, 46
"On Narcissism" (Freud), 61–62, 134, 135
Osborne, John, 144
Other, the: clichés and, 22, 40–41, 42; etiquette and, 21; Goldberg and, 39–43, 44, 141–42, 154; maternal desire and, 89; Oedipal complex and, 91; Sartre on, 113; Stanley and, 29, 30, 35, 37; state as, 145; subjectivity and, 120, 160; symbolic father as, 31, 33; violence and, 46–47; Wilden on, 20, 43, 119. *See also* Cultural power

Paranoia, 87, 88
Parody, 87
Parole (individual speech-act), 18, 19, 20, 21
Passivity, 73, 74
Patriarchy: family power and, 24, 77; female sexuality and, 50–75, 94; homosexuality and, 155; lesbianism and, 129, 132, 133; maternal role in, 84, 89; mimicry and, 76, 100; phallus/penis distinction and, 104; popular culture and, 120, 156; prostitution and, 77–78; scopic regime of, 101, 102; sexual difference and, 117, 118, 125, 127, 130, 133; survival of, 158, 159; wife/whore opposition and, 82. *See also* Fatherhood; Husband identity; Law, paternal; Symbolic fathers
Penis, 65, 103, 104–5

Penis envy, 62, 89, 134
Pessimism, 157, 158, 160
Phallic symbolism: in *The Collection*, 70; in *The Homecoming*, 77, 83, 90, 91, 106, 107; Irigaray on, 65; lesbianism and, 129; the penis and, 89, 104–5, 134
Philosophical Investigations (Wittgenstein), 17
Pinter Problem, The. See Quigley, Austin
Platonism, 15
Pleasure, 68
Poliakoff, Stephen, 143
Political themes, 23, 141, 145, 152
"Politics of Anxiety, The" (Bigsby), 143
Popular songs: Deeley/Anna relationship and, 132–33; Deeley/Kate relationship and, 136; Deeley's subjectivity and, 119; patriarchy and, 120, 127, 156; scopic desire and, 125–26, 128
Porter, Cole, 125
Power, 23–24, 125, 140; confession and, 68; Foucault on, 106–7, 143, 147; Max and, 85; representational, 95–96, 138; state, 145–52; subjection to, 157–58, 160; "truth" and, 51. *See also* Cultural power; Empowerment
Prostitution: as empowerment, 79–80; in *The Homecoming*, 95, 96; lesbianism and, 129; marriage as, 79; patriarchy and, 77–78. *See also* Wife/whore opposition
Proverbial formulas, 21–22, 40, 41, 42
"Psychogenesis of a Case of Homosexuality in a Woman, The" (Freud), 131–32
Psychotic persons, 92

Quigley, Austin: on *The Homecoming*, 77, 106; *The Pinter Problem*, 16–19, 20, 21, 22, 24, 25

Reason, 151, 152
Reed, Carol, 119, 121
Reference theory of meaning, 17, 18, 19
Representational power, 95–96, 138
Representational truth, 51, 58
Representation of gender, 118, 125
Resistance, 132, 140, 142–43; *The*

Birthday Party and, 48–49; female commodification and, 78; in *The Homecoming,* 107; mimicry and, 76, 101; political, 152

Rose, Jacqueline, 112

Ruth *(Homecoming),* 76–80, 105–6, 107, 159; Anna/Kate relationship and, 129; Lenny and, 93–96; Max and, 81, 87, 130; as mother figure, 91, 100–101; Stella and, 72; Teddy and, 98–99; as visual object, 101–2

Sabbath observance, 41

Sadism, 95, 126

Sam *(Homecoming),* 82, 98

Sartre, Jean-Paul: *Being and Nothingness,* 113; "look-looked-at," concept of, 108, 112–13, 114, 115, 124–25, 138–39; *No Exit,* 113, 157; on visual eroticism, 57

Saussure, Ferdinand de, 18, 52, 54

Savran, David, 138

Scopic transactions, 101–4, 108–40, 149. *See also* Audience gaze; Male gaze

Scopophilia, 101, 102

Secombe, Wally, 81, 83

Seduction, 69, 70

Self-concept development, 18

Self-definition, 32

Self-estrangement, 28–30, 91

Self-representation, 118, 138

Self-sufficiency: Freud on, 61, 135; of Kate, 135–38; masculine desire for, 134; of Stella, 61, 62, 63; symbolic father and, 31

Sennex, 87

Sexual difference, 117, 118, 125, 127, 130, 133

Sexuality, 105. *See also* Female sexuality; Heterosexuality; Homosexuality; Male sexuality

Silence, 73–75, 118, 155

Silverman, Kaja, 121, 139

Socialist playwrights, 143–44, 145

Socialization, 36, 37–38, 47, 81, 83

Song lyrics. *See* Popular songs

Specularity. *See* Scopic transactions

Speculum of the Other Woman (Irigaray), 131

Split stage, 58–59, 65–66, 114–15

Stage lighting, 59, 115, 138–39

Stanley *(Birthday Party),* 26, 28–40; Meg and, 20–21, 34, 38; as "mouthpiece," 43, 45; Stella and, 57–58, 76; surrogate parents of, 80; violence against, 46–47

State power, 145–52

Stella *(Collection),* 51, 52, 53, 54, 55–56; Anna/Kate relationship and, 129; attempted domestication of, 64; attempted seduction of, 70; audience gaze on, 56–58, 59–60; "confession" of, 68–69; Deeley and, 118; homosexuality and, 65, 66, 71, 72; Jessie and, 83; Kate and, 134, 135; as mimic, 72–74, 76, 154–55; Ruth and, 96, 99; self-sufficiency of, 61, 62, 63

Stoppard, Tom, 144

Subjection, 22, 26–49, 77–78, 157–58, 160

Subjectivity: vs. cultural coding, 154; "floating," 111, 116–17, 133–34, 139; in *The Homecoming,* 90, 98; "insecurity" and, 145; language and, 19, 106–7, 156–57; mimicry and, 155; Oedipal matrix and, 89; in *Old Times,* 117–18, 119, 120, 134; subjection and, 22, 26–49

Symbolic fathers: biological fatherhood and, 85, 86; in *The Birthday Party,* 30–32, 33; "fascination" attribute of, 101; in *The Homecoming,* 77, 82, 84, 87, 100, 106, 130; male paranoia and, 88; phallus/penis distinction and, 89, 104

Symbolic mothers, 86

Symbolic-real border region, 92

Symbols, 156

Tabachnik, Stephen E., 42, 154

Teddy *(Homecoming),* 77, 97–100, 106; "castration" of, 101; on Jessie, 81; Lenny and, 92, 93, 98

Television, 59

Theatre of the Absurd, 22, 143–44

Theatrical lighting, 59, 115, 138–39

"They Can't Take That Away from Me" (Gershwin), 119, 126, 129

To-be-looked-at-ness, 124

Totalitarianism, 47, 140, 145–52, 158

Tractatus Logico-Philosophicus (Wittgenstein), 15, 17
Tragic scenario, 28
Trial, The (film), 110, 112, 114, 121; audience of, 115; Deeley's subjectivity and, 119, 120
Truth, representational, 51, 58

"Uncertainty Principle and Pinter's Modern Drama, The" (Fuegi), 24–25

Vagina, 103
Victor *(One for the Road)*, 150, 151
Violence: in *The Collection*, 69–70, 71–72; male sexuality and, 91, 95, 137;

the Other and, 46–47; state, 150–51; verbal, 20, 34, 46, 87, 150–51
Visual transactions. *See* Scopic transactions
Voyeurism, 108, 128

Weber, Max, 152
Welles, Orson, 110, 119, 120, 121
Wesker, Arnold, 144
Wife/whore opposition, 50–75, 79, 82–83, 159–60. *See also* Prostitution
Wilden, Anthony, 20, 37, 43, 58, 119
Wilson *(Dumb Waiter)*, 139
Wittgenstein, Ludwig, 15, 17, 18, 19
"Women on the Market" (Irigaray), 64
Woolf, Virginia, 15
"Writing the Event" (Barthes), 150